**Conflicts in
Urban and
Regional
Development**
a series
edited by
John R. Logan
and
Todd Swanstrom

In timber country

Working people's stories of environmental conflict and urban flight

Beverly A. Brown

Temple University Press   Philadelphia

Temple University Press, Philadelphia 19122
Copyright © 1995 by Temple University. All rights reserved
Published 1995
Printed in the United States of America

⊛ The paper used in this book meets the requirements of the American National
Standard for Information Sciences — Permanence of Paper for Printed Library Materials, ANSI Z39.48-1984

Text design by Adrianne Onderdonk Dudden

Library of Congress Cataloging-in-Publication Data

Brown, Beverly A., 1951 Feb. 21–
    In timber country : working people's stories of environmental
conflict and urban flight / Beverly A. Brown.
        p.   cm. — (Conflicts in urban and regional development)
    Includes bibliographical references (p.   ) and index.
    ISBN 1-56639-272-1 (cloth : alk. paper). — ISBN 1-56639-273-X
(paper : alk. paper)
    1. Rogue River Valley (Or.) — Rural conditions.   2. Working class —
Oregon — Rogue River Valley — Interviews.   3. Urban-rural migration —
Oregon — Rogue River Valley.   4. Forests and forestry — Environmental
aspects — Oregon — Rogue River Valley.   5. Green movement — Oregon —
Rogue River Valley.   I. Title.   II. Series.
HN79.072R633   1995
306'.09795'27 — dc20   94-21274

Contents

In-migrations, timber, and owls: background to a transformation

In the country

In our lives

What kind of future?

Language, complexity, and power: life stories and a community in transition

An environmentalist reflection

Postscript

Acknowledgments

I am grateful for the support, encouragement, and critical evaluations of this book from my friends and colleagues. Special thanks to Cynthia Coleman, Tee Corinne, Paul deLeon, Kiko Denzer, Ann Hawkins, Helen Lewis, Mollie Owens-Stevenson, Boyd Peters, and Mary Raymond.

Jim Strassmaier at the Oregon Historical Society, where the original interviews are archived, provided invaluable technical assistance and enthusiasm for the project. Janet Fitchen of Ithaca College, Louise Fortmann of the University of California at Berkeley, and Victoria Sturtevant of Southern Oregon State College were available for consultation at crucial moments. The book could not have been finished without the expertise of Fran Cardoza, Daurel Coolidge, Marian Masters, Pat Mersman, and Mary Pierce, librarians at Rogue Community College. They helped me to gain access to national research material from our small rural campus. Librarians at Southern Oregon State College also provided guidance. Mary Bradford, clippings librarian at the *Grants Pass Daily Courier*, skillfully and patiently helped me locate information from two previous decades. The Northwest Women's History Project in Portland provided a small initial grant for a segment of this undertaking. My mother, Ann Levickas Brown Clark, saw the importance of documenting the transformation of her own once-rural community and my hometown — a part of the great "State of Jefferson" — and financially assisted the project.

The mixed-social-class consciousness-raising groups of the women's movement in Rhode Island in the early 1970s first alerted me to the importance of people's own stories. Professor Milt Barnett at Cornell University focused my interest on listening for larger themes in interviews with rural people. I am especially indebted to the Highlander Center in Tennessee, and particularly John Gaventa, who invited me to be an intern at the Center in 1986. There I learned the power of people's stories when they are shared as part of a deliberate learning process aimed at social change. Learning about the truly grassroots activism of rural people from Appalachia and the South, both as history and through personal experience, was an inspiration I have carried with me to all my subsequent work.

My office co-workers Mary Raymond and Barb Scholl provided insight, laughter, and perspective as I struggled to balance making a living with creating this book. Jerry Bryan was an important initial source of encouragement.

My deepest gratitude and appreciation go to my partner, T.A.C., who lived through my temperamental ups and downs as the project evolved; endured the piles of paper, tapes, and references that constitute my visually-based filing system, and provided a sounding-board for ideas on innumerable occasions. Thank you.

Finally, this project would not have been possible without the generous help of the people interviewed for this book, who for professional reasons must remain anonymous. The experiences and insights they offered pushed me to look at the Rogue Valley from new perspectives. To them: May our valley prosper with all of us as equal partners.

Preface

The central idea of justice is a matter not of rules, distributions, or correctives, but a matter of relations.

James Boyd White

Everyday life is central to this book. In the following pages, people speak plainly about their lives and their community, documenting how twenty-five individuals responded to the rapid transformation of logging towns into enclaves for tourism, retirement, and urban flight. Mostly poor and lower-middle-income people, none is intended to be representative of the entire population of the area, but they do belong to a large and crucial segment who are often presented as scapegoats or stereotypes: the liberal's "rednecks," and industry's and the right wing's "silent majority."

These interviews were recorded in Oregon's Jackson and Josephine counties between April 1989 and August 1990. During that time, debates over the Northwest timber harvest attracted national attention, symbolized by the spotted owl controversy. Lumber mill closures accelerated, and a regional depression foreshadowed the national recession of 1990–92. Nonetheless, local home construction and real estate sales prospered as retirees and professionals relocated to southwest Oregon. Professional medical positions and low-paid service and assembly line jobs replaced timber and military-related electronics work. Unemployment reached 8 percent by the end of 1990 and continued to rise. In February 1993 *Labor Trends* (a publication of the state's Department of Human Resources) reported unemployment rates of 12.5 percent for Josephine County and 9.5 percent for Jackson.

The goal of this project was to explore poor and working people's opinions about the changes taking place in the Rogue Valley region for perspectives that might differ significantly from newspaper, political campaign, and social agency versions of local affairs. Sifting through the details of lives, sorting out what is of real concern to people in a community, is a chaotic occupation. Nonetheless, without an effort to discover the core troubles on people's minds, public policy born of good intentions or theoretical purity will fail.

People were contacted through several friendship networks and asked to suggest others who would be willing to talk into a tape recorder. I was at least marginally acquainted with about half the interviewees; the other half were strangers. One of the interviewees in this book is biracial, passing as white; the remainder are of European ancestry. Essentially, and intentionally, this is a book about white working-class rural people.

Most of these interviewees are people who are usually not represented in public debate: primarily poor or lower-middle-income blue- or pink-collar people who spent all or large segments of their childhood in southwest Oregon. The few who have recently achieved middle-class status grew up in working families in the region. The last interview presents the narrative of people of blue-collar origin who moved to Oregon as adults and helped launch environmental activism in the Rogue Valley. Their interview provides a reflective counterpoint to the main body of the book.

At the beginning of each interview session, people were asked to talk about growing up, the changes they have seen in the area, and what they think of the changes. Within those parameters, men usually discussed public events, whereas women often described private lives. In our society, public events are traditionally considered the province of "history," while private events are placed outside history: Here, that distinction is rejected. This book affirms the commonsense integration of public and private lives. Consequently, the narratives vary from the tall-tale-influenced storytelling of Peter Alten and Larry Lyon, reflecting their passion for the land, to the more intimate histories of family violence and alienation in several women's interviews, especially that of Kathy Dodge.

History as related by any of the individuals here may or may not reflect what actually took place. Of the "facts" recounted in the interviews, some are accurate, some are inaccurate, and some are unsettled points of contention. In the unfolding of social events, what is perceived by many to be true is often of greater importance than what others may consider cold, documented realities. This book emphasizes local perceptions and does not attempt to pose as an authoritative history.

Although the emphasis here is local, state and national politics, the international organization of timber corporations, and the crises of U.S. cities all affect southwest Oregon in ways that become apparent in the following pages. Long-term community members are not passive recipients of change: Through family and friendship circles, poor and working people aggressively search for ways to accommodate to changes and turn them to their own advantage. Most build upon their own experience of the culture of the area, rather than adopting the new values of recent urban in-migrants.

As will be evident, considerable resentment, suspicion, and uncertainty color the local reaction to the middle-class, urban in-migration of the 1980s, which coincided with the disappearance of well-paid blue-collar jobs. There is nervousness about the increasing racial diversity of the area. People feel cut out of the process of change. Social networks divide further along class, education, and urban–rural lines. Unemployed and underemployed workers try to cope with a suddenly uncertain future. As Rhonda Marshall notes of displaced timber workers: "You have to realize that it's almost like a different type of world compared to what most people are aware of. In the valley, this is what I see: All the millworkers is one kind of a community, as far as their survival techniques. Then you have managerial people — their survival techniques would be totally different."

The divisions and tensions within the Rogue Valley area are hardly unique; they echo conflicts within rural and urban areas alike across the United States. A society increasingly divided along class, race, and gender lines is easily enticed, as ours is, to increasing segregation. The interests of poor and working people are often in conflict with those of groups who have the power to enforce their will, while lack of communication across cultural and social divisions exacerbates the general discontent.

Listening to real people tell their real stories, in all their complexity, is an essential ingredient for democratic change; theory, ideology, and "saving the planet" are no substitute. As Art Downing says: "You can become so acutely aware of how stupid the system is. How utterly wrong it is. Intellectually, logically, philosophically, you can be so hyper-aware of how wrong it is, that you can get into having the power of being right. And you end up taking extreme postures. . . . And you don't do yourself or your cause or the woods any good by alienating people — just because you're right. Just because you're right doesn't make it work, you know?"

As citizens of the United States, we are caught in a vast net of actions and consequences. Our Constitution promotes a concept of justice. For some, that means justice only as it relates to property rights, but for most citizens, justice extends to the social conditions under which people conduct their everyday lives. "Justice and friendship are about the same things, and occur in the same relations," wrote Aristotle in the *Nicomachaean Ethics*. In the following pages, people talk about how their everyday lives have been transformed during a time when the distance between rich and poor is increasing and neighbors no longer know each other's names.

Note on the interviews

The twenty-five people who tell their stories in this book generously gave me their time for what must have seemed a vaguely conceived project. I have tried to edit their stories honestly and accurately, distilling forty- to eighty-page transcripts into short narratives, while keeping their ideas in context and protecting their privacy. The internal sequence of each interview is intact, with a few minor shifts to maintain continuity. The original grammar is retained. All names, many places, and some circumstances have been changed to protect anonymity in all the interviews except the final one, that of Art and Paula Downing.

Glossary

AFS   Adult and Family Services—"welfare."

ASQ   Allowable sales quantity—set by Congress, the amount of timber a national forest or BLM district is expected to sell for harvest in a fiscal year. Previously the "allowable cut."

Binders (or chain binders)   A length of heavy chain with special cinches on each end, used to secure a load of logs on a truck.

BLM   Bureau of Land Management, under the Department of the Interior.

Bucker   Person who limbs fallen trees, then cuts the logs to the right length to haul on a truck. Works closely with the faller.

Camp White   A World War II training camp near Medford, Oregon.

Cat   A bulldozer used in logging operations. Short for Caterpillar, a brand name for one line of machinery, but used generically.

Catskinner   Someone who drives a "cat"—a bulldozer that "skids" (drags) logs out of the woods to the landing site where the logs are loaded onto trucks.

CETA   Comprehensive Employment and Training Act—a federal training and job-subsidy program of the 1970s.

Chip truck   Truck hauling an oversized hopper-trailer for transporting woodchips, which are used primarily in the manufacture of paper.

Choker   A heavy steel cable looped around felled logs so that they can be dragged out of the woods.

Choker setters   Workers who loop heavy steel cable around felled logs, preparing them to be dragged to the landing.

Claim   A parcel of public land, usually twenty acres, which is "staked" according to the Mining Law of 1872. The miner then has the right to use the land and resources upon it for the extraction of minerals. As of 1993, $100 must be paid annually to keep the claim current.

Clearcut   A method of logging in which virtually all trees and brush are cut from a harvest site, leaving it "clear."

Crummie   A vehicle that transports woods-workers to the forest worksite. Usually a bus or a modified truck with a passenger compartment where the truckbed would normally be mounted.

DEQ Oregon's Department of Environmental Quality.

EarthFirst! A very loosely organized national protest organization that usually advocates "preservationist" options—that is, no harvest or absolutely minimal harvest—on federal lands. In the Northwest, it is especially concerned with the protection of old-growth and late-successional forests.

Felling (or falling) Cutting down a tree.

FLPMA Federal Land Policy Management Act of 1976 (applies to BLM).

FSA Family Service Act—a welfare-reform program that allows welfare recipients to enter post-secondary training programs.

GED General Equivalency Diploma—a certificate pursued by many adults who did not graduate from high school.

Greenchain The area of a lumber mill where raw slabs of wood just cut from logs are sorted. Greenchain workers have one of the heaviest jobs in the mill.

Grubstake Food supplies that a miner buys in bulk to take to a mining claim in the backwoods country—usually enough for several months.

Gyppo logger A small independent logging or log truck outfit. Also the person who owns or works for such an outfit.

Hazel hoe A very wide-bladed hoe used as a hand fire-fighting tool.

Headwaters The most prominent and regionally focused public lands environmental group in the Rogue Valley. P.O. Box 729, Ashland OR 97520.

Highball operation Speeded-up operation.

High-lead logging Method of logging that uses a "spar"—a high pole, once a de-limbed tree, now a mobile unit made of steel—through which cable is suspended through pulleys to drag logs from the woods to the landing.

Hodges High school hangout for forty years in Grants Pass—a local landmark.

Hyster Forklift—from the name of the company that manufactures them.

Landing Wide place in the road where equipment is centralized and to which logs are hauled out of the woods to be sorted and loaded onto log trucks.

Landing chaser Worker who releases logs at the landing from the steel cable (choker) set around them.

LCDC Land Conservation and Development Commission—the governmental body that oversees Oregon's statewide land-use planning system.

Lookout Fire lookout station on a tall mountain in a tower (a "lookout") with windows on four sides. Lookouts are occupied continuously during the approximately five-month fire season.

NCAP Northwest Citizens Against Pesticides—an environmental group. Organized in 1977 and still active in 1994. P.O. Box 1393, Eugene OR 97440.

NEPA National Environmental Policy Act of 1969.

NFMA National Forest Management Act of 1976.

NRDC Natural Resources Defense Council.

O & C Segment of lands under the jurisdiction of the Bureau of Land Management. "O & C" stands for "Oregon and California Railroad," which had to return lands to the government when it reneged on the original land-grant agreement.

Preservationist Someone who advocates a no-harvest or a minimal-harvest policy on federal forest lands. Especially applied to those who oppose harvest of old-growth or late-successional forests.

Pulaskie Fire-fighting hand tool with a double-sided head: an adze on one side and an axe on the other.

RCC Rogue Community College, in Grants Pass, Oregon.

Select-cut Selective cutting of trees at a harvest site, leaving many standing (as opposed to a clearcut). Various methods of select-cutting are utilized, and considerable controversy exists over which ones are ecologically sound.

Shelterwood cutting Cutting method in which a partial harvest leaves many trees standing, followed by a second cut of the remaining tall trees several years later after young trees have begun to establish themselves.

Skidder Person in charge of the machinery to haul ("skid") logs out of the woods.

Skidroad Makeshift road left by a "cat" skidding logs out of the woods.

Slash Wood and brush left over in the forest after logs are trimmed and hauled out. Also, during the era of open burning and tepee burners, the scrap and sawdust at a lumber mill (now obsolete).

Sluice Slurry of water, sand, rock, and debris run over or through a course with low impediments that catch the heavier gold and heavy-metal sands.

SOC Southern Oregon College, the old name for Southern Oregon State College (SOSC). Many local residents still refer to SOSC as "SOC," pronounced "sock."

SOCATS Southern Oregon Citizens Against Toxic Sprays, founded in 1977 and surviving until a gradual decline in activity in the mid-1980s.

Socs A high school clique; slang for "sociables."

SOSC Southern Oregon State College, Ashland, Oregon.

State of Jefferson Mythical state proposed by a short-lived secession movement of the early twentieth century, generally described as stretching from the mountainous areas just south of Eugene, Oregon, to the mountains of far-northern California above Redding.

Tepee burners (also Wigwam burners) Conical incinerators about forty feet high, with a door to the open air and no pollution controls, in which sawdust, scrap, and bark were burned (now obsolete).

UGB Urban growth boundary. Area surrounding incorporated cities that is reserved for future urban expansion. Areas outside the UGB are mandated to remain rural.

Veneer (or veneer skins) Thin sheets of wood peeled from logs and used to make plywood. Plywood veneer is usually about one-eighth of an inch thick.

Watermaster The official in each Oregon county responsible for overseeing the rights to and use of surface water in the county. All surface water is owned and controlled by the state; individual users own "water rights," which are administered by the Watermaster.

Widow-maker Large unattached branch hung up in a tree. Widow-makers are frequently obscured from ground view and may fall unexpectedly. They are responsible for many deaths on logging sites.

Wigwam burners See **Tepee burners.**

Yarder A stationary machine that uses cables to haul logs out of the woods to the landing. Also the person who operates the yarder.

In
timber
country

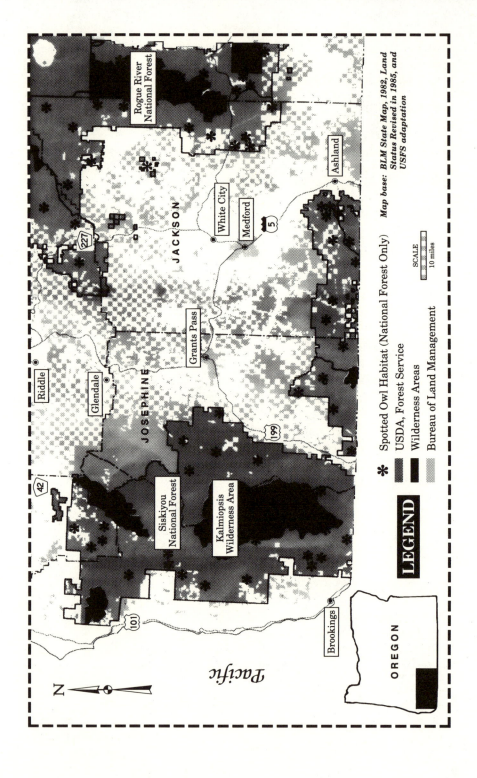

LEGEND

* Spotted Owl Habitat (National Forest Only)
USDA, Forest Service
Wilderness Areas
Bureau of Land Management

Map base: BLM State Map, 1982, Land Status Revised in 1985, and USFS adaptation

SCALE
10 miles

Rogue River National Forest

JACKSON

White City

Medford

Ashland

5

Grants Pass

227

JOSEPHINE

Riddle

Glendale

199

42

Siskiyou National Forest

Kalmiopsis Wilderness Area

101

Brookings

Pacific

N

OREGON

In-migrations, timber, and owls: background to a transformation

The struggle over land, culture, and the economy in the Rogue Valley of southwest Oregon reached its late twentieth-century peak with the convergence of four streams of events. The environmental movement found a popular cause in preserving the natural mixed-species forest cover of the Klamath and southern Cascade mountains. The Land Conservation and Development Corporation (LCDC), created by the Oregon Legislature in 1973, formulated a set of statewide zoning goals to which all local planning decisions — rural as well as urban — must conform. Urban tensions and the opportunity to cash in on inflated real estate values in California and Seattle initiated a migration of relatively well-off suburbanites to rural Oregon. Finally, national economic fluctuations affecting the timber industry undercut the traditional economic foundation of the region, and worsened the effects of a national recession.

These events affected the lives of all Rogue Valley residents, and their combined impact changed the cultural as well as the economic base of the Rogue Valley community.

THE CRISIS DEVELOPS

The Rogue Valley Region: a sketch The Rogue Valley region encompasses Jackson and Josephine counties, which sit side by side on the California border in southwest Oregon, occupying an area of 4,416 square miles, almost the size of Connecticut. The combined 1990 population for the two counties was 209,000: 62,649 in primarily rural Josephine County, and 146,389 in somewhat more developed Jackson County.

Southwest Oregon is a rugged, heavily timbered, mountain area, stretching from the Klamath Mountains on the west to the volcanic Cascade Mountains and the high desert beyond on the east. Most of the

3

terrain is mountainous; the slopes are covered with pines, Douglas firs, and cedar. At lower elevations, oak trees, madrone, and manzanita mix with conifers. Fire, an integral part of the ecosystem, usually breaks out during the hot, arid summers. The relatively mild winter climate in the valley floors (elevation 500–1,000 feet) is contrasted with heavy snow-packs above 4,000 feet. Mount McLoughlin, the local volcanic peak in the Cascade Range, reaches over 9,000 feet.

In the early nineteenth century, explorers from Spanish-controlled Mexico were among the first non-Native groups to move through the dense mountains; large parties of northern European-Americans arrived soon after (Gamboa, 1991). The original Natives, the Takelma Indians, were a small nation of approximately six hundred members, with a reputation among European-Americans of fighting fiercely in defense of their territory. Following battles between settlers and Natives in the 1850s, Takelmas who had not died of disease or been killed were relocated to the cold, wet, central Oregon coast, where few survived (Beckham, 1971).

Accounts of the population in the Josephine County in the mid-1860s vary, but they indicate that a quarter of the settlers were Chinese men who arrived to take part in the local gold rush (cf. Hill, 1976; Johnson, 1978). Whites harassed the Chinese, prohibited them from owning claims or other property, and finally ran them out of the region during the early 1880s, the era in which the Federal Chinese Exclusion Law of 1883 was passed. Some Hawaiian (Kanaka), Mexican, and Mexican American men also sought out the gold fields; several Jewish families set up mining operations and shops despite general anti-Semitism (Lowenstein, 1987).[1] In 1859 the State of Oregon legally prohibited Black immigration, although a few brave souls came anyway (McLogan, 1980). Gradually, settlements enlarged, increasing numbers of European-American families in-migrated, the percentage of women grew, and the miners moved on to Canada and Alaska. Gold mining diminished in importance, but never disappeared. Claims are still staked up canyons and along the rivers.

A farming economy anchored the valley for several decades after the gold rush. Pear orchards attained economic importance in the early 1900s and grew to a multi-million-dollar industry with a national market. Orchards and several fruit-related mail-order businesses hire thousands of seasonal workers to the present day.

---

1. See especially Lowenstein, 1987, pp. 32–34, regarding the late nineteenth-century Jewish commune of New Odessa in southwest Oregon.

The introduction of the one-person chainsaw and more efficient ways of getting logs out of the woods changed the nature of logging, just when the housing boom of the late 1940s and 1950s was feeding the demand for wood products. Extensive acreages of private industrial forest land were cut. As coal declined in Appalachia in the early fifties, many southerners migrated to southwest Oregon to heft a chainsaw or work on the line in a lumber mill. People from the border states and Oklahoma, who stopped off in Los Angeles during World War II, came north to settle in an area reminiscent of home. Highway construction cut new routes, and many road workers settled down when the roads were completed. Regional jobs with the Bureau of Land Management (BLM) and the Forest Service proliferated, gradually transforming the agencies' role from low-key caretaking to overseeing "multiple-use" forestry, including expanded recreation and the aggressive management of the forests for commercial timber sales as the volume of prime timber on private lands declined.

The roots of a local environmental movement As the energy of the Civil Rights and antiwar movements of the 1960s dissipated, concern for the environment grew in various segments of the protest generation. One idealistic set of European-American activists dispersed to rural communes in an effort to "live lightly" on the planet. The Rogue Valley hosted one of the largest concentrations of back-to-the-land migrants in the United States.

These "counter-culture" in-migrants arrived in an area that prided itself on its hard-working, hard-fighting, blue-collar, timber, mining, and farming identity. Land was cheap enough for local working people to acquire homesites that were widely dispersed throughout the forested area. Local people could balance their own interests with a boom and bust timber and mining economy by depending upon the mountains, rivers, and gardens — or stubbornness and simple living — to get by during the hard times. Few people were wealthy, but few were destitute.

Cheap land suited both locals and the long-haired newcomers, but cultural and political clashes over everything from the Vietnam war to public nudity and drugs kept tension high in the early years. The counter-culture communes lived apart from the established community. They started their own network of food cooperatives and seasonal tree-planting cooperatives, and many, but not all, participated in a marijuana-based economy. Even though many "hippies" worked hard toward their own goals on the land, food-stamp fraud, white-collar petty theft, and other

"scams" were common, as were checks from urban parents. With reduced need for direct employment and a knack for stretching low incomes, they attempted to create a marginal, but comfortable, lifestyle.

Counter-culture groups bought land in the mountainous regions
originally settled by miners and loggers — areas with poor soils and, usually, cut-over land. Although some of these parcels shelter pockets of
farmland, larger farms with productive soils had been settled early and
kept in commercial agriculture for generations (Casebeer interview,
1993; Owens-Stevenson interview, 1993).

Consequently, the counter-culture communities found themselves
near the areas that were "interfaced" with the public lands, either on the
edge of Forest Service land or interspersed within a "checkerboard" pattern of mile-square private and BLM lands, including many tracts of
industrial forests owned by timber companies. Some of the newcomers
bought out old placer gold claims and, using a broad interpretation of
the 1872 mining law, set up their homesteads within the public lands.[2]

The proximity of counter-culture homesites to forests clearcut by the
timber industry led the new settlers to challenge the wisdom of federal
forest policy, thus initiating a local environmentalist movement. Because
local environmentalist actions arose among the back-to-the-landers and
grew inside the back-to-the-land networks of the Pacific Northwest, with
only minimal attention to the concerns of the established local popula-
tions, the stage was set early for confrontation. At that time, however,
environmentalism presented no threat to the basic well-being of the
greater community, nor to the overall character of the region.

Land-use planning for the nation's public forests Forest ownership in southwest Oregon is a complex matter. The Rogue Valley region
contains two national forests. The Siskiyou National Forest lies mostly
to the west in the Klamath Mountains. It includes the Kalmiopsis Wilderness area and a roadless area referred to as the North Kalmiopsis. The

---

2. That 1872 mining law allows miners to stake claims on public lands and to live on
the claim as long as they are producing enough mineral to support a "prudent man."
Various individuals, including many counter-culture families, have set up households on
Forest Service and BLM land, where they are in a perpetual stand-off with public lands
officials. If they can prove that they are mining at a level to sustain the "prudent man" test,
they may apply for a "patent" on the claim, and the federal government must sell them
the property for $2.50 to $5.00 an acre. This law applies equally to the corporate mining
company and to the miner with a single twenty-acre claim. The law was partially revised:
$100 worth of work a year maintained the right to the claim until 1993, when an annual
cash fee of $100 was required instead.

Rogue River National Forest lies to the south and east, extending into the Cascade Mountains. The Forest Service, an agency of the U.S. Department of Agriculture, has authority over all national forests.

The area controlled by the BLM lies between the two national forests. The checkerboard pattern of BLM land is the legacy of the Oregon and California Railroad company land grant, which the federal government reclaimed when the Oregon and California promoters reneged on the terms of the agreement. These lands, which constitute the majority of high-production timber lands administered by the BLM nationwide, are alternately referred to as the O&C lands or, locally, as BLM lands. The U.S. Department of the Interior oversees the BLM.

Jackson County is 52 percent publicly owned land; Josephine County is 72 percent public. Through the 1940s, the Forest Service's role on public lands had been "essentially custodial" (Culhane, 1981, p. 50). Only after World War II did an expanding housing market create pressure to harvest the public trees, just when the use of national forests for recreation was increasing. Mining, grazing, watershed, and other users competed for their share, but in the Rogue Valley region, timber became king.

The Multiple Use Sustained Yield Act of 1960 attempted to balance competing interests in public land. Four years later, in 1964, Congress created a 76,000-acre Kalmiopsis Wilderness area in the Siskiyou National Forest. The 1968 Wild and Scenic River Act designated the lower Rogue River, flowing out of the high Cascades to the sea, as a Wild and Scenic watercoursse. The National Environmental Protection Act (NEPA) followed on its heels in 1969. NEPA instituted legal mechanisms to challenge federal or federally funded projects that might damage the environment. The intentions of the Multiple Use Sustained Yield Act, along with NEPA, provided the opening for counter-culture activists to challenge timber harvest practices in southwest Oregon.

NEPA requires the filing of an environmental assessment on any federal project with the potential to cause environmental disruption. If the assessment finds significant impact, the agency involved must write an environmental impact statement (EIS) detailing the likely environmental effects of the proposed activity. An EIS may be challenged on an administrative level, or, when that route is exhausted, may be challenged in court by any party that has established "standing" (Wondolleck, 1988).

Counter-culture land, as noted above, was likely to abut BLM land. Challenges to forest practices began with the BLM land and, for the most part, stayed preoccupied with BLM issues for more than a decade.

The local environmental group Headwaters began as an effort to force the BLM to comply with its own sustained yield goals.[3] Headwaters' suit involved NEPA provisions. After reaching the U.S. District Court in the District of Columbia, *Natural Resources Defense Council* [NRDC] *v. Kleppe* (1975) was settled out of court when the BLM agreed to write ten-year plans and comply with all NEPA requirements, including detailed EISs, which would be open to subsequent public challenge.[4] This set a national precedent for all BLM forest lands.

Meanwhile, in the Bitterroot National Forest in Montana and the Monongahela National Forest in West Virginia, environmentalists fought clearcutting on Forest Service land. Successes in the courts led to the National Forest Management Act of 1976, directed at the Forest Service (the Federal Land Policy and Management Act of 1976 filled much the same purpose for the BLM). National forests were to assemble land-use plans with a fifty-year vision and a ten- to fifteen-year design (Wondolleck, 1988). The plans, in the opinion of many professional foresters, elevated flexible multiple-use goals to inflexible legal obligations (Behan, 1990). Plans were fully subject to NEPA criteria, including the filing of detailed and voluminous EISs, and all the "ten-year plans" would be subject to challenge by individuals or organizations. Julia Wondolleck points out that the shift of paradigms in the Forest Service from "scientific land-management" to "political resource-allocation" (subject to challenge and dependent on the courts and Congress) meant that "no decision can be proven to be the correct one" — leading, inevitably, to a gridlock of competing interests in suits and counter-suits (Wondolleck, 1988, pp. 120, 70–71).

It is important to note that private industrial forest land accounts for vast acreages in the Pacific Northwest, including millions of the most productive acres. The regulations on private lands are very different from those on public lands: For instance, clearcuts are limited to 40 acres on BLM land and 60 acres on Forest Service land but can be as large as 120 acres on private land. With narrow buffers, this sometimes results in clearcuts of hundreds of acres.

Other events were evolving as these changes in federal land policy developed. Each had its own trajectory, but the effects combined with

---

3. See the interview with Paula and Art Downing, p. 261.

4. A second case from 1975, *Downing v. Frizzel* (U.S. District Court, Oregon, 75-1128) was never resolved but the content and merits of the case forced a change in BLM's sustained yield plans. Kent Frizzel was Temporary Acting Secretary of the Interior in 1975 and Undersecretary of the Interior in 1975. Art Downing was a Rogue Valley environmentalist (see n.3). Thomas S. Kleppe was Secretary of the Interior from 1975 to 1977.

far-reaching consequences in the late 1980s. In the next sections, I discuss Oregon's unique land-use planning laws, the exodus of urban-dwellers from the problems of the cities, the collision of land-use controls and urban flight, and the restructuring of the regional and national economies as discrete elements of change. I then outline how these events, compounded by an environmental crisis over the spotted owl and timber management, transformed the Rogue Valley.

Oregon's quiet revolution: comprehensive land-use planning on private lands By 1976 legally codified land-use planning was institutionalized on public lands by NEPA, the National Forest Management Act (NFMA), the Federal Land Policy Management Act (FLPMA), and the resolution of the Medford District BLM case. In 1973, the House of Representatives killed a National Land Use bill, halting a four-year effort to require states to implement land-use planning of private lands as well. Senator Henry ("Scoop") Jackson of Washington, then chair of the Interior Committee — whose staff was in large part responsible for the wording of NEPA — believed that a multiple-use approach implemented by scientific land-use planning in the private sector would rationalize the growth of industrial, residential, recreational, and other private land uses. The movement toward national land-use planning was influenced both by a belief in science-based management and by the Keiser, Kerner, and Douglas reports, commissioned by the government after Civil Rights movement protests, which concluded that the abuse of zoning and land use regulations was in great part responsible for increased segregation nationwide (Plotkin, 1987). The federal bill was watered down by the time it was killed in the House, but that same year the State of Oregon set a national precedent with the passage of Senate Bill 100, establishing comprehensive land-use planning for all land in the state.

Senate Bill 100 authorized the Land Conservation and Development Commission (LCDC) to establish statewide goals, regulations, inventories, and guidelines, and "review all local comprehensive plans and implementing ordinances for conformance with statewide goals" (University of Oregon, 1984, p. 1–15). A watchdog group, 1000 Friends of Oregon, organized with the support of Governor Tom McCall to advocate for the new bill in the courts and ensure that it would not be watered down or eaten away (Oliver, 1992).

The director of 1000 Friends of Oregon wrote in 1975, "Oregon's land use planning program can help harmonize environmental and economic interests" (Richmond, 1975, p. 1). Henry R. Richmond III, in

1976, further clarified the group's goals: "While agricultural land preservation and coastal planning issues are the most talked-about features of LCDC's program, the urban growth boundary requirement is really more important. . . . Generally speaking, only rural uses are permitted *outside* the [urban growth] boundary. . . . Working cooperatively with counties, cities are to include sufficient land resources *inside* the boundary to accommodate growth needs over the next 15–20 years" (Richmond, 1976, p. 1). In other words, new residential development would be confined within *incorporated* towns and the legally defined urban growth boundary (UGB) surrounding them. Exceptions would be made for rural lands already developed or parceled, for one single-family dwelling on land zoned "exclusive farm or forest" (usually twenty acres or more), and a small amount of rural residential land near already-developed areas. These restraints, by design, benefited commercial farms in high-production areas[5] and commercial timber producers (Salazar and Cubbage, 1990). LCDC has been challenged at the polls three times, but each time the urban corridor in the Willamette Valley, including the Portland metropolitan area, where the majority of Oregonians live, voted overwhelmingly to keep LCDC intact, overriding the majority "no" votes of rural Oregon.

In the critical area of low- and moderate-income urban housing, of which LCDC requires consideration by city planners, state planning has contributed to lower-cost options. The Home Builders Association of Metropolitan Portland and 1000 Friends conducted a study in 1991 which "found that housing was more affordable in Portland than in other major West Coast cities" (Oliver, 1992, p. 11). Rural zoning requirements do not provide for low- and moderate-income housing,[6] even though the majority of working people in the Rogue Valley are accustomed to living outside the city. In southwest Oregon, which has high poverty rates but also fast-rising real estate values, the relatively small areas within city limits and UGBs must find room for affordable housing for a local working population under increasing economic stress.

Not long after the creation of LCDC, the rural land market in southwest Oregon was shoved upward by an influx of suburban transplants who arrived in the mid- to late 1970s. As they competed among themselves for scenic forest, riverside, or secluded rural homesites, blue-

5. The conservative Farm Bureau was a prominent participant in defining land use regulations for farm zoning (Lang interview, 1993).

6. In fact, 1000 Friends of Oregon successfully sued Curry County to prevent even modestly higher density housing in unincorporated hamlets (Lang interview, 1993).

and pink-collar working people were edged out of the real estate market. Since the parcelization of rural land had slowed to a trickle of zoning "exceptions" since 1980, prices on land jumped far above values reflected by strictly forestry or farm usages. Zoning restrictions on new dwellings were tightened: A professional planner who prefers to remain anonymous told me that some Jackson County residents owning exclusive farm or forest parcels too small for use as farm or ranch land were prevented from building a house (interview, 1993).

Rural areas like the Rogue Valley include substantial acreages of economically marginal farm and forest lands unlikely ever to be managed in any commercial sense (but having, nonetheless, their own important ecosystems). On these lands, zoning laws have contributed to a proliferation of ten- to twenty-acre and larger "ranchettes" as well as extensive forested parcels (owned by individuals who employ sustainable forestry methods, as well as those who cut up the land and then re-sell it). An increasing number of large forested properties are being managed as, essentially, personal parks. Oregon provides tax breaks for large or small parcels under agricultural use or forests managed for long-term timber production; sophisticated land purchasers, buying primarily for residential uses but keen on tax shelters, could easily figure how to meet the minimum requirements. But strict building codes eliminated the old practice of saving up to buy land and then building a not-quite-to-code house over a long period of time.[7] Codes and zoning favored the upper-income citizen.

LCDC's support from urban Oregon, primarily the Portland region, is seen as reflecting a rural–urban split within the state. But the LCDC's most fundamental farm and forest goals have been met, and are supported by the rural and urban population alike, because they have protected high-production commercial agricultural and forestry land. The laws preserved open space and inhibited toxic industries and fly-by-night subdivisions from covertly bilking rural communities. Conservative groups balk at regulations of any kind as a "taking" of private property rights. However, it is the *unintended* consequences of LCDC requirements — such as the lack of provision for low- and moderate-income housing in rural areas — which have gradually "taken" lower-income people out of the countryside and contributed to growing social divisions in Jackson and Josephine counties. In southwest Oregon, the split cannot be characterized as urban Oregon versus the rest of the state (people

---

7. Fitchen (1992) discusses this phenomenon in rural New York in detail.

rarely migrate from Oregon cities to the state's southwest counties); here, support for LCDC comes from the many middle- and upper-income out-of-state in-migrants who have enjoyed the income-exclusionary benefits of Oregon's rural land-use planning.

Equity migrants and other "ex-urban" in-migrants Between 1985 and 1990, more than four hundred thousand people moved to Oregon, or more than 15 percent of the 1990 population. Of the 2.8 million residents of the state in 1990, only 49 percent were born in Oregon (*Grants Pass Daily Courier*, 1992). Californians make up one-third of the very recent in-migrants in the state as a whole (Frohnmayer, 1993), but in the southwest corner of the state, the percentage of California in-migrants is much higher.

In the Rogue Valley region, net growth did not match the extraordinary gains of the 1970s: Jackson County grew by over 40 percent from 1970 to 1980, but a mere 10.5 percent from 1980 to 1990. Josephine County had a growth rate, however, of 64.6 percent in the 1970s and 6.4 percent through the 1980s (Southern Oregon Regional Services, 1992). The lower growth rate does not represent a slow-down in in-migration so much as an increase in out-migration. Between 1985 and 1990, 15,675 people moved to Josephine County (*Grants Pass Daily Courier*, 1992), but the net increase in population was less than 4,000 (U.S. Census, 1992). That is, almost 12,000 people left the county. (In the high out-migration years of the 1981–83 recession, the county experienced a net loss of population.) Given Josephine County's total 1990 population of 62,649, the 1985–90 out-migration represents 19 percent of the current population, while very recent newcomers represent 25 percent. Most of the out-migrants were working-age adults.

In 1992, 28.6 percent of Josephine County residents over fourteen years of age were at or below 125 percent of the poverty rate; the figure in Jackson County was 19.0 percent (State of Oregon, 1992). Josephine County remained at the bottom of Oregon's thirty-six counties in per capita income (65 percent of national per capita income); Jackson County ranked between twentieth and twenty-eighth in the state (80 percent of national per capita income) (Anderson, 1992). The higher-income in-migrants have not counterbalanced a statistical rise in poverty, in part because some newly arrived retirees have low transfer-payment incomes (Anderson, 1993), whatever their financial or income-property assets may be, but also because of a net increase in poverty among working people.

Land inflation was driven by Californians who purchased homes sufficiently expensive to shelter capital gains from the sale of high-priced homes in California. Many then lived on (or subsidized their income with) the remaining capital gains — hence the label "equity migrants." Many of those who were not retirees were leaving technical and managerial jobs behind for an uncertain job future in a high-unemployment area (Adams, Badger, & Todaro, 1989). Newcomers were willing to take jobs below their level of skill and accustomed pay, and, thus out-competed the less educated, less experienced local job-seekers in high- and middle-range jobs. Mary Raymond of the RCC Employment & Career Center observed that middle-class newcomers often applied for very low wage jobs as an interim strategy (personal communication, 1992).

The migrations beginning in the mid- to late seventies brought people of middle and later years, accustomed to a comfortable income from skilled or professional work. They were settled in their ways and had few children of school age. By the late 1980s, in-migrants represented a sufficiently large group in southwest Oregon that, as Victoria Sturtevant, professor of sociology at Southern Oregon State College, remarked in a 1993 interview, "They've established who they are, they don't need to be accepted, . . . [and they] don't have to assimilate to get what they want." Margaret Shannon (1991) comments that these new migrants are involved disproportionately in local politics, where they tend to take high-profile roles.[8]

Equity migrations to southwest Oregon followed the peaks of real estate booms in California. In 1975–79, the time of the Proposition 13 property tax revolt, the value of modest homes in suburban California doubled; that of expensive homes quadrupled. Southern California homeowners averaged 30 to 40 percent earnings on equity per annum — three times the rate of income growth (Davis, 1991; also see Chapman, 1981). The second peak of real estate prices in California, coinciding with the 1987 slow-growth movement in the Los Angeles–San Diego megalopolis, was reflected in the late-1980s migration to southwest Oregon.

Land-use planning and urban flight: a collision course Zoning in the United States was originally intended to preserve neighborhoods of single-family dwellings and to physically separate those neighborhoods from early twentieth-century factories and the tenements that surrounded industrialized areas. As racial segregation became illegal in mid-century, deed covenants that excluded non-whites were replaced in

---

8. Shannon (1991) discusses this as a characteristic of ex-urban in-migrants to forest regions in general.

many white neighborhoods — especially upper-income neighborhoods — with zoning laws intended to exclude racial diversity as well as lower- or moderate-income or multi-family housing (Davis, 1991; Nelson, 1977; Plotkin, 1987). The malleable "pro-environmental" language of the sixties was appropriated by suburbanites who sincerely believed in preserving the environment, but were also protecting their neighborhoods from undesired development. A prominent politician in southern California argued, for example, "The middle- and upper-middle-class people who live in coastal neighborhoods feel settled, and are deeply concerned about preserving and improving the environment around them" (Davis, 1991, p. 178). Meanwhile, lower-income citizens, of any race, were restricted to crowded sectors of the cities by suburban housing costs and prohibitions on multi-family and high-density dwellings (Davis, 1991; Plotkin, 1987).

Although southwest Oregon still attracts idealists with an interest in social justice, the new migrants are, for the most part, white people from well-off out-of-state suburbs, equipped with a social and environmental concern that Oregon not become "like California." This universal statement requires some translation. Many people moved to escape pollution and congestion, but the growth of poverty and racial tensions (and their attendant problems) were for many also a strong incentive to move: Ex-urbanites sought places where they would not be required to experience social divisions face to face. The Rogue Valley's "sundown" laws (laws or traditions requiring African Americans to be out of town by sunset) were not rescinded until the 1960s and 1970s; and its tradition of racism remains strong, making the area attractive to white-flight suburbanites bringing their problems north.[9] Another, smaller but growing migration of Latino/Hispanic peoples has also come to the Rogue Valley. Persons of color are received with apprehension by many new white migrants. Recent in-migrants arrived in a state already prepared for a defense of zoning rights, including the defense of income- and racially exclusionary rural zoning made possible by regulations originally intended for environmental and open space protection of farm and forest land.

In their new civic roles, in-migrants separated according to their political proclivities. The more liberal ones provided the second wind for the public lands environmental movement. The conservatives, especially

9. Although no studies have yet documented the extent of this phenomenon, it appears in everyday collisions with in-migrant attitudes on the streets and on the editorial page alike. Employees in service jobs and activists report frequent encounters with overt racism among new arrivals in the community ("almost mandatory," a waitress working in a fraternal club told me), aggravating a history of racism in the region (personal communications; also KenCairn interview, 1993).

the more politically conscious migrants of the late 1980s, brought their tax-revolt and socially exclusionary ideologies with them, rending the politics of the valley. (The state's bitterly divisive anti-gay/lesbian rights initiatives of 1988 and 1992–94 were spearheaded by migrants from southern California.) But when it came to protecting the environment and property values of their *own* neighborhoods, the middle- and upper-middle-class base of both groups defended environmental restrictions on public property. This held true even when the more conservative members ideologically opposed the broader principle of land-use planning as a "taking" of property rights (Sturtevant, 1991).[10]

Because of statewide requirements, few uses other than single-family dwellings are allowed on these relatively restricted private parcels outside the UGBs. Small businesses, with the exception of severely restricted "home businesses," are excluded. Even temporary mobile homes set up to accommodate family members in need are prohibited unless two doctors verify that the occupant is medically unable to care for himself or herself. New mobile home parks are prohibited outside UGBs. New multi-family dwellings or densities higher than one dwelling per acre are not allowed (and areas with one-acre allowances are relatively rare: The goal in rural areas is parcels of 20, 40, 80 acres or more,[11] — both to promote commercial-size parcels and to enhance environmental values.

Although citizens' challenges to land-use changes generally do not rest on strictly environmental reasons (as they can on public lands), professional Rogue Valley planners report that a wish to preserve the environment is frequently invoked (personal communications, 1993). Opportunities to challenge specific land-use decisions are numerous in Oregon, because the appeals process for private land-use decisions is intricate and prolonged, much like the intricate ladder of appeals, counter-appeals, and lawsuits involved in the struggle (and gridlock) over public lands.

Neighbors, who frequently initiate challenges in Oregon's complaint-based system, are less likely to object to the "taking" of their *neighbor's* property rights when adjacent uses conflict with their own property or ideological values. When challenging zoning decisions, dust control, traffic, "visual pollution," open space, waterflow, and quality-of-life issues are commonly cited, along with forest and wildlife habitat concerns. As

---

10. Sturtevant found that ideologically conservative respondents supported more logging in forests "where people don't live," such as tracts adjacent to wilderness areas (personal communication, 1993).

11. Fitchen (1991, esp. pp.189–96) discusses the similar impact of related land-use planning regulations in upstate New York, especially the zoning out of affordable mobile homes.

Frederick Buttel points out, "The definition of particular conflicts or issues as being environmental ones is, in part, a social construction. A good example in this regard is (typically suburban) no-growth or growth control policies, which are rooted as much or more in defense of property values than in environmental concerns per se" (1992, p. 14). During a campaign against a rock-crushing operation in an increasingly middle-class rural neighborhood long zoned for gravel processing, alarm over a potential drop in property values became, in public, a concern for wildlife habitat and water. Several key individuals said the problem could be solved by moving the operation to a nearby hamlet, where, not coincidentally, poor people live (personal communication, 1993).

These kinds of objections to changes in private land uses have usually been raised piecemeal or at the neighborhood-association level: Public lands environmental organizations in the Rogue Valley have not formally entered the private lands debates. However, numerous "watershed groups" protesting against operations on the public lands in their backyards share the protective sentiment of neighborhood associations protesting against private usages. These watershed groups are strongly allied with public lands environmental organizations.

Thus, although many long-time residents were privately concerned about the mismanagement of public forests and the potential loss of the area's rural character, many came to distrust environmentalists as a group. The sentiments driving public land and private land environmental issues are perceived as similar, both being identified with the desire of economically secure newcomers to protect their own parochial interests. Although the public lands environmental organizations are rarely involved in LCDC actions, the core group of activists (who are, with rare exceptions, people who grew up outside the region) have not opposed the philosophical stance of LCDC and 1000 Friends. They have paid little attention to the concerns of long-term low- to moderate-income residents regarding either public or private land. They have shown only rhetorical concern for the distress of poor and working citizens caught up in the fundamental economic changes in the Rogue Valley. The public lands groups benefit from the broad support of the watershed groups and the non-activist environmental public, many of whom — whether actively or passively — support environmental and LCDC protection of their own rural neighborhoods. Here, though the zoning requirements were not originally *intended* to be exclusionary, they are very much so in practice. Increasingly homogeneous neighborhoods are created, concentrating higher-status socio-economic and cultural groups in a way that has not been typical of the rural Rogue Valley.

With the exception of a few controversies over extensive tracts of corporate-owned timber land in the Northwest, private land issues have never achieved the prominence of public lands debates, in part because their impact is not perceived to have the widespread immediacy of local mill layoffs, or the national economic significance of a drop in wholesale building materials and revenue-generating exports. As Henry Richmond of 1000 Friends of Oregon says of land-use planning: "It's like school board meetings. They're important but they're dull" (Oliver, 1992, p. 13). The level of political activism, or even voter registration, among rural working people who are directly affected is extremely low: They are unlikely to organize effectively to protest. The history of zoning battles since the turn of the century suggests a parallel: Then, well-off neighborhoods fought to be homogeneous and separate from industrial zones. Lower-income people, the third party with a stake in the outcome, had to make do with what was left. In the 1980s in the Rogue Valley, the polarized battle between industry and environmentalists (often understood as counter-culture or ex-urban people with higher social status) left poor and working people to cope with the fallout by themselves. Although this is sometimes discussed in terms of the loss of a romanticized ideal of "rural values," the crucial difference is to be found, not in nostalgia, but in a very real drop in status, income, and future possibilities for poor and working people.

As the impact of changes accumulated, chances to "get by" diminished: Low-income living strategies that were bearable, even pleasant, when buffered by a land-based informal economy were transformed when people were moved off the land and into the more rigid cash-only economy of the towns. As Mike Hibbard (1993) noted, just when lower-income people were being forced from a semi-informal economy into an entirely cash-dependent one, the national and regional economy pulled the rug out from under them.[12]

Rural gentrification in the Rogue Valley began within a twenty-minute radius of the towns and slowly spread to the outlying areas which today still contain significant poverty, an artifact in part of very low land prices twenty years before. The progressive exclusion of lower-income and blue- and pink-collar people from the land and their replacement with a much higher income group oblivious to, or with a stake in, restrictive zoning has raised no protest. Indeed, it appears that few groups even noticed the ongoing turnover in land demographics except for professional planners, a few county officials ("Yes, we know it's a big problem, but we can't do anything about it"), and poor or working people

---

12. Hibbard is an associate professor of Planning, Public Policy, and Management at the University of Oregon.

themselves. The economic disruptions hitting working people were magnified by the collision of in-migration, high land values, and restrictive zoning laws buttressed by environmental concerns. Still, the ill will generated by these trends might have been muted had it not been for a dramatic change in the economic base of the region, coupled with a restructuring of the national economy.

The economic realities: timber, recessions, national transitions A quieter stream of migrants entered the Rogue Valley alongside the counter-culture and middle-class urbanites fleeing the cities. Hundreds of Latino/Hispanic families settled in the greater Medford area each year, initially working in agriculture or service jobs or planting trees in the forests. They have met with varying levels of resistance and racial prejudice from the majority population.

Lower-income European-Americans arrived also, joining the majority of the local population who worked at blue- and pink-collar jobs. This migration attracted less attention, and the people apparently assimilated fairly easily. The interviews in this book, as well as the research of Janet Fitchen (1991) and Jonathan Kusel (1991), demonstrate that some of these people grew up in the region and returned as working-age adults dissatisfied with life elsewhere. Others sought a dream, or simply an escape: Fitchen has documented a movement of poor people, many on public assistance, who seek affordable housing and safer streets than they can find in cities. Local experience with welfare-reform programs indicates some migration from big cities to smaller towns in search of better living conditions, according to Mollie Owens-Stevenson (interview, 1993),[13] but affordable housing has proved to be a chimera in the Rogue Valley region since the late seventies. In 1989 Jackson County had the highest rents in Oregon outside the Portland metropolitan region (Rogue Valley Fair Share, 1989).[14]

Movement from an industrial to a more service-oriented economy throughout the United States was reflected locally in the decline of local timber and military-related employment, and a burgeoning of health-related, tourist, and other low-paid service jobs. The growing market for the area's orchard crops, especially pears, continued to provide jobs of long standing, though of varying quality.

13. Mollie Owens-Stevenson is Coordinator of Training Resources for Women at Rogue Community College, and master's degree candidate in history at Southern Oregon State College.

14. Dee Southard's research (1993) indicates that substantial numbers of homeless people move from site to site in the national forests, observing the fourteen-day camping limit, to have a cheap or free place to live.

The recession of 1981–82 undercut the new housing market and extinguished the demand for lumber and plywood—the two principal wood products manufactured in the Rogue Valley. Large wood products companies could shift their assets in and out of product lines—lumber, paper, pulp, chipboard, plywood—as well as move their operations thousands of miles within the United States or overseas. National and transnational wood products giants such as Weyerhaeuser, Boise Cascade, and Georgia Pacific began their movement from the northwest to the southeast United States in the late 1960s and 1970s (Clephane, 1978; Israel, 1980). Although overseas shipment of trees from public land is prohibited by law, a high proportion of logs from private industrial land owned by timber corporations was targeted for export: Statistically, one in four trees harvested in the Pacific Northwest was destined for a high-priced international market (Gregory, 1989b). Log exports aided the U.S. balance of payments with Japan, and exporters received tax incentives to continue raw log shipments abroad. The big firms automated and retooled their northwest plants. Mid-sized companies, like the majority of timber outfits in the southwest Oregon region, owned only modest parcels of timber, if any. They were dependent on trees from public lands (which cannot be exported), and their ability to automate and retool was limited.

As a consequence, the reorganization of the industry in the mid-eighties left fewer small to mid-sized companies. Automation alone accounted for a loss of 13,000 wood products jobs in Oregon between 1976 and 1986 (Gregory, 1990). In the Rogue Valley, several mills, and their accompanying timber base, were bought out by multinational companies whose main product lines were not necessarily timber-related. One of these companies devastated previously well-managed "tree farms" in order to acquire capital to satisfy debt, then closed down all but one of five mills. That company is now buying additional tracts of private old growth to supply a modernized plant. The smaller mills felt the effects of restricted credit, caused not only by national crises of debt and the savings and loan bailout (Gregory, 1990), but also by the increasingly restricted flow of logs from the national forests as a result of court injunctions and environmental regulations.

Regional development planners and government officials, realizing that timber was on the decline, sought out other options. Industrial parks near Grants Pass (in Josephine County) and Medford (Jackson County) attracted some manufacturing after intensive and expensive recruiting, but the cutthroat national competition among rural communities for business relocations put the Rogue Valley, nestled between looming mountain passes and remote from major markets, at a disadvantage.

Instead, business and development interests turned their attention to attracting upper-middle-income tourists, as a local development specialist told me (personal communication, 1993; see also Allen, 1987). Without a clear vision of an alternative, they organized with the help of the Oregon Economic Development Department (OEDD) to set the area on an upscale course. LCDC's statewide zoning, as it turns out, categorizes golf courses as "open space" (State of Oregon, 1993, p. 6) and "destination resorts" as one of the few uses permitted on certain kinds of forest lands (State of Oregon, 1993, p. 9).[15] Four major destination resorts were proposed for the two counties, one planner told me (personal communication, 1993), patterned in part on the wildly successful planned resort communities near Bend in central Oregon. As in all tourism development, however, the job structure is one in which entrepreneurs and some managers receive high wages, while the majority of service workers are at the low end of the scale and seasonally employed. The low-wage structure of the tourist industry is well documented (Ansell et al., 1992; Centaur Associates et al., 1981; Rodriguez, 1987; Smith, 1989). The Bend Chamber of Commerce and the City of Bend, in an analysis of Bend's tourist industry released in 1993, acknowledged that part-time or seasonal jobs accounted for 49 percent of the 3,275 jobs, and that the payroll was just $33 million. By contrast, the equivalent number of jobs in the wood products industry paid $74.7 million ("Tourism notable," 1993).

The income-exclusionary California suburbs from which many Oregon in-migrants came were hotbeds of support for the antitax measure Proposition 13. Oregon does not have a sales tax. Revenues are generated through a high state income tax and local property taxes, which, though relatively low in the Rogue Valley region compared with the rest of Oregon, are nowhere near the rock-bottom post–Proposition 13 rates experienced by many former residents of California.

The antitax campaigns of the late 1980s and early 1990s in the Rogue Valley, coupled with a statewide property tax limitation initiative passed by voters in 1991, froze or reduced property tax rates by establishing constitutional ceilings. Measure 5, conceived by Portland-area business owners and carried by Portland-area voters, lowered business property taxes proportionally more than homeowners' taxes. Farm and forest

15. A destination resort is "a self-contained development providing visitor-oriented accommodations and developed recreational facilities in a setting with high natural amenities." Unless on the coast, a destination resort requires a site of 160 or more acres. "Accommodations available for residential use shall not exceed two such units for each unit of overnight lodging" (State of Oregon, 1993, p. 9).

operations are shelters from some taxes, and large landowners, such as the timber companies, gained a windfall. But because Measure 5 demands that home taxes be assessed at true market value, residential tax rates in escalating real estate markets, like that of the Rogue Valley, still go up (Sadler, 1994).

Since the land base of Josephine and Jackson counties is mostly public land, both the BLM and the Forest Service contribute part of their timber revenues back to the counties in lieu of property taxes: 50 percent of receipts from BLM's O&C lands, and 25 percent of receipts from the Forest Service. The BLM funds are by far the most significant form of income to county governments in southwest Oregon, where O&C lands are concentrated ("Money from timber sales pays," 1992; Tollenaar et al., 1981; Weber, 1992). With a precipitous drop in harvests on BLM lands, both because of the spotted owl problems discussed below and because much of the prime timber has already been cut, O&C money plummeted and county budgets crumbled. School budgets, library services, law enforcement, health services, and recreational programs for youth and seniors all suffered. Voters from various political persuasions — both long-time residents and in-migrants — defeated increases in property taxes, some for ideological as well as economic reasons, others in a desperate effort to stop a personal economic free-fall.

As the new population arrived in the county, demanding high-end services, the willingness and ability to pay for them vanished. Blue- and pink-collar workers were caught in the crunch. High-wage jobs disappeared, replaced with a low-wage economy servicing an in-coming urban culture. The land-based informal economy of firewood and plant gathering, gardening, hunting, poaching, fishing, low-income home construction, and free leisure use of the woods was transformed, replaced by a gentrified landscape. Public support for schools and other public services, hobbled by an unwillingness to pay for them, discouraged better employers from either relocating or starting businesses in the area. Sensing a lack of effective legal oversight, however, heavily armed drug manufacturers did move into the area, turning southwest Oregon into a capital of methamphetamine production.

The members of 1000 Friends of Oregon opposed rural residential spread for economic reasons as well as environmental ones, arguing that communities cannot afford to subsidize services in rural areas. But subsidies already exist for school transportation, roads, fire service, and other infrastructure elements enjoyed by the higher-income rural residents and resource-based industries. Fitchen (personal communication, October 2, 1993) and Lois Levitan and Shelley Feldman (1991) observed that goods and services provided by the informal economy in rural areas, which enabled people to "get by" on their own, are now being provided out of the public till by social service and welfare agencies, often to people relocated to urban areas. As in developing countries, lower-income people are displaced from the land and find themselves in ever-growing cities. Better-off people enjoy the infrastructure and environmental amenities of the countryside. Subsidies still exist; they have merely shifted.

Southwest Oregon has a long history of contention over public lands, and a battle over private lands in rural residential areas has developed in recent years. In the gentrified countryside, citizens organize at a rural neighborhood or "watershed group" level, protesting against clearcuts, forest herbicides, and other issues. Local town-dwellers and ex-urban migrants to Ashland, Medford, and Grants Pass have neither income nor property interests in outlying rural areas and value the countryside for its aesthetic amenities. In contrast, a core of committed environmental activists has carried the struggle beyond the neighborhood and aesthetic level to address an overall ecological crisis, but still without addressing the fundamental economic or social dilemmas.

This book does not try to argue the merits of environmental protests, although I hope to make it clear that I believe most of these groups' efforts to challenge destructive forestry practices were shown to be justified by subsequent events and court decisions. This chapter should not be construed in any way as a defense of the more odious practices of parts of the timber industry. My purpose here is not to denounce broad concerns for the environment, nor to castigate LCDC, but to show that a cause structured by a mostly counter-culture and middle-class not-in-my-backyard ("NIMBY") movement (including, but not restricted to, groups with strong exclusionary underpinnings) and buttressed by an urban aesthetic of forest land ("not like California") cannot accommodate the core social justice concerns of the broader community. The paradigm is exclusionary at its core: Provisions for economic and social justice will always be tacked on as afterthoughts. A healthy environment will benefit everyone in the long run, and many better-off environmental supporters also support broader causes of justice. However, the local movement (as structured to date) does not realistically envision broad community well-being in its core agenda, nor has it attracted significant numbers of blue- and pink-collar allies who could enlarge its vision.

The interviews in this book do not always frame these issues in terms of the conspicuously competing interests discussed above. Yet this background of migration patterns, land values, and rural zoning regulations helps explain why poor and working people are angry at environmentalists and an environmental movement sustained by more affluent citizens. At the same time, the majority of poor and working people quietly support protection of the forest environment from clearcutting, overcutting, and other environmentally contested uses of public lands. We now turn to the history of the local environmental movement since 1976, and its face-off with changing social realities.

THE TRANSFORMATION OF A REGION

"Spray Wars" and beyond   As a result of the settlement of U.S. District Court cases brought by Headwaters and the Natural Resources Defense Council, the BLM agreed in 1976 to follow its own prescriptions of sustained yield. Instead of a permanent drop to a more sustainable cut at the rate of natural regeneration, the BLM used computer modeling to determine how much timber *theoretically* could be grown if herbicides, fertilizer, and genetically improved seedlings were utilized (Norman interview, 1993; SOCATS Staff, 1983).[16] The figures thus generated were used to justify escalated harvest levels. Both the BLM and the Forest Service were under pressure to keep the Congressionally assigned "allowable sales quantity" (ASQ) high. A booming housing market that extended from mid-1977 into the beginning of 1979 (Israel, 1980) kept demand for structural wood products strong.

As the computer-modeled, herbicide-dependent, high-cut policy swung into effect on BLM and Forest Service lands, environmentalists on the Oregon coast responded with a suit against the Forest Service for its failure to consider the health effects of the defoliant 2,4,5-T and its dioxin contaminant. This began a campaign later referred to as the "Spray Wars."

In the late 1970s, Rogue Valley environmentalists, a coalition made up primarily of counter-culture settlers and new migrants, formed Southern Oregon Citizens Against Toxic Sprays (SOCATS) in solidarity with Citizens Against Toxic Sprays (CATS), an antiherbicide group on the central Oregon coast. Cooperating through SOCATS, small, neighborhood-based "watershed groups" protested against herbicide spraying on a site-by-site basis. At that time, the filing of an administrative appeal with the Forest Service would halt all activity until the appeal was resolved. With a flurry of networking and cross-education, the various watershed

---

16. Such computer projections, including those on the Siskiyou National Forest, were sharply criticized by the House Interior Committee as being based on premises "totally unproven and purposefully blind" to limiting factors (Davis, 1994, p. 97). Computer projections of forest growth continue to be a contentious issue in the 1990s (Brock, 1993).

groups substantially delayed spraying each season, according to SOCRATS coordinator Phyllis Cribby (interview, 1993) and Headwaters activists Jack Shipley and Chris Bratt (interview, 1993).[17]

The antiherbicide campaign garnered wider citizen participation than any environmental effort in the region to date: Newcomers, long-term locals, and counter-culture members alike resented the idea of heli-copters descending on the slopes immediately behind their houses, spraying chemicals with unknown effects, turning the forest into hillsides of dead madrone trees with young conifers poking through. Effectively introducing a whole new public to the environmental struggle, the cam-paign won major press coverage for sit-ins featuring loggers and hippies protesting side by side.

In order to establish standing in the event of litigation, an environ-mental organization must follow every procedure available to it within an administrative appeal process. This time-consuming process was pur-sued, as is typical, by a very small nucleus of activists who educated themselves in the relevant scientific, procedural, and legal matters. Faced with the well-researched environmentalist appeal, the BLM shunted the entire question to the Secretary of the Interior, Cecil An-drus, effectively blocking any further administrative remedies. SOCATS filed suit, using a pro bono lawyer (Cribby interview, 1993).

The victory of local antiherbicide activists in *SOCATS v. Clark* (1983), decided by the Ninth Circuit Court and affirmed by the Su-preme Court, set a solid foundation for other no-spray victories, which blocked BLM and Forest Service spraying programs throughout the United States for ten years. It was the second court case with national implications to arise from the Rogue Valley environmental movement (following Headwaters' groundbreaking mid-1970s case against the BLM) (Cribby interview, 1993; Grier, 1984; SOCATS Staff, 1983).

The fight against the BLM and Forest Service spray programs at-tracted little of the type of resentment directed against the environmen-tal movement after 1983. Public opinion was against herbicides, and the new migrants had not yet gained sufficient numbers or political strength to remake the culture of the area in their own image. But by 1981, the area was headed for a deep depression. The wood products industry laid off one-third of its workforce in Oregon. Although timber harvests rose to

---

17. Jack Shipley is a member of the Applegate Partnership and Vice President of the Headwaters Board of Directors (Ashland, Oregon). Chris Bratt is a member of the Apple-gate Partnership, the Headwaters Board of Directors, and the Board of Directors of the Rogue Institute for Ecology and Economy (Ashland, Oregon).

record levels in the recovery of the late 1980s, the prerecession level of employees was never regained, mostly because of automation and streamlining. In spite of the economic hardships, and a net out-migration from the county during that time, urban newcomers continued to arrive, according to John Anderson, Regional Economist for the State of Oregon Employment Division in Medford (personal communication, 1993).

After a period of dormancy, Headwaters, the leading public lands environmental group in the 1970s, reorganized in the early 1980s to initiate new appeals against BLM forest practices around the Rogue Valley. The watershed groups that persisted after the conclusion of the Spray Wars consolidated under a Headwaters umbrella and provided support for the formation of new watershed organizations. By this time, the participation by middle-class in-migrants in these neighborhood-based associations was significant. Able to contribute a high level of technical sophistication and a face of social appropriateness to agency managers, most of these newcomers joined groups to challenge timber harvest in their neighborhoods (Shipley and Bratt interview, 1993), many in NIMBY forms of protest.

BLM sales were challenged one by one: One activist estimates that 20 percent of all sales in one large watershed were appealed. BLM records on reforestation were reviewed, and the agency was discovered to be in virtual noncompliance with their own regulations, resulting in a re-survey of all the lands to be reforested in the Medford District. The struggle proceeded in this piecemeal fashion until 1987 (Shipley and Bratt interview, 1993).

Conflicts on the Siskiyou   The next environmental battlefield was on the Siskiyou National Forest, where a long effort to include the North Kalmiopsis in the Kalmiopsis Wilderness area led to confrontations between the Forest Service and the in-your-face radical activist organization EarthFirst! The Kalmiopsis Wilderness is one of the West Coast's few low-elevation untouched forests. The wilderness area was expanded in 1978 to include 179,850 acres, but the North Kalmiopsis roadless area, which contains some dense stands of old growth, was excluded in a political compromise that embittered environmentalists. When the Forest Service planned to construct a logging road deep into the area in 1979 (in order, it was suspected, to exclude it from future wilderness consideration), the ire of environmental groups was aroused again (Davis, 1994).

Road construction began in 1983, precipitating a series of Earth-

First! demonstrations that were highly publicized in the local press. At that point the discovery that spikes had been driven into the trunks of the old-growth trees infuriated the local working population (Fattig, 1987a). (When saws hit a spike they shatter, endangering loggers and millworkers.)

In the early eighties, the real effects of state-controlled comprehensive land-use planning were beginning to sink in. The group 1000 Friends of Oregon appealed Jackson and Josephine counties' plans, arguing that they included too much farm and forest land in rural residential categories (Lang, 1993; professional planner, personal communication, 1993). The appeals were successful, and both counties found the stock of rural land on which new dwellings could be sited severely limited.

Just before this development, the counties had decided to beef up their enforcement of building codes. Jackson County was relatively successful, but a loud, angry crowd of many persuasions at a now legendary gathering at the fairgrounds in Josephine County made it clear that citizens were unwilling to back any politician who would demand building code compliance. The lower-income strategy of building a house incrementally was temporarily preserved.

During the confrontations on the Siskiyou National Forest, a new environmental group, the Siskiyou Citizens' Task Force, was fortunate enough to encounter a computer science professional who had relocated to the area to be a professional river guide. Julie Norman (now Projects Coordinator for Headwaters in Ashland) undertook a review of FOR-PLAN, the computer modeling equivalent of the BLM's forest simulation programs. Like the BLM program, FORPLAN included many untested assumptions that boosted the theoretical rate at which trees in the Siskiyou National Forest would regenerate. Moreover, the Siskiyou National Forest is, for the most part, a low-regrowth forest on marginal soils, and the formulas in the program were keyed to high-production sites further north (Norman interview, 1993).

The forest planning process with which the Forest Service was charged by the NFMA in 1976 was gaining momentum in the early eighties. Local forests were just completing comprehensive inventories and preparing to assemble their ten-year plans when President Ronald Reagan appointed John Crowell Assistant Secretary of Agriculture in charge of the Forest Service. As a former attorney for the lumber giant Louisiana-Pacific, he was sympathetic to the Reagan administration's desire to get the logs out of the woods. Crowell demanded a national reinventory of the lands to increase the timber base, precipitating a two-year delay in the planning process (Davis, 1994; Norman interview, 1993).

Cutting continued at close to a record level, while distress grew among people sympathetic to improved forest management.[18]

1987: a pivotal year In 1987 federal forest land and local community issues exploded. In June and July EarthFirst! conducted a series of high-profile demonstrations in the North Kalmiopsis. One protestor buried himself up to his waist in the path of bulldozers entering a formerly untouched area to build a road; others chained themselves to gates, blocked the bulldozers with their bodies, and instituted "tree sitting." A young man perched for several days on a platform high in a Douglas fir was almost felled with the tree by an angry logger who fired up his chainsaw and punched out an undercut (Fattig, 1987b). In May of that year, a millworker in a Louisiana-Pacific plant on the north California coast was maimed when a spike shattered sawteeth, which then penetrated his safety helmet and face shield. Although most Earth-First!ers renounced tree spiking, a local paper had quoted one protester in the North Kalmiopsis as saying, "We discourage that here . . . but next year it would be a lot harder to say 'Don't spike trees'" (Fattig, 1987c). Not surprisingly, local people took his statement as a threat.

Earlier in the year, the Oregon Natural Resource Council, backed by local environmentalists, proposed that the entire disputed Kalmiopsis area be declared a national park. An aggressive promotional campaign argued that tourism would be a commercial boon to the region, and a source of jobs to replace reduced timber employment. Oblivious to local distaste for low-wage service jobs, and the failure of the same strategy in the Redwood National Park just over the California border, the promoters took their case to a national constituency.

On August 28, 1987, the Forest Service released a proposed ten-year plan for the Siskiyou National Forest that included high levels of timber harvest throughout the forest, including the roadless North Kalmiopsis (Davis, 1994). Headwaters promptly appealed the plan.

This was, in addition, a peak year for the influx of a key set of migrants. The housing market had jacked the selling prices of California homes literally hundreds of thousands of dollars above the prices of ten years before (the time of the previous large influx of California equity migrants). These late-1980s migrants practiced conspicuous consump-

18. This is reminiscent of the FARR (Forest and Related Resources) process during the Nixon administration. Unable to expand the allowable cut in the late 1960s, timber industry representatives are alleged to have worked through presidential assistant Charles Colson to arrange a 50 percent increase. The Forest Service adopted FARR in 1970, bypassing the legislative process (Culhane, 1981, p. 57).

tion and boldly proclaimed their desire to escape the racial, poverty, and congestion problems of southern California and the Bay Area. Changes in the character of the region reached a critical mass: The mood of the counties shifted. "No Trespassing" signs, once rare, became common-place on the LCDC-protected no-growth lands. Accustomed routes to public fishing sites, swimming holes, blackberry and mushrooming areas, and informal access to public lands across private parcels began to be cut off by landowners.[19] Social groups segregated themselves with more conscious design (Fitchen, 1991; Kusel, 1991). Long-term locals felt beset by people from an urban culture who called them "rednecks."[20] People in cars with California license plates were surprised and angry when locals made obscene gestures as they passed by. The new middle class basked in the low-tax, tourist-fostered environment, and environ-mentalists considered recreational "user's fees" for hiking and other ca-sual use of public lands (O'Toole, 1988). Locals found nothing to praise in a national park proposal that promised more close-to-minimum wage jobs, or user fees that would help exclude the growing numbers living at or near poverty levels. Gradually, however, as middle- and upper-middle-class migrants grew in influence, low-income residents were not per-ceived as part of the community, but as part of a "problem."[21]

On August 30, 1987, nature touched off a pivotal event. A dry-light-ning storm hit the entire Rogue Valley, igniting deep forest duff parched to tinder flammability by several years of drought. The high columns of smoke that arose from several large forest fires mushroomed out when they hit cold air thousands of feet above the ground. By the next after-noon, the Rogue Valley was surrounded by a half-dozen mushroom clouds, and it looked as if the area had been hit by a nuclear strike.[22]

The Silver Complex Fire was the largest and longest of the fires, flaring up in the Silver Creek drainage, in the contested North Kal-miopsis forest, and eventually burned close to a hundred thousand acres deep into the wilderness area. After two months of firefighting efforts, the fire was extinguished by fall rains. When the foglike smoke cleared from the Rogue Valley, a prolonged battle over salvage logging developed into

19. This phenomenon is also discussed by Shands (1991) and Fitchen (1991, esp. pp. 99–100).

20. Locals may use the term "redneck," usually to refer to an individual (with either affection or disapproval) but rarely to condemn an entire social class or culture. This is in contrast to the blanket use of "redneck" by new migrants as a broad term of condemna-tion of local working people.

21. For related discussions, see Southard, 1993, and Chapman, 1981, esp. p. 92.

22. Personal experience of author.

a symbolic fight for the cultural as well as the economic destiny of the region.

Enter the spotted owl   The northern spotted owl, *Strix occidentalis*, an eighteen-inch-high bird that feeds on woodrats and flying squirrels, nests primarily in the old growth forests of the Pacific Northwest. In 1987 a tiny, previously unknown, Massachusetts-based group named GreenWorld petitioned the U.S. Fish and Wildlife Service to list the northern spotted owl under the Endangered Species Act of 1973. Environmentalist groups throughout the Northwest, and the nation, were taken by surprise (Norman interview, 1993; Peters interview, 1993).[23] The consequences of this listing eventually changed the universe of forest management throughout the western Pacific watershed.

The owl had in fact been a subject of discussion for almost two decades. Between 1968 and the mid-eighties, its status had been central to state and federal discussions over harvest of old-growth forest, and planned set-asides of owl habitat ranged from 70 acres in the mid-seventies to 1,000 acres in 1983.[24] In 1986, the Forest Service proposed setting aside 2,200 acres for each nesting pair of spotted owls (Fattig, 1986). (By contrast, the set-aside on private industrial land was still 70 acres in early 1994.) Oregon's Governor Victor Atiyeh angrily counter-proposed bringing an equivalent amount of wilderness back into the timber base for every acre set aside for spotted owls (*Grants Pass Daily Courier*, 1986). Local mill owners held press conferences to explain their dependence on public land timber, and the consequences of set-asides. Tensions mounted throughout the Pacific Northwest.

When environmentalists met in early 1987 at the Environmental Law Conference in Eugene, Oregon, lawyers for the Sierra Club Legal Defense Fund, like many other people in regional environmental organizations, were hesitant to petition for the listing of the spotted owl under the Endangered Species Act (Norman interview, 1993; Peters interview, 1993). They doubted that they had the political clout to carry through with such a listing. Said one: "It potentially could breed a firestorm we could not control. It could generate a backlash that would undermine any judicial success" (Peters interview, 1993).

The paperfront GreenWorld pushed them over the cliff of indecision. Recognizing that GreenWorld would not have the resources to

---

23. Peters was President of Headwaters in the mid-1980s.

24. The early history of southwest Oregon's spotted owl controversies and set-asides is well documented in the clippings files of the *Grants Pass Daily Courier*.

defend its challenge to list the owl, twenty-six national and regional organizations joined the petition, jumping headlong into the effort to include the owl under the protection of the Endangered Species Act (ESA) (Norman, 1989).

The national struggle over the Pacific Northwest forests The tactics and counter-tactics of the judicial, administrative, congressional, industry, and environmental players in the drama of the spotted owl deserve a history of their own. A detailed account is beyond the scope of this book; an outline, covering events up to the election of Bill Clinton in November 1992 must suffice. The primary decision-making entities were the BLM, the Forest Service, the Fish and Wildlife Service; National Marine Fisheries Service, the Congress, the Bush administration, and the federal courts. The full force of the executive, legislative, and judicial branches of the federal government was brought to bear on a problem with billion-dollar consequences.

In December 1987 the U.S. Fish and Wildlife Service denied the original petition to list, sparking a lawsuit by conservation groups (Norman, 1989). In November 1988 a Federal judge, Thomas Zilly of the Seattle District Court, instructed Fish and Wildlife to reconsider, basing the ruling on a broader set of evidence. In March 1989 Fish and Wildlife proposed to list the bird. By this time the scientific evidence in favor of listing was compelling to decision-makers (the timber industry continued to dispute the findings), but the Bush administration stalled the process as long as possible. Nonetheless, by June 1990 the spotted owl was officially listed as a "threatened" species (Fattig, 1990).[25]

Environmental groups had already brought a suit against the BLM, and in 1988 they brought another against the Forest Service, charging each agency's ten-year plans with not providing adequate protection for the spotted owl in compliance with NEPA, ESA, and NFMA (Caldwell et al., 1994; Daniels, 1994). In March 1989 Judge William Dwyer of the Seattle District Court imposed an injunction halting Forest Service timber sales in spotted owl habitat. In reaction, Northwest politicians led by Oregon's Senator Mark Hatfield convened a "timber summit" with environmentalists, held in Oregon. When these negotiations went nowhere, Hatfield spearheaded passage of a rider on the 1990 Interior Appropriations Bill (Section 318), which voided the injunction for one year and severely restricted judicial review of 1990 fiscal year sales. (It also re-

---

25. The following paragraphs are a compilation of information from Julie Norman (1993), Steve Davis (1994), the *Headwaters Journal,* Steve Daniels (1994), Lynton K. Caldwell et al. (1994), and the clippings library at the *Grants Pass Daily Courier.*

quired the Forest Service to re-examine its spotted owl guidelines and in response the Forest Service appointed an Interagency Scientific Committee to develop a "credible" conservation plan for the spotted owl [Caldwell et al., 1994; Daniels, 1994].) All environmental appeals were dead in the water until late 1990, when the Hatfield rider was declared unconstitutional (in part) two weeks before it expired — a ruling that would be overturned by the Supreme Court in 1992 (Davis, 1994; Dan Stottard, Headwaters staff attorney, personal communication, 1993). Intensive logging continued in the interim.

In May 1991 Judge Dwyer imposed a second injunction, expanding the stoppage of owl habitat timber sales. The ruling required the Forest Service to present by March 1992 a plan that would preserve the spotted owl. He imposed a third injunction in 1992 when the Forest Service released its new spotted owl EIS, which Dwyer ruled inadequate. In response, the Forest Service appointed a Scientific Analysis Team, whose report confirmed the negative impact of proposed Forest Service logging plans on both the owl and the old-growth ecosystem, and included a cross-agency criticism of BLM harvest practices (Brothers, 1993). It also expanded riparian protection to preserve salmon habitat (Daniels, 1994).

In late May the House Agricultural Committee and the Merchant Marine and Fisheries Committee commissioned the Scientific Panel on Late-Successional Forest Ecosystems to evaluate forest practices in the northern spotted owl region from an ecosystems protection approach. The panel was known as the "Gang of Four" after the four prominent forest scientists assigned to the team.

Injunctions halting BLM timber harvests in owl habitat had begun in 1988. These were less comprehensive than the Forest Service injunctions, but were accompanied by considerably more local turmoil. In early 1989, the Federal Appeals Court denied a request by timber interests to lift the ban, but a series of political maneuvers, including the Hatfield Section 318 rider, lifted the injunction overall. By February a number of BLM sales were again closed, and later the overall injunction was reinstated. BLM harvests supplied large amounts of money to the thirteen "O&C counties." Short of funds and in the midst of a tax revolt, those county governments and the state governor involved themselves in the cases on behalf of the timber industry. In June 1989, Josephine's commissioners proclaimed it a "yellow ribbon" (pro-industry) county (Huntington, 1989).

When the Fish and Wildlife Service officially listed the owl as threatened, Oregon's Senator Bob Packwood pressed for the convening of a "God Squad," a special committee that, by the provisions of the

Endangered Species Act, could allow certain species-threatening actions if other considerations were proved compelling. In 1991, to great fanfare, the God Squad exempted thirteen BLM timber sales from the ESA, but the ruling was moot, since the overall injunction against the BLM was still in effect.

Since 1986 the BLM had refused to prepare an EIS on the spotted owl. In 1991 federal Judge Helen Frye of the U.S. District Court in Portland agreed with the BLM that under the 1937 O&C Act, BLM land was to be managed for timber production. In 1992, however, in the face of scientific evidence, she permanently enjoined BLM timber sales in owl habitat until the agency drafted an adequate EIS.

Political resolutions of the conflicts were attempted, but failed. In Congress, most of the delegation from the Pacific Northwest, with the prominent exception of Oregon's Representative Peter DeFazio, finagled to increase the ASQ quotas the BLM and Forest Service must try to meet, and to prevent appeals through the courts. As the issues reached national prominence and court remedies appeared tenuous, environmentalists found allies in members of Congress from outside the Northwest and lobbied intensely for the strongly preservationist Jontz Bill, H.R. 4492 (H.R. 842 in 1992), originally introduced by Rep. Jim Jontz (D.-Ind.), and the somewhat more moderate H.R. 4899, the Ancient Forest Act, introduced by House Interior and Insular Affairs Committee Chairman George Miller in the Spring of 1992.

The Bush administration obstructed all efforts at compromise that would acknowledge the ecosystem destruction evidenced by spotted owl declines. The Ancient Forest Act, which was gaining support, was quashed by last-minute pressure by Senator Thomas Foley of timber-rich Washington State on key members of the Interior Committee (Davis, 1994; Norman interview, 1993). The convening of the God Squad opened a campaign to gut the Endangered Species Act—a goal that became explicit in Bush's presidential campaign of 1992. Even attempts by regional organizations such as Headwaters to persuade the BLM and Forest Service to conduct thinning and other lower-impact logging sales in *non*–spotted owl habitat (and therefore outside the injunctions) was rejected by local forest administrations (Norman interview, 1993). Pressure to refuse legal and environmentally sound timber sales appeared politically contrived to maximize public distress over the injunctions throughout the Pacific Northwest. Representative DeFazio's and Headwaters' charges that this was precisely the Bush administration's strategy were lost in the confusion (*Grants Pass Daily Courier*, 1991; Norman, 1993).

All credible scientific evidence, court cases, and even traditional pressure from the Northwest Congressional delegation failed. In the spring of 1992, Secretary of the Interior Manuel Lujan announced the formation of a new independent task force, dominated not by scientific expertise but by six powerful political appointees (Gregory, 1992a). This eleventh-hour attempt to ignore the spotted owl recovery efforts initiated by agencies, the scientific teams, and the courts was acknowledged to be dependent on a Congressional agreement to bypass the Endangered Species Act, the National Environmental Protection Act, and the National Forest Management Act. It was deflected by the presidential campaign of 1992, and ultimately defeated by the election of Bill Clinton.

Cultural and economic shift   If the above rendition of events, streamlined by hindsight, is difficult to follow, the day-to-day unfolding of events was bewildering. Confusing the picture even more, newspapers offered wildly different estimates of the impact of owl or old-growth protection. Some environmentalists calculated that fewer than 20,000 jobs would be lost, while the industry insisted on of more than 100,000 (Gregory, 1989).

In the Rogue Valley region, arguments over the salvage of timber burned by the Silver Complex Fire in the North Kalmiopsis provided the symbolic basis of the local battle over old growth and the northern spotted owl. After highly publicized maneuvering, which included national attention from major environmental groups and high-profile members of Congress, a compromise was negotiated by Representative DeFazio. Only three-tenths of a mile of road was to be built, and helicopters would be used in the logging of a somewhat reduced volume of timber, reducing environmental impact on the soils. In exchange, no environmental appeals would be allowed on timber sales in the fire area (Davis, 1994; Norman interview, 1993).

One important result of these negotiations was the intensification of public debate. Inspired in part by timber supporters' demonstrations elsewhere in the West, pro-industry groups such as the Oregon Project and the Southern Oregon Resource Alliance (SORA) orchestrated the Silver Fire Roundup, including a convoy of fifteen hundred log trucks to the Josephine County Fairgrounds in summer 1988. Yellow ribbons symbolized support for the Roundup and the timber industry: Josephine County was a sea of yellow ribbons that day. Cheering crowds greeted the log trucks on the main street of Grants Pass, and the fairgrounds were packed.

For many people, the rally was less a rubber-stamp endorsement of the timber industry than a celebration of solidarity among people who identified themselves with their rural and small-town communities, and with a culture that included timber harvests, but was not solely defined by them. As divisions among residents accumulated, spurred by conflicting visions of the area's cultural and social future, area residents were speaking from the heart when they told me, "It's good to see the community pull together over something." Interpretations of the meaning of the event varied widely, but few people provided the carte-blanche endorsement the pro-timber interests desired. A few months later the timber industry asked people to fly yellow ribbons again, this time specifically in support of timber, during a visit by the governor. On this occasion, which had no element of community solidarity, few yellow ribbons were to be seen. That same year, the Oregon public revealed its disapproval of forest industry practices when voters from all parts of the state, including Josephine and Jackson counties, voted 90 percent in favor of an advisory measure to prevent any export of logs from state lands (Fattig, 1989).

The Silver Fire Roundup was probably the last large gathering to celebrate Josephine County's blue-collar rural heritage and land-based informal economy. The animosity between people who flew a yellow ribbon and those who did not deepened the gulf between residents that had opened up over the preceding decade. A 1989 event with similar repercussions but a different design marked a watershed in Jackson County. At a public meeting convened at a local high school to discuss the timber crisis, two thousand angry timber workers, organized by their employers, faced fifty environmentalists. "It was rancorous," said Brett KenCairn, a participant, "It was almost a brawl" (interview, 1993).[26]

In 1989 and 1990 several large mills shut their doors, beginning a long series of mill shutdowns that closed the majority of the locally operating mills by late 1993. "Dislocated workers" took their chances in federally subsidized, state-run "retraining" and "relocation" programs. In a job market featuring low-wage service jobs on one end of the spectrum and highly technical/professional jobs on the other end, state policy assumed that large numbers of poorly educated Rogue Valley workers who needed "family-wage" jobs would choose to relocate. Many felt pressured to leave, but a significant percentage were determined to stay in the region (Job Training and Partnership Act and Rogue Community College employees, personal communication, 1992). Of the men who

---

26. KenCairn is Executive Director of the Rogue Institute for Ecology and Economy, Ashland, Oregon.

opted to keep their homes in the Rogue Valley, many chose mobile jobs, such as long-haul trucking, contract construction, or short-term work in Alaska. Women made do with lower-paying jobs near home. Low-income, two-worker families — as in the rest of the nation — became the norm.

Core members of the public lands environmental groups were too single-minded in pursuit of environmental goals to consider what was at stake for working people in these overall regional transitions. Indeed, one often sensed that many of the counter-culture and middle-class environmentalist allies would be glad to see the previous lower-income, land-based rural culture disappear, assuming it to be uncritically pro-timber. Certainly the collision of high land prices and LCDC restrictions on rural lands — rationalized in terms of environmental concerns — foisted on the population an unintended and far-reaching program of land reform in favor of the region's better-off citizens. Public lands environmentalists gave poor, working, and displaced workers no compelling reasons *not* to identify the environmental movement with urban migrants who too often looked upon low-income or local people with contempt. The declines in high-wage jobs, prohibitions on strategies of living close to the land, and the political ascendancy of newcomers were decisive in changing the course of the region. Rather than an evolution incorporating strengths from the past, the dislocation and wholesale replacement of the older land-based culture and resource-based informal economies was well under way. And this local phenomenon mirrored the experiences of other areas with recreational and aesthetic amenities valued by urban migrants (see especially Rodriguez, 1987).

It was in this atmosphere of flux that the interviews in this book were conducted. Disaffection among social groups in the Rogue Valley has led to a bitterly factionalized community. I initiated the project in curiosity: How were the issues being defined among low- and moderate-income citizens, a group which usually was excluded — or excluded itself — from the public debate? It is through their stories, as well as those of politicians, industry leaders, and environmentalists, that the social and cultural changes under way in 1989 and 1990 in the Rogue Valley region must be evaluated.

In the country

PETER ALTEN and LARRY LYON   (age 40) Two big, hard-working men sharing a few beers with friends. They aren't afraid to argue with one another, or with the men and women sitting with them, loudly disputing facts without trespassing the boundaries of goodwill. The rugged lives of their parents and grandparents are typical of the histories of many long-term Oregon families. Pete and Larry were both born in 1949.

Pete   My great-grandparents moved here to the north part of Josephine County. My grandfather grew up there. My mom grew up there. A whole mountainside out there used to belong to my grandfather.

I never could find my way out of the valley. I'll probably die in this valley. I've tried to get out. My dad was a truck driver. Drove for K&C for a number of years.

Larry   A forest raper. Oooh!

Pete   Save a logger, kill an environmentalist.

Larry   Hey, I work on log trucks all the time. I've got nothing against logging old growth. Nothing against it.

My father was career military. I'm a fourth-generation Oregonian. My great-grandparents came here and settled, homesteaded in the Applegate Valley. As close as I can figure, they were out Mule Creek out there. High up on the hill. They got here after the Applegates took the valley. And anybody that came after that got the sides.

I guess they had a dirt farm. They grew real good rocks. And they had three sons and three daughters. The three boys, which was Thomas, Clyde, and Tom, all turned into prospectors. They founded about eighty percent of the old claims in this area. They've prospected Rough and Ready, they prospected China Creek, they prospected all up and down the Rogue, all up and down the Illinois. But the problem with them was they were typical Oregonians. They would find it, get a score, come in, sell the claim, get drunk, bum enough money for a stake, and head back out. They never kept anything.

"Roscoe" is another name around here. My grandfather couldn't stand Roscoe. Those two fought all the time. They were always arguing over what claim was where. In fact, my grandfather, the three of them, and Roscoe found and sold the Deadman's Claim out on Rough and Ready Creek.

There's a story. They found it, panned it, got their stakes, came in, paid off their grubstakes — which they always did. They always paid their grubstake. Then they got drunk and partied.

So, anyway, the two guys they sold the claim to went out there with an old concrete mixer — used to run a lot of your sluice through concrete mixers. And it was a real good claim. In fact, Grandpa and the guys brought out more money than these two guys were bringing out, and they were just panning.

So both the guys that bought the claim decided the other guy was ripping the other guy off. So one night one of them stood up in the middle of the night, shot the other one through the head, grabbed all the gold, and split.

And the claim stayed there and changed hands about four times. And all they did was took this concrete mixer and threw it off to the side, then they started bringing in real equipment to work the claim. And a couple of people made a lot of money off of it.

But, anyway, some people all went together and bought the claim. They were out there, and they said, "Well, throw that old cement mixer away."

And the guy says, "Yeah, well, we can't haul it, so let's cut it in two and we can put it in the pickup. And they cut it in two, and found almost a quarter of a million dollars trapped in the veins. That was the gold that both of them thought the other one was stealing. It got caught in the veins because the veins in the old concrete mixers were so high-pitched that it would hold the gold. Anyway, a guy lost his life over a concrete mixer.

But Grandpa went up China Creek, when the Chinese were up there running it. And they would pan the dredge that the Chinese would let come through, and then go up about once a month and rip the Chinese off. You know?

That's where Thomas died. And then Clyde was stomped to death by a bronc out in the Illinois Valley. And then my grandfather was stomped in front of the Corral Tavern by an irritated husband. It knocked him down, he hit his head on the curb and killed him. He was fifty-nine when this husband walked in and caught him messing with his wife, and took him outside and beat him up. Well, Grandpa, he had nine children. He was never one to pass a lady by.

But then my dad, he kind of grew up on a shoestring. He was born on a homestead out in Wilderville. Grandma was alone — except when Grandpa'd shoot through and make another kid and then split up for the hills. So she was having a real tough time. All the kids worked all year round. And she just come to the point where she couldn't support all the kids, so she farmed out the boys. My dad ended up on a ranch.

He learned horses and all this, so when he was about fourteen, he took off and joined the rodeo. He was a professional rodeo rider until December 7, 1941, when him and another guy that got bucked off and busted up were sent to the bar to heal, 'cause they had to ride again that night. And they heard about the Japanese attack, and they said, "Well, let's go fight." And they said, "OK." And he said, "What'll we join?" And they said, "The first recruiting station we show up."

And the first thing they ran into was an Army one, so they joined the Army, and my old man ended up spending twenty-five years in the Army. And just like the rest of us, he kept returning to the valley.

Pete   This valley's got like a suction on it.

Larry   Yeah, it's like a magnet. My mother almost had me in Germany. Then she said, "Oh, I won't have a Kraut." So she dashed for back here, because it's the only place she knew. And I was born up here in Josephine County.

My mother grew up here, but she was born in Long Beach, California. Her people moved up here when she was seven. Grandma was from Alabama. And Grandpa was from Massachusetts. And the only thing Great-Grandma and Great-Grandpa could say was, "Why did you marry that goddamn Yankee?"

But she married him, and they ended up here. My parents met right as Pop was taking his ninety days at the end of World War II. Grandma never forgave my mother for doing it.

Pete   My dad comes from North Dakota. When they built I-5, he was working on the highway. He met my mom out at the local inn, and they got married shortly thereafter. She never got out of the valley until she was past fifty, when she finally moved. Now she's living in Montana.

Larry   Ran most of us out. I don't plan to retire in this valley. Too many people. It's just grown up too much.

When I was a kid and I lived just down from Roosevelt School? I could get on my bike after school and ride two minutes, and be out by myself in the wilderness. I could go to the old granite pit out there. No one around you. Sneak cigarettes. Do whatever you were going to do. Just be a kid. Get home, drop your books, grab your twenty-two, throw it on your bicycle, and in two minutes you were out in the sticks. Now you can't drive two minutes and be away from people.

What killed me was—OK; I graduated in 1966, was drafted prior to graduation. Left nineteen months, going through training in the military, and then pulling a year in 'Nam. And I came back, and this place had exploded. I came back and didn't recognize it. I went, "What the hell is this?"

Now you can't drive an hour and get away from people. We were driving the other night, out to Williams. I said, "Look at all these houses! When I was a kid, there was probably two houses in this whole area." And they didn't care if you hunted their property, as long as you didn't shoot their cow.

Pete You could do just almost anything you wanted around here. It was nice.

Larry And you go up Thompson Creek or something like that now, you try to fish, and there's barbed wire strung across it. In the old days, you could walk up through there, and as long as you didn't destroy anything, just left everything alone, just fished the creek, you were fine.

I remember my dad and I went down with Hank Shephard, down the river. We blew out one of the ripples so you could float through it. I was probably six, seven years old.

Hank would pull up next to a rock, and he was oaring, and my old man—because my old man was military, he knew explosives—he'd strap some dynamite together and chuck it in next to this thing. He said, "Well, the water's going this way, and there's a downer right there." And they'd get right next to that downer, he'd drop that dynamite in, and then old Hank would just pull like a son-of-a-gun, trying to get away from that dynamite.

All of a sudden, *Boom!* And that rock would fall over, and then you had a passage through. That ripple, when I was a kid, was non-passable with a boat until they blew that thing out.

Pete You was damn lucky to be able to pass in an inner tube without getting beat up.

Larry Yeah. And I remember Rainie. We'd float on down after we cleared that ripple, we'd float on down and pull up just before

Rainie Falls. The old cabin there with Rainie in it? Meanest old man I ever met.

Pete   He was an ornery old fart, he was.

Larry   Ornery! That man had a mean streak in him worse than a polecat. I mean, he was just flat mean. "What do you two want? Why'd you bring that damn kid with you?"

Hank would go, "Aw, shut up and feed us!"

"Well, I guess I got to."

And then we'd go and eat, and he'd go, "You just tell that kid to keep his mouth shut."

Boss Taylor wouldn't let you by. Old Boss Taylor was about four miles below Rainie Falls. You'd come by in a boat, he'd almost shoot you to get you to come just sit down and talk to him. He'd feed you. He'd pour booze — he used to make that corn whiskey. Oh, Lord!

By God, you didn't stop, though, he'd fire shots on you. He needed somebody to talk to. Anybody coming down the river had to talk to him.

There was some crazy people down that river.

Pete   There were some good old guys. If you looked at them now, they were just lonely old guys that wanted somebody to spend a little time with from time to time. When I was a little kid, you'd see them, they'd scare the piss out of you.

Larry   You couldn't blow them off the claim with a stick of dynamite. Yeah, they were crusty old people. But they were good. They would give you the shirt off their back. And if you were out'n by yourself and in trouble, they'd die rather than see you get hurt.

Pete   They'd do anything for you, those guys. That was back when they cared.

Larry   They were some good people, and they were rough and mean. And there were some awful bad people out there.

Pete   Uncivilized types. There was a lot of them old loners like that up there. You know, Grandad used to tell me about a lot of the old boys. And I mean, that old man, I thought my grandfather was an ornery old fart. I'd grown up with all the reputation of him.

Out there in the northern part of the county, I guess I was about nine or ten, I was sitting out there — he just stopped back on the way in, he'd pick me up. He was going in and have a few beers. Somebody slapped him around in the bar, and threw him out.

Well, this was his town. They pissed him off. He went outside, got his old chainsaw out of the back of the pickup, fired that baby up, and cut the door hinges off the place. Walked in and chased them boys out. And I thought, Now, this old boy, he's one mean hoser. But old Grandpa, he was real kindly to this old boy.

Larry There were some pretty bad people up in this valley. I imagine there still are out there in them hills.

Pete Hey, out there around Takilma and everything, up there on Skull Mountain. There's some crazy assholes up there even now.

Larry Most of the new ones *think* they're crazy. The old guys *were*. They had been up on those claims and up in the timber so long that they actually went batty. The new ones like to *think* they're crazy. I've ran into a lot of the Takilma people, either here in Grants Pass or over in Cave Junction, that really would like you to believe they're crazy. But, it's like Grandpa. My dad would rile my grandfather in a minute, just to see him. When he got mad, you could see it in his eyes.

You know, as a small child, it was hard to define in your brain, but you just knew, Ooh! don't get around that dude. And my old man, my dad, to the day he died said, "Well, you know, your grandpa was a little wild, but he wasn't crazy."

I said, "But, geez! The way he used to look!"

And he said, "Yeah, but that was just being mad. There were crazy people out there — they had that look all of the time." They'd come out of the mountains once every six months for their staples. And they walked out with that look, and they walked back up with that look. The best thing that happened to the world was they went back up. Just mean. And right now I imagine there still are some real bad folks up there. But most of the new people . . .

OK. We got a whole influx of mountain folk from the sixty-hippie generation. Who would like you to believe they're crazy, and like you to believe they're bad, but, really, they're here every month for their welfare. These other people come out every six months so they can have a spot of sugar.

Pete My dad was a highway heavy-equipment man. Then when he married my mom he got into the logging, driving truck for my grandfather. My dad's kind of a toad. I loved him in a way. I ain't got much respect for him. He took off when I was nine years old.

My grandfather owned a logging outfit. That's back when Charlie Crumble started burning down forests.

Bystander [To B. B.] You never heard about the Crumble brothers? They're the ones that whacked off a piece of I-5.

Pete   When the state built the freeway through, they made the families sell this property through it. Well, they forgot, in their estimation of the lines and everything, the Crumbles ended up owning twelve inches from side to side of I-5. The full distance. The state wouldn't go ahead and buy it, so they just set up roadblocks and started charging toll.

Bystander   And they sold square inches of it.

Pete   Hell, they got more out of that one-foot width than they did out of all of the land they had to give up. They didn't realize that they still owned any of it until it was brought to their attention because they were having to pay taxes. That was back in the early sixties, late fifties.

Larry   Great-Grandpa, who was out in the Applegate, he homesteaded hundreds of acres. And when you had hundreds of acres in this country, you had trees. And you made your basic living off the trees. It's not like you could plant two hundred acres of wheat. Especially when you're on the side of the Applegate Valley. You had a garden enough to support the family, and you took the deer out for your meat. Like Grandpa used to say, "We fed some time on Applegate beef."

Then, after the timber industry really boomed, and people started realizing, "Hey, I can make a lot of money off the sides!" All of a sudden, the sides with the trees were making more money than the flatlands.

And in my case, my family's case, we never really had a pot to piss in or a window to throw it out of. Windfall! Big bucks! Because at that time, there was a huge valley here that we could go anywhere. That's when they moved out towards where Wilderville is now. My grandfather was the only one of the three married, so he just threw his family out there and said, "There's your homestead. There's your place."

My dad's older brother was the only one that wasn't farmed out, because he cut the wood, did the land, did everything. My dad's second-oldest brother, he got farmed out, and then my dad got farmed out. The girls were even farmed out. One of my aunts was maid-attendant at twelve years old for a doctor here in town. She cleaned house, she got room and board and education in town. That's the way you did it back then if you had no bucks.

My grandfather, exact words, when I was a young man sitting there listening to him talk, he says, "Well, I ain't worth a shit anymore."

I'd go, "Why, Grandpa?"

He says, "I used to be able to pick up a gun, some ammunition, a little bit of food, and walk. A man could walk for fifty years and never go hungry." He says, "You can't do that no more."

And that was back when the first deer I ever shot in my life, I shot right out of Devil's Slide, because they were *there*. Now Devil's Slide is all houses.

I had friends that grew up in this valley, they'd all say, "Well, come on, let's stay the night."

"Why?"

"I'm sick of venison. Your parents have *beef!*"

Pete The fifties and sixties is when it was good times.

Larry The early sixties. About sixty-five is when we started seeing the retired California influx into the valley.

Pete There about sixty-eight you start seeing the hippie influx.

Larry Well, I didn't know that, because I was drafted in sixty-seven.

Pete Yeah, well, me and you both left about that time. We were both sent to Vietnam for a few years.

Larry My graduating class, I'll bet you one out of eight went to college, could afford to go to college. The rest of us were draft-meat. We either joined the service, or we were drafted into a service.

In high school, I got called in because I had my hair pulled back on both sides and over the top, a long Princeton, or "ducktail," whichever you prefer, and told, cut my hair or get thrown out of school.

And then I come home from 'Nam eighteen months later, and guys are walking around with hair down to their butts! And they're not saying a word to them!

When I left, and what I came back to, was two completely different worlds. We heard of pot in the sixties here in Oregon. But the only thing most of the sixty-seven graduates knew of pot, that if you smoked it, hair would grow out of your palms. And you'd go blind.

Pete And you'd kill people.

Larry I come home eighteen months later, people are smoking it right and left in the halls of Grants Pass High School.

Pete You could walk down the streets of this town —

Larry — taking deep breaths. The whole thing had turned around, done a big flip. Now of course California progressed into the drug culture several years before, but we were so backwards up here.

Pete You went out Redwood Highway, there was hundreds of acres and a house, hundred acres and a house. Now you drive out there, there's nothing but houses.

Larry I wanted to get out of this town! [*Laughs*] I wanted out so bad I could taste it. When I left high school, I had no intentions of ever coming back to this valley.

Pete Me either. It was too slow. I wanted some action.

Larry I wanted the big city. I wanted everything an eighteen-year-old kid wanted. Ended up spending two tours in 'Nam. Got popped real hard in my second tour. Ran all over the world, had a good time. By the time my third tour rolled around — one night in the jungle it hit me. I went, "I've been in every free country in the world, and some communist countries, and I never saw a place I liked better. I just want peace and quiet. I want to go home."

So I came home. It wasn't what I left. But it was better than what I'd seen. It was still quiet. It was still, at that time, fairly crime-free. I don't hunt anymore. I haven't since 'Nam. I don't like guns anymore. I don't play with guns at all. They're a killing thing, and they belong in the killing world, not in my world. But this place was as close to quiet and peaceful as I could find. I've been back for about ten years, and I'll probably never leave either.

I may not retire here if the cycles keep happening. The cycle is just too many people. As the people come, the violence comes. I'm lucky enough to be able to raise my kids in a pretty good environment. I don't think they can raise their kids here in a good environment.

Pete It's the old Rat Syndrome.

Larry When I was a young man, I had no intentions of going to college. Long before I did, I read a bunch of papers because I was bored to death in Vietnam. And a study by this man, he took a rat, and he put it in a six-by-six box. The rat was happy. He put two rats in. The rat was happy. He kept adding rats. Pretty soon the rats changed. All of a sudden they were irritable, nasty to each other. They kept adding rats. Pretty soon they became violent.

And to me that's called the Rat Syndrome. The more bodies you shove into a small area, the more the Rat Syndrome takes over. We are right now saturated to the point where the Rat Syndrome is taking over. The people that are coming up used to be, "Thank God I'm up here where it's quiet!"

Pete People accepted you. And liked you.

Larry Now somebody comes in and they go, "Well, we could change this."

"Why?"

"Well, we had it this way in California, and it was so good . . . "

"OK. Why'd you come up here?"

"Because this is better."

"So what do you want to do? Make it like it was, which you wanted to leave?"

But they do it. They do it and they do it. I'm probably going to finish my working life out here. Because I'm kind of committed financially and everything else to this valley. But if I'm going to retire, I want to retire into the Tetons. Or into the Canadian Rockies. Somewhere where I can get up in the morning, and your biggest hassle of the day is throw rocks at the deer to get them out of your garden.

I'm old now. I'm forty years old. My body is shot up, tore up, been cast away several times. I don't want to hike to find that peace. I want to wake up and find that peace. It's like the old mountain men. Go up to the high and lonesome and just get away from the people that can't stand the high and lonesome.

Pete I can still find it here in Oregon. I can go up in Antelope Valley, La Pine area. There's still some really nice area up there that isn't heavily populated where you can walk out your back door and scream at the top of your lungs and tell the world — and nobody hears you.

Larry Around here it was all an artificial economy to start with. When I was a kid, half of the people I knew were unemployed. All year.

Pete Or working part-time. Work a month or two here, work a month or two there. Everything.

Larry I have never seen this valley prosperous. The one time I did see it is when I came home, and then all of a sudden everybody was making good money and everybody was having a good time. And I went, "Well, what are you doing? You're ripping the area. You're doing your human locust thing for a short time, but it's going to fall down on you." And it's fallen down on us.

This is not an area to become a millionaire in. It never was. The only difference now is, not only can you not become a millionaire, you cannot have any peace and quiet either.

Pete It's like in this area, like the bull they're running up on us now. The spotted owl. "You can't kill the old growth." I'm a firm believer in killing them. Because you let it grow up, you let it rot. It's got a disease, therefore all the young trees that's coming up is going to get the disease, too. And they're all going to die.

Now, I believe in using our forestry. I don't believe in raping it to where there's nothing going to be there. I believe in cutting them down and replanting them. We got our East Coast people coming back on us and saying, "You can't do this." Well, is it my fault that you idiots paved over all your forest back there, and now you're telling us how to run ours back here? We do a good job of doing reforestation back here.

One thing I don't agree with is selling the logs to the Jappos. The raw logs bullshit. You want our timber, you buy it in the finished product. They send it out, just shitloads of raw logs.

Larry   They're shipping out millions of board feet a day. And the millworker's setting there going, "There goes my job."

And you don't hear an environmentalist scream against that. If you honestly believe that the old growth has to stand, then you've got to stop the Oregon logger and you've got to stop the Japanese logger — who isn't carrying a chainsaw. He's unloading a ship and cutting it up. OK?

B. B.   I heard the Japanese bought the Jebson mill.

Larry   Yeah. Because they know that pretty soon we're going to stop them from shipping them. They're also trying to buy MXF Woodproducts. Because they know, sooner or later, we're going to wake up and say, "No! You're not getting no more logs, you're going to buy lumber." And they're going to say, "Fine! Through my mill."

They're just coming at us from a different direction now. And they will beat our socks off. They will undercut you every time, because they have no defense budget, all this stuff we're doing, so their government's money can turn right around and resubsidize their own people and beat our brains out.

And all I'm saying is, Fine! That's fair. But if it's fair for you, it's fair for me. You're not getting any more logs. Because if you let the Japanese go, you're going to look out one day, and there's not going to be a tree left on these mountains. Because they don't care what this country turns into.

Companies like Weyerhaeuser has planted a billion more trees than they ever cut. They will guarantee the future of this area. They will guarantee that my grandchildren can go out to Indian Mary Park and look at a tree. See a squirrel.

Pete   See a spotted owl if they want.

Larry   While the rest of the world doesn't care. When we grew up here, there was Spaulding and Son. They were local people. Out of Cave Junction, there was the old Buell mill.

Pete   Which is Rough and Ready. Robert Dollar out in the Glendale area.

Larry   The guy up at Glendale right now. Those were locally owned peoples who tried to make a buck, OK?

Then you got Conrad, MXF — these big conglomerates coming in, buying this stuff up, going in debt, then figuring out, Hell! The guy who runs MXF lives in San Francisco. He doesn't live in Grants Pass, Oregon. He doesn't care any more than the Japanese if this whole valley's stripped. He makes a fortune.

Pete He could care if it looked like San Francisco tomorrow. "Well, I don't see any trees out my window. Why the hell do you need to?"

Larry That's his idea: "What I need to do tomorrow is show a good profit because this million-plus a year that I'm making through this corporation — " And that's what's killing us.

Pete Short-term interests is what it's called. What they can get in the shortest term. And nobody thinks anymore — especially the big business — they don't think in the long haul anymore. Because they're out to get the money *now* to make their livelihoods and say to hell with everybody else. And a true Oregonian — I'm a conservationist. I want to see the deer out in the forest there.

Larry I want to see the streams there.

Pete I believe in keeping the spotted owl. But, God, they lie to us so much. They've already spotted them breeding in madrone trees and in the second-growth forest. What the hell does old growth have to do with it? The spotted owl is going to go where it's got to go. When it starts getting endangered, OK — you got to bend to it a little bit. But you don't have to say, "Well, this thousand acres is not going to be farmed on because there's a pair of spotted owls in it."

Larry You got a bunch of . . .

Pete Big business.

Larry . . . conservationists who don't care about anything except their thought. All right. They can foresee down the road, the world stripped. Which, if you allow money and big business to take over, yes, it will be stripped.

And you're looking at the logger here who says, "I can do this and I can do this." No one wants to compromise. No one wants to say, "OK, wait a minute. Back up. I'll plant trees, so the world is insured that by the time this last old growth is cut, the second growth is already standing tall."

The conservationists don't want to look at that. The logger will not look at the conservationists and say, "Well, we've got to save the spotted owl." He says, "What's an owl compared to my job?"

The American species — that's what I wanted to get at — radically changed during the sixties. Before the sixties, you had a nation that jumped up at World War II and destroyed half the world because they were angry over what people were doing to other people. Now you've got a nation that: "As long as I'm comfortable, the hell with the rest of you." And when you start thinking so much in creature comfort, which we are today—

It's like, when I was a kid, my mother would get all flustrated when I would grab my fishing pole and my bicycle on a Saturday.

"Don't go through town."

"Why?"

"The farmers are in—too many people."

All right? But you could ride downtown on a bicycle when Sixth Street was two-way.

Pete Back when the Caveman Bridge was a two-way bridge. And on both ends of that bridge—now, this is something I remember from a little teeny kid . . .

Larry Yeah, I remember it.

Pete . . . and it's strictly prejudiced. Which, I'm not that way. I believe everyone has their own space, and I've got a lot of colored friends. But you remember the old signs on the bridge? "Nigger don't let the sun set on you here." And it meant it. It was a nasty town in some ways. And in other ways it was real mellow.

Larry This was a Klan town.

Pete In fact, if you go up to the City Hall, and go up in and look on the walls there, you'll see the Ku Klux Klan marching in the Rose Festival Parade.

Now, I'm not that way. My dad was a Klan member. And I grew up hating coloreds to the max. Until I went to Vietnam and had one save my life, I never even thought twice about giving them other than slave status. That's all they were to me. That's what I was brought up to believe.

Well, a friend of mine, Brother Johnson, he's a colored man, he saved my life in 'Nam, and we got real tight. And I classify him my brother. And if he wants to come to Grants Pass, I'll introduce him to Larry and all my friends, and I will expect my friends to accept him.

Larry What I'm saying is this: My mother used to get uptight because I wanted to ride through town to go fishing on a Saturday, because of the amount of people. Today it took that guy sitting right across the table from me twenty minutes to get from Sixth and "I" Street, across this bridge. And how many people cut him off, flipped him off, screamed at him, because they were in the wrong lane and decided, "Well, I've got to get across the bridge! I'll *turn*."

And in those days all you had to do was turn your turn signal on and say, "I would like to get over there." And someone would stop and let you in.

I remember a cat. My parents were driving out of town, and a cat got hit on the Sixth Street bridge, and you couldn't see the poor thing, because of all the parents that stopped their car, jumped out, and tried to revive that cat.

And now you could fall over on that bridge with a heart attack, and everybody would go, "I hope you're not going to fall in the street. I'm in a hurry!" You know, whole different world.

Pete   Families, long-time families of the Rogue Valley, who no longer live here are living in Alaska, because they went to Alaska to find what they've lost here. Because it's still backwards like Oregon was twenty-five years ago. You can walk up to your neighbor and say, "Hi!" Just talk to somebody. They don't stick their nose up in the air at you. In this town, everybody's out for themselves anymore. And it's getting worse all the time.

Larry   These conservationists who are out here spiking trees and doing this — they cannot believe that their idea is not worth the cost of the whole valley, is not in the best interest of the valley.

Their idea is a great one. If the worst-case scenario happened, if the Japanese bought all the hills around here — which becomes private land, no longer controlled by the federal government — they could strip them. And they could kill off the spotted owl. The deer. Everything. And ship it all to Japan. That's the worst-case scenario that you can come up with.

OK? I see that point. But what they're fighting is already federal land. That cannot be bought up by private property. That will be re-planted. That will not allow the spotted owl to die, the deer to die, anything else to die around here. The timber will come back, every-thing will be here.

Maybe not in as abundance as it was, because of the number of people. It's going to come down to where environmentalists are going to say, "Fine! That's all the people that can move in this area." Be-cause that's what's killing everything around here. I walked up Mount Baldy as a child. Remember the mines — where people had been? But there's nothing out there. All right? Now you walk up there, there isn't half the trees that used to be there, *because* they're all houses now. And people want their lawns and want this and want that. So they cut the trees down.

Sooner or later you're going to have to get off the logger, get off the miner, get off the oil producer, and say, "You want to keep having kids? Keep them in the city. Keep them out of the wilderness."

That's what's destroying it. Not the logger, not the miner, not the oil prospector, not anybody else. It's just that you're moving out there because you have the money. You can buy this seven acres and strip it! 'Cause you want to be able to look out and see the stars. That's what's killing the Rogue Valley.

Pete   See, the logger never will kill the Rogue Valley. The logger has always looked to the fact that there always has to be trees there. That's why we reforest our section of the country. I mean, the old growth is just a figment of everybody's imagination.

Larry   No. It's there.

Pete   What happened in the last forest fire?

Larry   We lost a pile of the old growth.

Pete   We lost more than we could have logged in five years in one year's fire. So why not build the roads up through there? You need roads to even protect against forest fires.

Larry   The deal of it is, the environmentalists — it's like the Rogue River. We got the Rogue River from Graves Creek to Taylor Ferry closed. Right? You've got to have a permit to go down. Why? Because someone from Portland wants to come down here with his permit and float it without looking at someone else. Not that it's harming the river. Or harming the environment around it. He just wants to be able to float it without seeing something else. And he and his buddies have the money to fight it.

Pete   That's taking away my right. And I have to apply for a permit? I've applied for four years and have not received one yet. I should be able to float it whenever I want. If you want to make permits to somebody from out of the area, OK. But why should I have to?

Larry   When I float the river, I don't particularly want to see a bunch of people, either. I'd rather enjoy the river myself. But do I have the right to deny you the same right that I'm enjoying? Do I have the right to tell that man from Portland, "Get off my river?" No. No more than he has the right to tell me to get off my river. But he did.

When I was floating the river, nobody wanted to. It was dangerous then. It wasn't fun. It was to us a natural thing, but to people up north it was, you know, "Why don't you just jump out of an airplane?"

The Californians came up here because it's so much better than what they had. But it's *not* what we used to have. The difference was, what they used to have, they hated, and what we used to have, we loved. Yeah, I'm guilty as everybody else going, "You California son-of-a-bitch!"

Pete "Californians" is a way—we just call it that. It's just they don't believe in the way we think.

Larry Back then, they didn't come up here to change it. They came up here to enjoy it.

The local people have a good concept. The problem is, no one in today's society is ever going to say, "Meet me halfway. You take care of the trees, I'll take care of the spotted owls, and we'll both can do this if we work together."

But, like I say, I love this area, but I would love more, I think, to find a place where I could relax. Just live quietly and peacefully. This area is not quiet and peaceful anymore. The more society insists on being the way it is, the less quiet it is. It's all going to just follow the part of gobble, gobble, gobble.

BARBARA ROLAND (age 51) Barbara Roland's Oklahoma roots
are shared by many southwest Oregonians. Emigrants from Arkansas, Oklahoma, and southern border states typically spent a handful of years in central and southern California, where they worked on farms or in war
industries until the late 1940s, then migrated to Oregon, an area that
seemed more like home. Farming, ranching, and other experience with machinery translated easily to logging and truck-driving jobs. She and her husband divorced, and now she is heading out on her own.

She is gray-haired and outgoing. We sat in the park on a spring day,
talking quietly between pleasant silences and watching people go by.

I was born in central California in 1938. My parents were transplanted Okies. They came out during the Dust Bowl to California.
They were many generations in the same county in Oklahoma — I
think it was C—— County. But they just got to where they couldn't
even eat. Things were so bad during the Depression that they had to
go to California like all those other hundreds of thousands of people did.

They lived in places up and down California, just following fruit,
following crops. They were the Okies that you see in the movies. They
finally settled in a place that was west of Bakersfield. It was almost all
relatives that lived in that little town — they moved C—— County out
there.

We lived in a tent when I was born. It was a two- or three-room
tent, but it was a tent. A little welfare baby. My dad worked for a
rancher there until I was twelve. We came to Oregon on a vacation in
June. And we went back, sold our house, and moved back in August.
All of us fell in love with it. It was like we finally came home. We had
transplanted friends there from down south. And they talked my folks
into coming back up. My dad bought a logging truck. He was a gyppo
logger for years. With absolutely no knowledge at all of the roads here,
how dangerous it could be. And my dad, at that time, was probably
about forty-seven years old.

Corners was a wonderful place. There's something about Corners,
it's always had a connotation of a little bit on the — not really sleazy,
but the wrong side of the tracks type thing. Yet I loved it. There were
good people. I was safe there. We would be out walking at midnight
on summer evenings. There was no fear of attack or danger back then.
I don't recall ever feeling afraid of being out.

The kids in Corners were all there to immediately pull us right in.
By the time school started, I knew every kid. My best friend Jenny's
dad was a millwright. Her mom stayed at home. Beth's dad worked in

a mill. Her mom stayed at home. Seems like Mr. Williams was maybe a county worker or something. But for the most part they worked in the woods or in lumber.

You see, back in that time, you worked in the lumber all summer, because you made good money. Then you got a mill job in the winter to get by. Because it was more than unemployment. But it was less than logging.

I remember the first job my brother, who was seventeen, ever had was logging. He made excellent money. He opted not to go back to school. Not that it ever really seemed to make a big difference, because he stayed in the logging industry and still is.

My dad was always gone. And so when we moved to Oregon, the long logging hours — it was no difference to me. It's just that he was driving a big truck instead of a piece of farm machinery. I can remember the first time I ever went with Dad on the logging truck. We were coming down a hill loaded. And he said, "Now, sister, if I tell you to jump, you gotta jump right then, and don't wait. Because I have to wait until you're out."

"Out? Why?" You know, I was terrified.

He said, "Well, if for some reason it gets away from me, you've got to jump so I can."

When we got up to the landing to get those logs, it was terrifying. It was like a scene out of hell to me. All that huge machinery. Dust everywhere. Huge logs rolling around. I wouldn't get out of the truck — I'd just sit there and stayed as small as possible.

My parents had no church affiliations whatsoever. No clubs. My dad wasn't interested in any men's groups. He was just a hard-working, work-all-day, sleep-all-night, and on the weekends tinker with machinery.

There was a pretty large Grange hall there in Corners. In high school we skated a lot. We spent a lot of time down on the creek. Sometimes we'd stay overnight. The mills burnt slashing right out in the open. Not even in those tepee burners. It was just piles of it — acres and acres of it that would burn. We would go out there and stay all night long at those fires. They would have one or two guys tending. We didn't even think of the danger.

The boys were expected to go into logging, woods, or the mills. Unless their parents were education-oriented, where they were expected to go to college. Very few people could afford it. And back even then, the thing to do was to go to L.A. Go to the Bay Area. Get your feet wet in the big city. But so many of them either never made it or they came right back home with their tail between their legs. Big cities were terrifying.

I wanted to leave. And I've lived out of the area quite a few different times. But it's home. I always come back.

I quit high school. I didn't finish. Corners and Grants Pass is like there's this huge wall, and there's one species on one side and one on the other. The "townies" and the "countries." When I got into high school it was rough. Because I didn't dress the way they did. All of us found that out from Corners.

I didn't like high school. I felt out of place. A lot of it had to do with money. If you lived in Corners, chances are you didn't have money. Now it's a kind of status-y thing to live out there in some of those nicer subdivisions. They're beautiful homes out there. But at that time there was old ramshackle old farmhouses. Town people just seemed like they were cooler than us.

I dropped out of high school in junior year. I got married. But I was back home in three months, getting a divorce. And I worked this job, that job. I lived with my parents until I married my children's father. I was nineteen. It's been back and forth to California, you know, chasing a dream. Good job and you go down there, and it ends up not being good. And you come back. We did that over and over. He's an excellent foreman. He did a lot of farm work when we would go down.

B. B. Were you working during that time?

Barbara No. Just having babies. I ended up with four. They're all grown now. It was rough during those years, never having any real security or anything.

During the years that I was a young mother and wife, I was so busy that that's a blur to me. It was all I could do to keep food on the table. Any other outside issues just didn't mean a thing to me. I spent my time trying to keep my kids warm and clothed and fed.

I have noticed now that I can walk down the street and not see a face that I recognize. It's disquieting. I feel like in some ways a big city has moved in on me rather than the other way around. People are in too much of a hurry to even look you in the eye. I feel like it's my town, but I also feel like a little invasion took place there for a while. Even though I came from California myself. In the real early fifties.

There for a while I did resent. I resented having them move in with a lot of money willing to put it onto property that really wasn't worth that much, and therefore raising the value of everyone else's property that did not intend to sell, but had to pay taxes on that raised value. I resented the hell out of that. It was just the whole county felt that way. People didn't even want to say they were from California there for quite a while. I think they feel a little freer now, a little more loose about it.

I think it's just the fact that people finally got used to what was happening. They got used to paying high taxes. So they quit blaming and just kind of buckle down and do it. But it was a way to vent their anger, to blame anybody that moved from California.

The thing that was voiced was taxes, but I think it might have had to do with being afraid that the town was going to get bigger and change when we didn't want it to change. Wanted to stay small. And that maybe they would bring things that we didn't want here. That they would have a right to bring those things simply because they lived here.

I felt lonesome, to walk down my city street and not see a face that I recognized. Not knew, but recognized! And where did all these people come from, and where are all of the real people? You know. That's what I would think.

The newcomers are making major changes in this area. Maybe I'm one of these people that—I'm not really willing to do an awful lot to make change, but I resent bad change that other people make. I'm not one to pick up a flag and march on Washington. Or even march on the courthouse downtown. But I resent other people coming in and making major changes that I think are for the bad. I love this town. It's home. It's my children's home. And will probably be my grandchildren's home. I would like it to stay a decent place for them.

B. B. Does it affect local people's networks?

Barbara I think it does in the fact that we're all just deluded. We've got so much outside influence that is insidious. We don't realize how much something is affecting us until the change is already made.

Look at our school system. It sucks. Back when I was going to school, there was plenty of money for school. I think it's the property owners that got sick and tired of taxes in California, and they don't have any kids in school now, and they don't want to vote on these taxes. And just so many people don't bother to vote, too. That could make the difference in the other direction. And our children are the future. And what are we leaving them? We're leaving them a filthy planet with filthy ideas.

I resent the change that's taken place in this town. Because this is what I relate to, is the changes in *this* town. Not the whole world, you know. And it all works together to work, but I think probably everybody in every little town resents things that have happened.

I don't feel safe at all. I don't feel safe in a locked home, now. Let alone walking a dark road at midnight, five miles long. The crime rate — I don't know that there's more maniacs in the world, just that there's much more people. So maybe they are just so much more apparent, because there are so many more of them. The only thing that I can think of is that, well, the moral values of the whole world have changed. In the last twenty years, they've dropped so drastically. Little kids that are taught really good Christian values, they're considered little weirdos. And now, sign your name to a contract, and you can still get out of it some way. You can cheat! Even with your name written down.

People are starting to realize that they have to pull together to make a difference. That they *have* to make a difference even. I think the way the government is trying to control our woods — there's ways of protecting the animals that need to live there and at the same time still get a living from them. You know, the government was not supposed to own land. And yet they own so much of Oregon that's just inaccessible to us to use as a livelihood.

I feel like the government is very sneaky with us. I think that people find out things after the fact, when there's very little they can do about it without a huge effort. And they're starting to get pissed because of that. And we are the people. But it doesn't work that way anymore. Without this huge effort. And then a lot of times *that* doesn't even work. And I think Grants Pass is starting to resent the intrusion into our area by Big Brother.

That's all I hear. My best friend works in a mill. And he comes home mad every day. Because he keeps hearing these rumors the mill's going to have to shut down, simply because they can't get any more wood. And it makes him mad. He says, "Go boil an owl!"

Well, that's the wrong attitude. The owl has nothing to do with it. That's just the excuse that they're using to shut us down even more.

I think it's wonderful that we have an arm of the government that is responsible for keeping and cleaning up our land. But not to the point where it ties people up where they can't make a living. That they've got to move.

They are. They're moving. They're leaving because they can't live here anymore. There's people that have lost their homes. They're having to move to an area where they don't want to have their children raised in. And it's not fair. So people are going overboard in their blame. 'Cause they really don't know what to do. Except gripe.

I feel like Grants Pass is kind of dying on the vine here. I think the heart's dying out of the town. It seems like the real heart of the community is dying and falling off in chunks. And yet there's more people moving in that don't have to depend on the trees. I don't know what kind of people they are yet. I don't know if they're people I want to live with. So I don't know where I'll be in a few years either. I may end up abandoning the town.

We're going into such a technical world that the old one is just losing its footing. It's stepping in the grease and sliding out from under itself. [*Laughs*] You know? There's not enough for people to do anymore, there's too damn many machines doing it. [*Laughs*] People say, "Well, you know, we don't like it, but there's nothing we can do." You know, the government's just too big, too strong.

B. B.   What about feelings towards the industry?

Barbara   Well, the mill where my brother works, he comes home in the evening and he'll say things like, "Well, the owner" — who only leases the mill — "says it's no big deal to him. He can pick up and move somewhere else. All he has to do is . . . " You know. And here's four hundred guys out of work. So it's a coldness. It's cold.

I have one feeling is that our town got bought without us selling it. You know? [*Laughs*] It's still ours to live here, but it's not ours anymore. I don't know. That's just the way I feel. Just that one little sentence.

B. B.   Do you have social organizations you're involved in?

Barbara   Yeah. Several. There's the Christian groups. A network of support groups. But I don't have a religious life, I have a Christian life. Which is a real big difference. A Christian is a Christian, and a religion is a regimentation. I tend to church-hop. So I'm not really a member of any one church. I go wherever I want to hear their program. [*Laughs*] I'm more interested in God and Jesus rather than a written-out set of rules. Not just take it out on Sunday morning and then gouge however possible all your workweek.

If I had to move, chances are I would move to a larger city simply because of the job opportunities. But by choice, I'd probably move downriver into a cave. [*Laughs*] If I didn't have to have money.

It's just a question of whether I'll be able to support myself in Grants Pass. And if I can't, I'll have to move. There's nothing else available to me. I'm too old for welfare, believe it or not. [*Laughs*] I mean, I don't have any little kids. When you get old and need welfare, you can't get it.

B. B.   We've got people moving in with a lot of education. What does that do to the balance of the community?

Barbara Well, the balance of power goes to the educated. It means that we'll end up being the peons. [*Laughs*]

I see my young cousin, eighteen, dropped out of school. What he writes you can't read. And he reads like a first grader. Very halting. He can't get a job. And he's so into dope and things that I can't get him motivated enough to get into school. Our school system just tosses 'em out now. Defective. Run them through, toss them out.

We're losing good people to teach. They don't pay anything! Being a teacher is the last thing in the world I would ever want to do. Especially these days. When they don't have any respect for them.

B. B. What about drugs in the community?

Barbara Oh, heavens. When I was a young kid, I remember when somebody was caught smoking marijuana. The guy went to prison for years! I don't remember anybody else. I was so unaware during those years, though.

I have friends that have kids that are so into drugs that their families mean nothing to them. Family and friends both. Yeah. No family is untouched. I can't think of one family. I might have thought of one up until a year ago, when I found out two of my more than perfect young cousins were in a drug program.

I see one of my close friends who works in a mill, he's fifty-five, and starting to drink a lot. He never drank a lot when he was young. Then all of a sudden, his drinking's getting to be a problem with him. Ties have got to be there, to everything that's happening to us. I just can't see some of them.

The town we came from in California, there were lots of Mexicans. My very best friend was a Black boy. We moved to Oregon — there's no Black people. This was in fifty-one. No Black people. In fact, some of the things that I remember hearing was, "No, they can't stay in Grants Pass overnight. They have to be out of town by the time it gets dark." And I don't know how much truth there was to that. But I heard that a lot. And I took it as the truth.

I've never had real racial issues. Because I feel we're just all the same. Just happen to be a little bit different. But the lack of color here then was as racial as treating color badly. I remember when they first set up the Fort Vannoy Job Corps, which is now the Rogue Community College campus. The town went completely nuts. Because they were going to be bringing in people from big city ghettos, and they knew that they would be Black and brown and whatever. The town went totally crazy. They would not let any of the young men come into town without a person in control of them. They weren't allowed to go into the stores unless they were in a group with someone in control of them. And it was simply because the town was scared to death of the color.

George Foreman was one of the boys. You know, the boxer? I remember seeing him a couple of times. He was not really famous, but he was well known as a boxer even then. Very handsome man. Young man. You know, every one of them were polite when you would encounter them on the street. They didn't bully you off into the gutter like the town seemed to expect.

I do very little downtown shopping. For one thing, it's mostly exclusive shops. There's a Penney's, but I don't even shop much there. For one thing, I hate the parking in downtown. But I think they're so overpriced — who's going to pay ten bucks for something when they can get the same darn thing for two by just driving a half-mile to Fred Meyer's? Plus all the other things that are available all under one roof. I think downtown Grants Pass just priced itself out of business.

There was little businesses coming and going — little cottage industry type businesses. But they never made it. Because you've got to have a good flow of money to keep those specialty places in business. There's just not that kind of money here, even yet.

And that hurts. If Oregon would loosen up a little bit in some areas, they could let some clean light industry in here. That would make a real difference. It would keep people that want to stay here, here. That are willing to settle for a little less high living, and still keep the beautiful place to live.

B. B. What about the great hippie revolution, when it hit here?

Barbara Yes! And I loved it! I worked at one of the little stores — they sold everything from jeans to kitchen matches. Kerosene. And those hippies bought a lot of kerosene. That store was their second home. There was jillions of them lived nearby. I mean, they were everywhere out there, under every rock, behind every tree.

But you know what? They were fun people. They'd come into the store, laugh and joke. Pop a bottle of wine in the cooler with my boss. Sit in there, and everybody get drunk on wine in the cooler.

They were good. They weren't out to hurt anyone. That's what I liked about them. Lot of people hated them. "Get a job!" You know. "Get off welfare!" For the most part, I cashed an awful lot of checks from the Bay Area for those people. Their parents were sending money, I guess — to stay out of town is the way I looked at it. Back then, like a five-hundred-dollar check a month? You know, like their dads were doctors and whatever.

My boss would take a very large amount of money once a month and cash checks for these guys. But they ran huge bills with him, too. And they would have their Twinkies right along in there with their nutro-grain. [*Laughs*]

I know one couple that live up Fern Creek. They were some of the original hippies. I've seen them up Fern Creek when I go up to get wood, or go up to see old Bob, which is an old miner that I know. I go up and pan for gold on the weekends in the summertime.

He's one of the old ones. He's been up there forever. Him and the BLM hate each other. I mean, he shoots their tires — terrible old guy! [*Laughs*] He's got a nice little mining operation up there. For the most part he ate deer meat and made biscuits and gravy. That's the way he ate, three times a day.

We met Bob in seventy-six. We were looking for a place to get wood. That was about the time they really started clamping down on places to go get firewood. You were having to go clear up miles and miles and miles. I mean, you may as well buy it.

And my ex-husband could talk to anybody. He struck up a conversation with Bob because he was walking along the edge of the road one day up there. And as it turned out, we got a lot of wood. Off of his claim. [*Laughs*] We weren't supposed to. He was supposed to be able to cut firewood, but not sell it or give it away.

He would talk about what it was like to be a miner in the good old days, when they left you alone. And let you provide the United States with gold. He's real bitter with the BLM and the Forest Service. He got sick, and had to go in the hospital. Came back, and his cabin was burnt down, and his animals were in the pound. He'd go build another one.

And the guy worked! He's sat hours by the creek bank with me, showing me how to pan. That's one of my favorite things to do is pan for gold. It's so soothing to me. To be there with just a babbling creek and people you really like — or nobody at all.

To me, Grants Pass has got its own smell. And when I'm away from Grants Pass, and something will bring it to mind? I can smell it. It's a combination of river and woodsmoke. And it's one of the most wonderful smells in the world to me. You know, I love the way Corners smells. Because I was so happy at the time that that smell was getting into my brain, and staying there forever. And it was definitely green, wet, woodsmoke. For the most part it was the wigwam burners and the slash they burned wide open, and all the woodsmoke in the homes.

I can remember the smell of my dad's, what he called tin clothes?

"My tin pants and my tin coat." That was a kind of a rubbery canvas, real heavy thing. When he would come in he always hung it behind the wood heater, and it would get a hot rubbery smell, also a dirt smell, a smoke smell. All of it. It was real soothing to me.

B. B.   Have you known anyone who got hurt or killed working in the woods?

Barbara   Yeah. My brother's best friend was killed. A log fell on him and hit him in the head. He died in my brother's arms. His truck was being loaded when a log slipped and fell off and hit him.

My brother was in a very bad, possibly a dying situation. He lost his brakes coming down a hill loaded with logs. We have pictures of what the truck and the logs and everything looked like down in the bottom of the canyon. He jumped. They measured his footprints, and they were gigantic, from one footprint to the other. He was like flying through the air. He jumped out of there really moving. He didn't die, but we saw how close he came to it. It's a dangerous profession. There's always logging deaths, every year.

My husband, when we first got married, worked as a landing chaser. Which is, he unbuckles logs, makes sure the cable's not tangled, kind of tends to the yarder, too.

They're proud of their work. I think it takes a lot of guts to work around that much dangerous machinery and logs hauling through the air and dirt flying. It's just a dangerous way to make a living.

I think that if my brother had his choice, he would stay in a mill. He enjoys it. He enjoys his cronies that he grew up with. He has coffee every morning with kids he went to school with when we first moved to Oregon. It means so much to have those long relationships and to mean something to each other.

[A man with beautiful long hair walks by] My boy has hair like that, only it's brown. Nice hair. Beautiful. I was going to Blind George's after work the other day, for some popcorn. And there was two skinheads sitting on the bench out front. So I walked way around. I mean, no need to ask for trouble. And as I walked around them he leaned out and blew his nose. Tried to get it on me, you know.

I was telling my son about it when I got home. He said, "Let's go back. I'll kick their asses!" I said, "No. They'd just as soon cut your throat as look at you, dear. We're not going back."

You just don't put yourself in a position to be hurt by them. You avoid them. But, you know — they're such a disgrace. To want Nazism. My God! It just makes my heart ache to think that their life is going in such a direction.

KEVIN SJORN   (age 20)   In the face of massive layoffs in the mills, Kevin reflects the optimism of the young. A slow-talking, muscular man, he is philosophical about the lack of empathy environmentalists demonstrate for timber workers. He is wry about the less-than-truthful reasons given to the public for the closure of the plywood plant where he worked.

Most of the laid-off millworkers who graduated from high school do not have high-school-level skills, and many are at or below eighth-grade level in math or reading. Kevin will probably fare well, going on to school with support from state and federal funds, but many of his older co-workers may have a difficult time.

We met in the back classroom of a school where he had just tested for his GED.

I was born in Medford in 1969. I'm Swedish and American — English American, I guess. European-American. My mom was born in Idaho, I think. My grandparents were from southern Illinois. My grandpa worked building mills — my mom's dad. He just kind of worked building mills, worked his way west. Was in Idaho for a while. Moved here.

My dad was born here. I don't know a lot about my dad. They got divorced when I was one. My mom got remarried, and I thought my stepdad was my real dad. She never told me and didn't like my dad and didn't want him to see me.

My grandpa, he just seemed stable. Everything was more unstable in my immediate family. It was like, you go to Grandpa's and Grandma's, and what's there — it didn't really change. Even when they moved, it still smelled like Grandma's house. We went probably every weekend.

We lived in Medford on a little farm when I was three to six. We had cows, we had a horse for a while. And chickens and goats. It wasn't real big — probably an acre. It's all subdivision now. Then we moved to a house that was probably a mile away.

I guess my stepdad was from around here. I think his mom died. He went to Vietnam, and he had to come back because his family got in an accident. I've got one half-brother. Then a bunch of stepbrothers and stepsisters. My half-brother — when my mom got married the second time, she had him. My dad's been married five times. The first time he had me. The second time he had my half-sister and my stepbrother Jim. Then the third marriage, my stepsister Joanna. The fourth marriage I had stepbrother Mike and stepsister Tanya. Now he's married and she has two kids. Frank and Cindy.

[*Coughs*] I'm going to cough some more. [*Coughs*]. I worked last night, and we broke down these metal plates. And there's a lot of formaldehyde fumes. [*Coughs again*] I wore a respirator. But it doesn't do a lot of good. I'm sorry.

I didn't really see my real dad very much. When I did, we didn't talk a whole lot. We went out and went bowling and went to movies and stuff like that.

My rabbit bit me one day, and my stepdad got mad and killed it. All I remember is him chasing the rabbit around the house. He was really mad. He was chasing it around the outside of the house with a two-by-four. Then he hit it and threw it in the field next door. And I went out and looked for it for hours and never found it. So I decided it must have lived. It ran away.

I don't remember a lot. Just bits and pieces. I remember all about our animals. And getting in trouble for things. I had just a little group of friends. I was really interested in science. I guess that didn't attract a lot of kids. I read all the books in the library on UFOs and the pyramids and Bigfoot and Atlantis.

My stepdad was a trucker at that time. It was just like a nine-to-five, driving a chip truck. It didn't really seem like he ever went to work, because he would leave before we got up. The only times I remember him coming home, he came home with friends. He was kind of a hippie. And he had a lot of hippie friends. He had—I think it's called a hookah. It's like a big bong, and it's got all the hoses coming off of it? He had one of those with like eight hoses, and he'd have all his friends over. Smoked a lot. He made me smoke it once. I didn't want to, and he made me do it. Like once. I coughed my brains out. And after that I guess I didn't have to—I don't know what the deal was.

They both smoked pot, and I don't know what else they did. They had a lot of friends that all had long hair. And they were all real friendly, and real happy. [*Laughs*] I know a lot of songs from the seventies and the sixties. I don't remember ever really seeing them smoke it except that one time he made me. He must have been stoned or drunk or something. But I think my mom had a big part in keeping us away from that.

My mom was a housewife. And she started going to school to get a degree. My mom would have me read to her a lot. Like out of the newspaper. She'd have me read her the ingredients off of cereal boxes.

We didn't go to church. The only time I had ever been to a church was for a funeral. I don't remember going until Mom—I think what happened was, she and my stepdad were fighting. And then these real religious people she knew told her all this stuff, and she got real into it. And now she's really into it.

I was probably six or seven. She was probably twenty-eight. My mom and stepdad got divorced when I was probably six or seven. After that she had a couple boyfriends. They were athletes. I'm sure they must have tried to get me to do sports. And got frustrated. I just didn't see the point. [*Laughs*] I wasn't real interested in hitting a baseball. Plus, up until that time, sports were really frustrating for me. Like in PE. It's like, "All right, we'll take the kid with the Coke-bottle-bottom glasses, and you take the science kid." That's just kind of the way it was.

My mom was real involved in church. A lot of different people wanted me to do a lot of different things. My grandma was real concerned with my education. And mom wanted me to get good grades, but she didn't want me to pursue a career. She wanted me to go to church a lot. There were a lot of things I wanted to do in school that I couldn't, because it interfered with church.

There was one elder, he thought I had the potential to excel in the church. I remember one time we were sitting in the car talking. I was wearing this blue polyester suit, and it was probably a hundred and four degrees outside. I was sweating really bad. And this elder and my mom and this friend of my mom's, they were all kind of arguing about what I was going to do. And I'm just kind of sitting there.

I decided it wasn't what I wanted. I kind of had a double life, because once I decided that that wasn't what I wanted, it was a year before I started acting on it because I knew it was going to cause some big, horrendous problem. And during that year I made a lot of friends at school. We had this group, four or five people, and we'd go sit on the front steps at lunch and discuss anything that came to mind. And we wrote it all down in notebooks. And we played Black Sabbath and Iron Maiden. I was kind of the ringleader.

It was hard, too, because there were kids in school that were in this church. Most of them kind of led a double life. It was different at school. It reminds me how they say people who went to Vietnam, you were all of a sudden taken out of this structured environment and put in one that didn't have any structure at all. It was kind of the same thing. Because you didn't feel like you had somebody watching all the time. So I looked forward to going to school. And I wanted three o'clock to come around so I could get out of school, but I didn't really want to go home. I did. I couldn't go anywhere else.

My friends from high school, the one's in the army. He's going to go to college after that. One of them got married. I don't know what he's going to do. Seems like he was working in an auto shop or something. There was a girl named Lucy, she is working at some kind of motel, cleaning rooms, saving for a pickup truck.

Nobody's really done a lot. The one guy that got married—I guess that's what he wants to do is get married. Seems like his wife wanted to go to college, but she'll probably end up having a kid. And then won't do it.

I think everybody graduated but me. I chose not to do my English. [*Laughs*] I sat in my English class, and it was when I was having all the problems with my mom. That I wanted to go out and be a real person. I would sit in English and write about how I felt. I've got the notebooks at home. Those were just for me, and nobody else has seen them.

I just didn't have enough credits to graduate. I stayed until the end of the year. And it was really hard because at the beginning of the year I was working at a market in Medford, and I was working like forty hours. I was living in Corners with my dad. I would drive to Medford and go to school. And then I would go to work. And then I would drive home. And then my dad and his wife would fight, and I would be up most of the night. That was pretty much continuous. And then I'd go to school the next day. It was real hard to do my homework. I had to share a room with my stepbrother, and he had bunk beds that were too small. And it was a mess. So it made things really hard.

I could have done it if I would've. If I would have been smart, I would have just transferred to Grants Pass High and worked in Grants Pass. But all my friends were at Medford.

For what I was supposed to grow up to do, there's nothing wrong with this area. For a normal person this area is kind of under-developed. There aren't enough activities. Well, it depends on who you are, too, because there are a lot of things here that I like to do. I like to go do things outdoors. I'm pretty laid back.

I have a diverse group of friends. I've got friends that drive low-rider pickups and have five earrings and weird hair. I've got a friend that's kind of a hippie, that's got real long hair and smokes a lot of pot. I've got a friend who's forty that is really knowledgeable as far as mental health goes. He works at the mill with me. He's like three terms away from his A.A. degree.

The guys that drive the low-rider pickups wish that it was easier to find drugs. And there were more parties and less police. My friend that's forty always has something to do. He's really into music and he collects books. And my friend that's kind of a hippie, we can talk about music. Like Pink Floyd. Especially Pink Floyd.

But it just kind of depends on who you are. It's a nice area for older people. I don't mean like sixty, but I mean like after you're out of college.

I just worked. I was being a box boy. I took a job at one of these convenience stores. One time I worked like three twelve-hour shifts in a row. It was three dollars and fifty cents an hour. It was real low pay. But it was pretty ridiculous. So I quit.

Then I got a job at another supermarket. And then RoguePly called me. My cousin works there. Our other uncle got him a job there. And then he got me the job there. That was about fifteen months ago.

When I was working at the supermarket it was: Have a job, be alive. Buy beer to go to parties. And then I decided I wasn't really accomplishing much and I wasn't very happy. So I decided to go to college, so I put in an application at RoguePly.

When I started working at RoguePly, it was like living hell. It was really, really hard work. Harder than I've ever worked. I was working harder than I ever had, and I still wasn't working hard enough to do the job.

I was grading veneer. We buy veneer from a lumber mill. And it's wet. And then we run it through dryers. And they're huge — they're as big as the house I lived in. They've got thousands of rollers in them. The wood runs in between the rollers, and we've got a furnace that blows hot air through there. It dries the wood and it comes out of the dryer onto a belt. And then it dumps it off onto a big round table and it goes around. According to the size of the knots and the quality of the wood, we have different grades.

So then we have carts to put it in. You wouldn't think that would be real hard. But it goes really fast. And there are different kinds of wood, and different qualities of wood. When I first started, we were doing a wood called "white speck." It's wood that the tree had fungus on it. And it eats a lot of little holes in the wood. So when you go to grab it, it just crumbles in your hand. So there's a special way you have to handle it to keep it from doing that. And it's really hard to learn it that way. We did that for like two months.

There are different sizes of wood. There's sheets that are fifty-four inches wide and eight feet long. Then we got "twenty-sevens" that are half as wide but just as long. "Fishtails" half as long. And different widths.

You have to look up the table at what's coming down towards you. If you miss it, it comes back around. But it'll pile up. And then you're in trouble. Because you're wearing big leather gloves. And if you're smart you wear mittens over those—they're just kind of a tube that goes over the leather. And that keeps you from getting slivers. 'Cause the gloves will wear out, and we've got guys that get slivers clear through their hand. It's not good.

Once you know how to handle the wood, it's kind of like driving a car. When you first start, you have to look to see where the pedals are? And then after a while it's just kind of automatic. It's not like you're driving a car, it's like you're going somewhere.

That's what I started to do. Then they trained me on a lot of other things. They've got hot presses. The veneer that I grade out, they take it to the spreaders. It's a big machine that you feed the wood through it, and it puts glue on both sides. So they'll take a big fifty-four. And they'll feed fishtails through this machine, and it puts glue on them. And they'll lay it down on top of this fifty-four. Then they'll put another fifty-four on top of that. Then more fishtails.

What they do is, one guy is feeding it through the machine. It's got big rollers, so it shoots them out, and there's a guy catching them. He just catches them and lays them down. They go really, really fast. They work on a production bonus.

So then they run it down a conveyer belt to a press. I don't know how many tons of pressure. It just squeezes it all together so it all sticks. Then they load it on these little shelves—it's called a charger. Then these like bicycle chains with little hooks on them, it'll come up, and they push the wood into the press, which has these big hot plates. And then it all compresses and heats up, and the glue melts and kind of combines with the wood. And makes it into plywood.

Then they take it down to the finish end and saw it out and sand it and putty it and do all kinds of things to it.

So I can help the spreadermen. I can help the press operator. I break the press operators when they go for their lunch break or whatever. They trained me how to run the furnace. I can grade. I can feed the dryer. That's when you stand at the end, you take the wet pieces and put it in one end, and it sucks it into the dryer. That's entry level.

Oh, and I can plug. They take big sheets of veneer, and where it has a knot, what it does, it punches out a football-shaped piece. And then it puts a good piece of wood in there. It looks like what it does is, it cuts a groove in the inside of the veneer, and then pops that thing in so it'll stay. A Raimann plugger. It's not real hard on you. It's real boring. And it sounds like a jackhammer. And it vibrates. But it's not really that bad.

B. B.   Did you have intentions of staying in the mill?

Kevin   No. Especially after I started working there. I had a foreman that was like a drill sergeant. That guy was a jerk. I didn't mind the hard work. I wondered for a while whether I was going to be able to do it. But that guy really pushed me. Now I'm pretty good at it.

But I didn't intend to stay. I didn't think they were going to ever call me. So I was just going to work at the supermarket. And I had decided I wasn't going to take the RoguePly job if they offered it. Because they had already started the spotted owl thing. Trying to make it an endangered species and stop them from cutting old-growth timber. Plus, you know, it's not a real good job. But as far as the money goes it's a good job. But as far as the work, it's not. It's dusty and dirty and hot and bad on your body. And I decided I wasn't going to take it, but they called, and I thought, Well, I'll just go in and see. And I went in and I thought, Well, this is my ticket to college. As far as money goes. But it wasn't like immediately. Now it's immediately. Because of the layoff.

Why they did it? They said it was because of the spotted owl. The immediate layoff is because of a DEQ regulation that says they have to put a scrubber on the stacks. At three hundred thousand dollars. They say that they can't see putting three hundred thousand dollars into a mill when they don't know if the supply of timber is going to last.

So that's what shut them down. But there are a lot of things that could be affecting it. There's the scrubber. There's the spotted owl. There's also, he just opened two mills in another region. He only has to pay the workers five dollars an hour. So that cuts his labor cost. It's all college kids. And so he can get away with it.

Nobody has really doubted that they're closing down because the scrubber costs too much. They're all pretty much already riled up about the spotted owl. And the environmentalists and all that. They think there's more to it, but they're not really sure what.

The only thing they know is working in the mill. Like the spelling down there. I have a good time going around picking on people's spelling. Not to be rude or anything, but it's kind of funny sometimes. During the winter we want to keep all the doors closed so it doesn't get really cold inside. Somebody put a sign up on the doors. Said, "Please keep the door closed." And they spelled door D-O-R-E.

It's kind of sad. Because they're people that could accomplish more, and make more out of their lives than just being alive. I think the people settle for the money. Or make poor choices and get trapped in the situation. Would get married and have a kid. Buy a car.

A lot of them have already gotten jobs at other mills in Medford and Glendale. Pretty local. The spreadermen aren't having too much trouble getting work, because that's considered really skilled labor. My job to me and to the other people who have my job is skilled labor. To management it's not. If they considered it a skill, they'd make a lot more money. Because half the people that do my job now would be fired, because they don't do it right. They would pick up a lot more money if they had more people who were concerned with doing it right. I started at seven dollars and sixty-one cents. I got a raise to nine sixty-seven.

It's not going to do them much good to move to another mill. 'Cause they're just postponing the inevitable. I think the layoff's good for some people. It's good for the people who see it as an opportunity to go to school, or to move to a different area.

As far as the spotted owl is concerned, I don't think the spotted owl is the reason. I think it's the tool to keep the timber from being cut. Because the environmentalists have decided that there isn't enough.

Which I can understand. But I also think that you have to weigh the consequences. There are good things and bad things from both viewpoints. As far as how it affects my life, for me it's an opportunity. Because there are programs to reeducate millworkers that have been laid off. And I'll get some money for college. But the guys that are fifty, fifty-five, even if they are a spreaderman, they're not going to get hired anywhere. And I really wonder what they'll do. Some of them are too stubborn to go to college. Too much pride.

I can see a lot of people moving away. It doesn't seem like the environmentalists that are behind it are from this area. They seem like they've come in from somewhere else. And they don't—it's like they don't understand how much the economy is based on timber. Or that—but I'm kind of biased, because my dad's a logger. So I grew up thinking that timber was the world. There's life after a plywood mill. I hope. [*Laughs*] So my dad'll be out of work before too long, too. He's really in debt. Has a house and truck and credit cards.

It's like if the environmentalists had grown up the way I did, they wouldn't be environmentalists. You know what I mean? That's why they seem so distant. Because they haven't had the experience that I have. They can sympathize, but they can't empathize. It's like, somebody that's never seen glass won't be sensitive to the fact that it'll break. So they won't be careful around it. Does that make sense?

It's like the glass is the timber industry and the economy of the area. And these people come from a different area where they don't have glass. And they say, "Oh, what's this?" And hit it with a rock to see what it'll do. And it breaks. And that's what they're doing right now.

They say they're doing it because they want to protect the earth. I guess that's why. I can't think of another reason to do it. I mean, I can't see a group of people out to destroy a town, or out to destroy a group of people's lives. Or deliberately turn things upside down.

I think they're kind of going overboard, though. The forests are being replanted. I think that part of it has to do with politics, too. Because there were all these studies of old-growth timber, and they found spotted owls. And they said, "Well, spotted owls only live in old-growth timber." Well, this guy over here went and looked at some new growth and found spotted owls. And it was in the newspaper. Then after that you didn't hear anything about it. But there were more old-growth studies.

As far as being able to sit here and really know what I'm talking about, as far as being able to say, "Yeah, there's plenty of old-growth timber to last," I can't say that. I don't know that.

I know how it affects the people in the area. It's kind of like all these people, like the people from my mill, and the people from GP Plywood. All the ones that have shut down, they move to National. And then National shuts down. And then they move to this other one until it shuts down. And then pretty soon there's not going to be anywhere to go. And there's going to be a lot of people that are having a lot of problems.

What changes have I seen? Well, all the fields around the farm in Medford are subdivisions. They're just building tons of them. And every time I go over there it's like the city's gotten bigger and the country's gotten smaller. I went to San Francisco about three weeks ago, and they had houses everywhere. And I thought about it. It started as a little town. And they just built. They kept expanding and expanding. And Medford could be that way someday. That would be really weird.

Medford used to be kind of like Jacksonville. A bigger version of Jacksonville. It was like people built houses, not like contractors came in and put together houses. Now it's kind of impersonal. Because tract homes, they all look the same. And condos. Townhouses and apartments. There's no individuality. It's kind of like, I look at Jacksonville or Medford and I see individual people. I go to San Francisco and I see a mass of people. It's a big difference. I can drive through town in Grants Pass and see five or ten people that I know. I could drive through San Francisco for a week and not see anybody. Even if I lived there all my life. People are rushing around to get places. I don't like to rush around. I like to take my time. I get there when I do. [*Laughs*]

I like to go camping. I'm going to go camping tomorrow if the weather's decent. I like to backpack, back in the woods where there's nobody. And it's just a sense of — it's like a condo is real fake. They're all alike. And there's this place called Circle Lake that I go to, there's a big cliff on one side. I climb up to the top. And there's this old scraggly tree. I sit by this tree and look out. This lake that's big when you're down there, it's really small when you're looking down on it. And you can see all these trees. And a couple different lakes. And mountains.

It's kind of like — in Grants Pass or Medford, when you're in town, I feel like I kind of live my life in two dimensions. Like I'm on a map. And when I get out in the woods, I get up on that cliff, and all of a sudden there's three dimensions. It's like, I'm out here, I can please myself, and be myself. And there are a lot of places to do that around here. Places to hike and fish and float the river, and ski if you're into that.

I didn't plan on the mill closing and people offering me money to go to school. It just kind of happened. It's kind of like the end of an era. You know, you have your colonial era. And then you have your gold rush era. And then you have your Old West era. And now you have the timber era, and that's ending. It's kind of like it's sad to see it go, but I'm curious to see what's coming.

I know it's not that way for a lot of people. They're just worried. Too bad they can't see more than that. It's not like they're going to die. There are programs to help them out, and if they want to do something better, they can. It's their choice.

Part of the 1,200-truck convoy at Silver Fire Roundup, a demonstration in support of salvage logging of wildfire-burned timber

Timothy Bulla

Logging operation in Siskiyou National Forest

Environmentalists hold drum ceremony on Sugar Loaf Mountain in North Kalmiopsis roadless area

Timothy Bu[...]

EarthFirst! protest at Siskiyou National Forest Headquarters

Rally supporting timber workers in Grants Pass, Oregon

Timothy Bullard

Contract logger sharpens the teeth on his chainsaw

Timothy Bullard

Gyppo (independent) logger with log deck and branding hammer in Rogue River National Forest

RIGHT: **Tree sitter protesting plans for salvage logging in roadless area**

Northern spotted owl juvenile and adult

ROSLYN SELLERS (age 38) Until the 1980s, relatively few jobs were available to women in the Rogue Valley. Now there are more, but not enough, and so there is stiff competition for the new low-paying, no-benefits service jobs. Women like Roslyn, with a strong work ethic and only a high school education (or less), often find themselves on welfare when they cannot successfully compete in the employment market to support their family. Until the "New JOBS" program was mandated by federal welfare reform and pioneered at the state level, women on welfare were severely penalized for attending college, including vocational programs.

Roslyn and I spoke a week before she started a new clerical job with moderate pay and health insurance. She was upbeat and excited.

I was born in Prineville, Oregon, in 1950. My mom was from central Oregon, and my dad's family was from northern Wisconsin. My mom's family were ranchers. My dad's folks died when he was young, so I never even got to know them. We've lived here for twenty-five years. My mom, she still lives in the same place that we lived in since I was five.

My dad basically moved out here trying to do construction, which is what he did some of in Prineville. But he ended up working in mills. Cheney Studs? Which is not even existent under that name anymore. And then Conrad for many years. That was considered a real good place to work. That's what ten of us arrived on, a mill job.

We only had a two-room house — they called them Camp White Houses. Through the years, what was our front porch ended up being our kitchen. And ended up being a four-bedroom house. Many, many bunk beds and kids piled up four high.

I was second to the youngest of eight kids. All but one brother of mine live in this area. One sister lives in Portland. And the rest of us are all still in the Rogue Valley. Two brothers and one sister own land here.

I really admired my dad. Very close to my dad. I was his baby girl of three daughters, and he really spoiled me. It had an impact on me, on what kind of man I was going to pick. Really. You know how little girls look up to their daddies. I wanted somebody that was a hard worker. My dad would come home so tired — had put in his day at the mill. And I ended up picking a husband that I thought was that type of guy [*laughs*], but that didn't work out.

My dad, seems like all he did pretty much was work. Our family, all the brothers and sisters, worked in a lot of the JoJo Chickens, at the Bill's Hamburgers. Some of them don't even exist now. We'd get on at each other's restaurants. That was handy. I got a lot of my first jobs because, either my sister two years older than me or my brother four years older than me got me in. And my mom did work at Nadine's Restaurant in White City, there on the highway. They had all the business from the mill.

That's where I was different than a lot of my friends. A lot of my friends didn't work as young as I did. I kinda had to grow up fast in ways. Because when they were going to proms, I was working.

We still had a lot of fun. We did a lot of stupid things. [*Laughs*] Well, like cruising. And doing the Chinese fire drills? Where you pull up to a light or a stop sign and everybody opens their door and gets out and runs through the cars? You've *never* heard of a fire — ?

To try pot was a big deal. At least in my crowd. I hung out with what they considered the hoods. Which were people that didn't mind admitting that they did that stuff. And then there was the Socs that, as far as I'm concerned, did it anyway, but claimed they didn't. But the people I hung around with the most, drinking was more of a big deal than the pot. That was fun to do on a Saturday night. I can really say that hard drugs just weren't a problem at our school. Drinking was what you did to be cool. We used to skip class and go get a bottle of Strawberry Hill.

A lot of my closer friends, their dads were in business on their own. I remember being proud that my dad worked in a mill. It's not like now, where everything is so iffy about whether people are going to have jobs. [*Laughs*] I thought, I'm going to find me a guy that works in a mill, and I'll be with somebody that makes good money. That kind of thing. [*Laughs*]

I knew I wasn't going to get a white-collar type of person. I wanted somebody that was a blue-collar worker. But knowing myself, I always pictured myself in a plush office, you know. Control. [*Laughs*] Not controlling things, but being needed. Feeling like I was making a difference.

The plan was that I was going to work and go to school and become a teacher. I went to Linn-Benton Community College. I love Linn-Benton. I went one term there. Started my second term, and just — I met my husband. My later-to-be husband. I quit school.

He was only sixteen, here I'm seventeen. But living on my own. He encouraged me to stay. I'd been working three jobs. A work–study job as a security person, working at Bill's Hamburgers up there, and a nursing home job. In the kitchen of a nursing home. Which is where I met my husband. He worked the next shift.

So I was in love. I felt I'd had a lot of pressure put on me, and I was the one eager to — "Let's just move." So we moved down to Brook-ings. I worked in a theater, and we just lived this real simple life. He worked out of the fisheries.

We moved around a lot, though. And still did, many years to-gether. I almost felt like a gypsy lifestyle. What I like about my life a lot right now, it's very my idea of normal. I'm trying to get real stabi-lized where I live, and now with a job coming up . . .

We moved to Red Bluff. My husband's job was picking up the lot at the drive-in and all that stuff. And I helped him. But we, you know, we weren't married at that time. We were still just living together. Then we moved up to the Medford area. And moved to Grants Pass. Then we got married, and we decided we're going to do things right. He was going to go to welding school. Got all A's. Now this is a guy that's never been past tenth grade.

Then we moved around and moved around. We moved to Salt Lake, and I managed a Jiffy Burger for a while. He did construction work. All kinds of jobs. But Salt Lake was the furthest we ever moved away. Mostly it was just northern California to Portland. Always com-ing back. We're both pretty family-orientated, so we kept moving to-ward the family it seemed like. And away. [*Laughs*] They were really happy years, but it was a lot of moving around. Finding out who we were.

And then, almost two years ago, I just got tired. I was growing and my husband was staying the same. And he's still doing what I thought was a lot of fun ten years ago. And it's not fun anymore. I hit my thir-tieth birthday this year. I thought, I want more out of my life. And so we separated. My husband's still in Jenner. Kind of going to some bad directions, which I'm real glad I'm not there to be a part of. For me or my girls. I came over here and started training in a joint program be-tween the local college and welfare.

B. B.   Was it hard for you to have to deal with welfare?

Roslyn   Yeah. We had a couple times before. I mean, growing up having it hard, I mean, I wasn't — so proud. Let's put it that way. But what I did is that I moved from Jenner. Got emergency help to get my kids, and I got a house. And got a job the same day. I moved into my house and started my work the next day. So, actually, my idea was, I'm having them help me out, but I'm not going to be on it. But, of course, wages at the MicroMart weren't enough to keep us going. It took almost a month and a half till I got any help. And I kept working at the MicroMart, and trying to get my life together and my head straight after splitting up with somebody.

B. B. So you didn't have to deal with the AFS [Adult and Family Service] system for very long?

Roslyn Well, at first I did. Sure, I did—you know, beg and borrow and steal is my feeling of it, just to get help. I mean, my car was a piece of junk that didn't run very well. I got a lot of help. I mean, they were good with me, but I really had to fight for everything I had. Just like it seems like I've always done. [*Laughs*]

And luckily, with my background, and with my schooling that I've had before, and my attitude, they thought the short-term training was just perfect for me. And there was a year. And I'm just completing my office technology certificate and already hired to go to work. So—I mean, I'm going nowhere but up.

Going through the program, I mean—women have been beaten. Women that take verbal abuse. That was a terrible situation for their children. Or have their children stole from them. And I figure, yeah, my husband started living a bad life and walked out on us. And I could set here and mope about things weren't perfect for me. But I wasn't beaten.

I started thinking, it wasn't as bad as it could have been. [*Laughs*] And we had many good years together. I can go on. I don't regret living with the sucker. [*Laughs*] The way I hear a lot of these women. But I feel good about my life.

B. B. What kind of changes have you seen in the area?

Roslyn So much seems the same to me. Except for the population. Growing up just outside of Medford was so small when we moved here. Where there was the schools there was just fields and fields and fields. And there was nothing else. Now there's just subdivision after subdivision. I just can't believe the growth.

The mills are still crucial to this area. Of course things are shaky now. Back then it was just, oh, yeah, you had a mill job. You knew you were set. You were going to have it made. You weren't going to hurt for nothing. 'Course now, it's a whole different story.

I have three brothers at Southwestern Mill. My other brother works at the Transco mill. Which they are already hurting. Real bad. From this spotted owl thing and stuff. Because they have that older-growth timber coming in there. That used to be Crown. And that's Transco now.

Southwestern, somehow I don't think they're touched by it right now. None of those three brothers are really worried. It's the one that has already been cut down to four days a week at Transco. And lots of people have been laid off and everything there. So.

But, see, in that way, to me, this area hasn't changed at all. I grew up with a dad that worked for years in mills. And now four of my brothers are still working in the mills. And several of those brothers, let's see, three of those have had college education. But they can't make the money doing what they went to college for—and how good of money they make right now at the mill. They love this area. They're here for life.

About the spotted owl, I think my family's torn between it. Boy! I've done a lot of thinking about it, and I tell you, if somebody told me I had to decide one way or the other, I couldn't do it. Because the reason those very same people in my family live here is because they love this area. And they love the nature. They're almost all of them involved in nature one way or the other. And they love the land, so they know the importance of keeping our environment, keeping the trees around. And yet, like I said, four brothers work in the mills. That's their income, that's their family.

My brother that's hurting the worst, the one that works at the mill in Central Point—him and my mom get talking, and she's, you know, really into the birds. She's saying you can't kill everything off. And of course Joe was going around with a bumper sticker, "We dip our spotted owls in Exxon" or whatever. [*Laughs*]

So. I'm real torn. I've got brothers that need that as their income. And of course I don't want to see them lose their jobs. And I've got an area I love to live in that I hate to see everything ripped out. Just for the sake of money. And a livelihood. Even though it is important.

I don't know what to think of the whole thing. I don't know enough of the real issues. I don't know if, you know, is this just pumped up to try to get more money? I mean, is the mill barking up the wrong tree? Or were they getting down on these people for the spotted owl, which has nothing to do with it at all?

I saw on the news last night, they're out there counting how many of the owls there are. And they got seventy guys on the job full-time. And I keep thinking, will they find there are a lot more of them than they thought? Because I lean towards being an environmentalist. Definitely. But when you have four brothers that work in the mill, you don't want to see them out of work. [*Laughs*] You know?

B. B.   Do you have any thoughts on the influx of people into the area?

Roslyn   I can't blame people for wanting to move from California up here. It's so beautiful here—they want what we already have! [*Laughs*] But I do keep thinking, Are we going to end up like a California? Is our woods going to keep being, you know — are we going to start losing more of our nature stuff? Are we going to get so overcrowded that we're going to end up to be city-like? Are you going to be able to drive by and see twenty-acre fields? And I think if people keep coming at the rate they do, we're not going to see that. And that's a lot of what I like about this area is space.

People come here that have never ever lived anywhere but in an apartment complex. I mean, as a kid! It's like a culture shock to me. I can't imagine living that way. I have to hand it to them. I couldn't do it. Boy, I sure can't blame people for wanting to come up here.

B. B.   What about the economy of the area?

Roslyn   I think if people want to work they'll find something. They might have to give in a little bit, to work into what this area offers. But, yeah, I think this economy's been scary for a lot of years for a lot of people. I don't know — I just think that's a reality of living here. I can remember people talking about the economy and worried about it when I graduated. And it really hasn't gotten any better. I look at people that really want work, and they find it. Like what I got. It's not like I just took whatever came along. I do think you may not get exactly what you want. [*Laughs*] In this area.

And the mills are very important. And that is scary to me: What is going to happen if these mills start shutting down right and left? Because that is what's keeping these businesses going, a large part.

B. B.   Some people talk about retirement and tourism as being some replacement.

Roslyn   I think that is a very realistic thing. You know, the worse cities get, and the bigger they get, the more city people need to get away, even if it's just as good old "tour-i's." I know they're counting on that right now to pick up the slack from mills and other things not doing well.

That Mall was such a plus for this area. I wish I had that as a teenager here! That's what I see different! I mean, we cruised, but I want to cruise on my feet in the Mall and look at the good-looking guys when I was sixteen instead of when I'm thirty. And look at all the jobs that brought in.

I think without an education down the line you're going to be nowhere. And you're going to be caught up in the welfare zone. For this area, if they don't get some education behind them, and hands-on experience. And they're not going to be able to support themselves and their family. I mean, for their needs — not even luxuries. But just to survive anymore.

I mean, most women, sure, they may enjoy their work. But they do it because they need to anymore. There are a lot of them that are single parents. My college has opened up places I wouldn't have gotten to be.

B. B.   The area used to be ninety-nine percent Anglo.

Roslyn   We are still so massively white here. [*Laughs*] That's not even funny. I mean, I remember having one Black girl in our high school. Now, I can't say that it's that much different. Just because of lack of seeing, my younger daughter will turn and look at a Black man because they're different.

When I walked into a McDonald's in downtown Portland, I was the only white person in the building. The only white person. All the workers were Black. All the customers were Black. And I was the only white person. And for the first time ever, I got to feel what it felt like to be the minority. I'll never forget that feeling. I felt like turning around and walking out. And yet the people were nothing but friendly to me. But I was younger, and I felt real intimidated by "I'm different, they're all the same" kind of thing. [*Laughs*] It was funny. I'll never forget that feeling of walking in there. I mean, there was no reason to feel that way. Just, you know, growing up in an area where it was white. Very white.

But it is changing a bit. The Mexicans have definitely increased. Or at least my knowledge of them — maybe it's just that I'm older. But where I lived, there's the orchards all around us. So it's something that I do think I noticed. Because I lived so close, growing up around them. I'd like to see us more culturally versatile, instead of being so white. Like I said, when a child looks at a Black person like they're so strange, you know?

B. B.   What about drugs?

Roslyn   With two kids, raising them right now, I'm scared to death of this area, and any area you're in. I feel safer being over here than where we moved from. I didn't like what was going on there, but it's going on everywhere. It's just not as obvious.

It's crazy now. I don't remember anything like methamphetamine labs going on when we were growing up. Sometimes pot plants. That was a big deal back then. People getting caught with pot was a big deal. Can you imagine? Now it's everything. Now it's crack.

Growing up we never locked doors. We never ever in my growing up ever had a locked door in our house. And now you're crazy not to lock your doors at night. Especially if you live closer into town. I mean, I live on Grady Street now, and lots of traffic going by, lots of

people walking. I always double-check my locks. And I'm not a paranoid person. But you can't trust anybody anymore.

I remember when we were growing up, riding our ten-speeds into
the Medford Shopping Center. You never worried. Even though we
were fairly young teenagers, we could be let go that far. I mean, I
worry about leaving my ten-year-old three blocks from where I'm at.
That's real sad. And we'll never get that back. Our kids will never see
that.

I know the economy being poor here — you know, people being
out of work makes people look for quick money and the drugs. And if
you get involved in drugs, you need more money, and crime gets
worse. And I do think if the economy gets worse here we're going to be
dealing with worse problems than we are. I remember where if you
heard about a murder or something like that here once in five or seven
years — ten years is a big deal to hear of someone getting murdered in
the entire valley. And now, what? Three, four people. I mean, the girls
found up in the bleachers in Ashland. This is just so unheard of. It's
no big deal to read in the paper about somebody blowing somebody
away.

But I don't have any answers. I wonder: Why does it have to be
this way? Times are rough — do people have to get involved in this?

I went through it in my own life. Watching my husband. Why
does a good guy, a good family guy, in a time when he could be with
a family and in a productive situation, choose to be off with people
that, you know — I hate to sound judging, but people that are going nowhere with their lives, and don't really care where they go with their
lives. Why would somebody like that? And how many think like that?
How many don't give a shit? [*Laughs*] Really. And this get-rich idea? I
mean, it happens to the best of people. I've seen it.

And now, look at kids. I mean, look at my own life, you know? I'm
with someone that doesn't have his two kids right now. That hasn't
even seen them for over a year. Because the mother took off with
them. Then I see my husband, that could be a part of my kids' life,
choose not to be. And you look at how crazy it is. Now my kids are living with another set of kids' father. Just how the plot thickens.

We didn't have that growing up. I think in all the friends I had,
one girlfriend, her parents were divorced. Shhhs! Hardly anybody has
their own parents anymore.

B. B.   What would you like to see for your kids and for the area?

Roslyn   Maybe somehow it could be a littler safer. I remember
riding my bike on the bike trail as a kid. Now, a woman's, couple years

back, raped. I mean, a beautiful place right now to be able to jog or do something. And I won't do it. I'd be afraid to do it.

The big picture is that maybe they can have the nature and all the stuff I got to enjoy as a kid. That the lakes will be clean enough. And camping! I hope they can go out and camp somewhere and it doesn't have to be in a little line with a bunch of people.

VERA and CHUCK CARTER   (ages 58 and 60) Each of the Carters radiates a sense of familial warmth and generosity. The family's two generations represented in this book (see interviews with Gary Carter and Theresa Carter) enjoy a wide circle of friends, with whom they gather frequently in their modest, inviting rural homes.

The long hours Chuck spent driving truck decades ago are still the norm for log truck drivers, and independent haulers put in many more hours on truck maintenance as well. Each job in the forest demands a level of physical exertion and danger alien to most workers in the United States today. Although Chuck's stint on the slopes was over years ago, his disproportionate upper-body strength still fits the physical profile.

Vera's stories of berry and mushroom patches disappearing because of rural residential development are now typical throughout southwest Oregon. Local family or counter-culture mushroom gatherers are in fierce competition with caravans of permit holders of various ethnic backgrounds, often of southeast Asian descent, seeking out high-price fungi for the international market.

Vera   I was born in Los Angeles in 1931. My folks moved back up here when I was two years old. They had been here before, because my mother had graduated from Medford. My dad was originally from Minnesota. I don't really know what brought them here. My dad was the youngest of ten children.

We came back up here and we lived up close to Preston. Up Ten Gulch Road, in a log cabin. I believe ours was the original family commune, because we had a cabin that we lived in, and down the road was my Uncle John and Aunt Louise, and then across the creek was Uncle Ken and Aunt Mary and their family, and some of the other members I think lived for a while in the barn.

We had a root cellar that went under the cabin that we kept a lot of the food in. We grew it, and then, of course, we'd have venison. We had dandelion greens and lot of the things that we went up in the field and picked.

When I was younger, there weren't too many girls that lived around close. It was usually just Ted and I playing around on the hill and collecting snakes and spiders and things. Most of our entertainment was homemade type. We were home feeding the chickens, working in the garden, and things like that.

After we were married, my husband needed to learn a trade, because we married while I was still in high school, and he was just out of high school. We went down to California and he took his apprenticeship in Electricians' Local down there. We were down there for five years, and I *hated* southern California. It's just freeways and cars.

Then we moved back up here. He said, "I don't care if we starve, we're going back to Oregon."

A lot of people have said this area is for a retired person that has a lot of money. Or you kind of scratch. [*Laughs*] I worked for Harry and David* for somewhere around twelve years. Just part-time. I started out packing Christmas baskets back in the sixties somewhere. They started back in the thirties sometime with just a fruit stand, so they just sold their extra produce from the orchard. Now it's worldwide.

That was the only outside work I did. I worked basically as a housewife except for when the Carter family had a rabbit ranch. We had a rabbit ranch just right next door for about five years.

Chuck's folks bought this property in the late fifties. There was just a little two-room cabin, and they added on to that. We rented different places, and then we moved into the house there. His folks built a house down the other end of the property. There were forty acres. So when they decided that was enough rabbit, we got eleven acres here.

But this is where we wanted to be. I said, "I want to live the rest of my life right here, looking at the mountains." When I told a friend from Arizona that, he said, "You do?" Like, you know, that was strange. And when I go to town, and have had a hard day in town, as soon as I turn up Clear Creek, it's home. It just seems to relax me.

The church down here, the boys went to Bible school. And when they got older they went to church so they could play basketball and whatnot.

B. B.   Has church been important to you?

Vera   Not really that much. I go occasionally.

So many houses are going up. In places that there used to be just a house here and there. Now it's even on Clear Creek. Somebody will say, "Well, do you know so-and-on lives on Clear Creek?" I say, "I don't know most of the people that live on Clear Creek anymore." Just the old-timers that live here. But you drive along and it's just one house after another.

We used to know most people on the road. Especially when our boys were in school. That was the community focal point, was the school. You had pancake breakfasts. Of course you always went to all of the programs that the children put on.

I can remember now when I was a kid growing up here. You could go down to the river anyplace and go swimming. And be the

*Harry and David's is a nationally known mail-order fruit, gift, and plant company that employs over a thousand Rouge Valley workers, most of them seasonally. *B.B.*

only ones there. Now you can't find a place on the river that it's not full of people. Even when we lived in Medford, the whole family would get together, and we would go up around Louden area and have picnics and swim and whatnot. All the places along the river that we would come out, we'd pick blackberries anyplace, and go gather mushrooms. Now, you go to one of your favorite mushroom spots, or blackberry spots, there's a sign: NO TRESPASSING. Or somebody's built a house right in the middle of it. [*Laughs*] People that move in, they seem to put up this wall around them, or fence — "Nobody trespasses on my property!"

And before, the old-timers, you'd just say, "Is it OK if I go through your field and go fishing, or go to the river, or pick blackberries?" And they'd say, "Sure." But not anymore.

I think you're losing a lot of the family closeness, families doing things together. Different families would get together for picnics and get-togethers at the different homes. I think there's a lot of people, seems like everybody's at odds with everybody else. They have so many different ideas as to how they want to run things.

It seems like that, after the children got out of school, we kind of lost contact with a lot of the neighbors. Somebody that lives just down the road, you very seldom see them anymore. Because you're not in contact, doing things at the school. The school and the church were the hubs of the community. At first it was basically a lot of the families were farm families here. They worked on the farm. And then, as other people moved in, they had both parents worked, and they worked in town, and they didn't have time. I think that was a lot of it. Land prices have gone up. Especially if it's along the river. They just go out of sight.

When Chuck and I met and were first married, his dad and Lou Sidel had a little sawmill right down here at Blaketon. And then Chuck drove a logging truck for a while. It was an old truck, and he'd get up early in the morning and drive, and then he'd come home and he'd work until almost midnight repairing it. Get up again. Drive.

Now, a lot of the clearcutting is not really too pretty. I can see where some people object to that where it's right in their backyard and that's what they look at. But I understand that it's not economical for the logging companies, sometimes, to go through and just pick. I think that if they harvest when they need to, and then the trees are replaced, that it should go on. But the logs should stay here for the lumber industry here.

Of course we have some people we know that are for shipping all the logs to Japan. Um-hmm. Money. Some that belong to the other political parties, shall we say? [*Laughs*] One is a part owner in a mill.

It seems like the people with more money come in and buy out and then everything seems to go downhill. Maybe it isn't, but it just seems like once they're sold to this big company from wherever, they are no longer business that has been in this area and kept people going for so long. [*Chuck comes in.*] She was asking me about the logging.

Chuck Logging, huh? I've worked sawmills and woods. I don't agree with the way they clearcut. I don't think there's any need to go on down and cut a twenty-, thirty-year-old tree just because it's easier to log.

They tell you it's too steep to log. You got to do it that way. I can remember years ago, wasn't too steep. And they select-logged everything. So, it's a mystery to me. They've got their version, and ecologists got their version, and try to meet someplace in the middle. Opinions are like noses, everybody's got one. But I don't like the clearcuts. I've never liked to clearcut.

Just take a look at all these mountains in here. [*Indicates*] That isn't clearcut damage. That's all fire damage. Years and years and years ago that all burnt off. Underneath those laurels and what have you there's a million little fir trees growing. But they're shaded, and they don't get the sunshine like they should, and the laurels eat up most of the moisture and the brush and what have you. But that was heavily timbered at one time. And it was never logged. Fire damage. That was way before I moved here. But the mountain's burned off twice since we was here. I can't ever remember being any trees on there.

And then a lot of these places. Like up back in here. We got a bunch of oak groves and stuff in there. And that's the soil. The soil won't support a fir tree. So nothing grows there. Rock. You can see rock outcroppings all through there. And where you've got a bunch of rock outcroppings, you don't have enough soil for a fir tree or a pine or something to grow on there. So the brush is going to grow.

There's a lot of people say, "Well, they clearcut that. Look at it." And it never was clearcut. There was never nothing ever there to start with.

This community's not like it used to be. There's more people. That's the main thing. There's just more people and you just don't know everybody.

I don't think it's less community — I think it's more a group of communities. A lot of people will get together, and they'll think that this school should be one way. And another group will be this way.

And another group will be this way. And it used to be the whole community would get together and discuss the whole thing. I don't think they have a discussion like that anymore. I think it's, "I'm against you and you're against me, and I've got my support and you've got yours, and that's it."

But you got a lot of people that—'course I came in from California, a lot of years ago—but you've got a lot of people that come in here and the first thing they'll want to do is start changing things. And 'course, your old locals here, they say, "Whoa! Wait a minute. Time out." You know, we're not against a change, but we're going to have to do this gradually. You can't come in and tell these people that've lived here for years and years and years that this is the way you're going to do it. Because it's just not going to work that way.

But there are so many people here—on Clear Creek alone. There are five hundred residents on Clear Creek alone. Scary. I can remember when there used to be about twelve.

There's nothing the matter with California. I come from there. Some people who've moved in, they think we're a bunch of yokels. They think we're a bunch of dummies never been to the village. I've been traveling all over the United States for the last twenty-five years, and I probably know more than they do. [*Laughs*] But I think they say, "Awhh—bunch of hicks. The world's about forty miles wide and that's it."

I'll tell you another thing. When I first moved here, this valley was very, very clannish. I mean, they just didn't welcome you with open arms. I mean, they weren't rude or anything to you, but it took a long time before they would accept you to their fold.

Right here, we don't have any pressure. We just don't let it get to us. I've got these trees over here, and we're pretty well isolated. But we're not hermits either—don't get me wrong. I have worked and lived in the cities so much that if I never go to a city again, it'd just suit me fine. 'Course, see, I've traveled and worked all the way from Florida to Prudhoe Bay. And I've never found a better place than right here. Weatherwise. I don't like flatland at all. I went down there in Louisiana working, and that bunch of flatland swamps down there didn't do a thing for me. Here you have your four seasons, but nothing real drastic.

Vera I can just sit in the front room and look out the window and watch the trees. We feed the birds. We have nests—boxes for the bluebirds and the swallows. I spend about three weeks putting yarn out for the mama oriels. For their nest. Throw seed out for the quail and the doves. If you're very still, the quail will come in and eat right just a few feet from you.

Chuck   We're still working on the garden this year. We have a little bit more to get in yet.

Vera   If the quail will quit dusting where I have my melons.

Chuck   Some of your melons have started to grow. I checked this morning.

The area's not going to grow a great deal now, the way LCDC is now. They won't hardly let you build a house on your own piece of property. I don't think you're going to see that much change until they change some laws. The way they got it now, you can't divide anything anymore. Well, it's pretty near an impossibility to divide anything. Farmland, you can't divide that. Can't subdivide that. Now the forest, they want everything in at least forty-acre plots. So I don't think you're going to see that much growth.

You know, forty acres anymore costs a lot of money. This forty, my dad and brother and I bought this forty, and we gave five thousand dollars. I don't think you could buy it for that now. [*Laughs*]

Across the road here they cut back the banks, put mobile homes up there, and the people is a-screaming and a-crying and a-groaning. And I said, "Hey! It's their property. They can do whatever they want with it." This six acres they're not going to build on. That's mine.

But that's the way I've always been. I mean, if it's your property and you want to do something with it, that's your right. It isn't the community to tell you what you can do with it. And that's what LCDC's doing today, is telling you what you can do with your own property. But you're paying taxes on it. And that's just the way I feel about it. Right now, the way it is, nobody can move closer to us. Which suits me fine. If I wanted to live close together, I'd live in Medford.

Vera   A few years ago there were some people that moved into the trailer park just down the road, and they complained about the dogs barking and the noise of the cows. They shouldn't have moved to the country if they didn't want to hear those noises. 'Cause that's country noises.

Chuck   It's like, there used to be a dairy right up here. And of course, you know, when the wind was coming down this direction and the rainy season, hey, it'd get a little smell, but it would just smell like a dairy. People say, "Boy, that stinks." I said, "It smells just exactly like country."

We first moved up here in forty-four, my dad and my brother and I were milking thirty-six head of cows. The hard way. Women did the gardening. Men didn't work in the garden. Didn't have time. Busy haying and whatever. Picked wild blackberries and made jam.

First year we come to Oregon, we ate those wild blackberries until we pretty near turned black. I was like twelve years old. My mom said, "Go pick some berries," and of course the berries were then tall, bushy wild, until they sits right on the creek bank. I picked about a three-gallon bucketful. We sit down to dinner that night, we had blackberries, bread and butter, and milk. We ate the whole three gallons.

Vera The last couple years, the creek's dried up, and our blackberries down there have just dried up and we haven't had as many.

Chuck That's another thing I don't like about clearcuts. I think they dry up your springs. And soil doesn't retain the water. Creeks dry up. When I was a kid, this creek run full all summer long. Doesn't anymore. 'Course, you got a lot more people up there using it, too.

In all these mountains, the trees cover springs and what have you, and anytime you cut the growth down around the spring, it's going to dry up. And you take a little spring here, and a little one here, and a little one here, and you got three or four hundred springs, they run a pretty good flow of water. Once you clear the growths around them, they'll dry.

B. B. What do you think will happen as the lumber jobs dwindle down?

Chuck Hmm. That's when the revolution starts. The next one the United States is going to have. They're going to have one, they keep going the way they are. I'm just talking about the United States in general.

The big companies that come in, they could care less. They're going to come in, and they're going to get every dime they can out of whatever it be. And when it's all done, they're gone and: "See you people."

They could care less. But what concerns me is the federal government lets them do it. And it doesn't make any difference what party it is. We're talking Republicans, Democrats, or whatever. They're all big money. They could really care about the small person. It's all money.

Georgia Pacific, they've moved pretty much all their operation down to the South. Well, I think the main reason they went down there — I don't think it's mainly the timber, because I've seen some of the timber. I think the main reason they moved down there is wages there. That's why all your shoe factories and all your clothing factories and what have you, they're all in the South. Because the union isn't down there. And of course I'm a union man. I've been one all my life. But unions down there are a dirty word.

They tell me—when I was down in Louisiana, people used to tell me you could live cheaper in the South than you can in the North? That's a whole bunch of malarkey, too. Poor. You're talking poor people down there. You drive out through some of those places, and it's a disgrace to the United States. It's just like these migrant farmers, some of the camps they live in. It's a disgrace to the United States to even see something like that. Yet they'll sit back there, them fat cats, and say, "This is the land of plenty." Well, where is this plenty? That's what I want to know.

I think the worst thing that's happened to logging—well, everybody talks about this spotted owl is costing jobs. The spotted owl is this, the spotted owl is that. I'll tell you what's costing more people work in the sawmills and what have you is them boatloads after boatloads after boatloads of timber going to Portland, Coos Bay, headed right straight to Japan.

But here they are, your big logging companies, they say, "Watch this spotted owl over here. It's getting endangered." And while you're watching this spotted owl, they're floating them logs out of here by the boatload. Day after day after day.

B. B. The environmentalists—

Chuck Don't get me started, please! [*Dogs bark, someone pulls in, Chuck leaves.*]

Vera Our well is down a little over a hundred feet. We have a very good well. We had it witched. It was just something that you did, you know. Like eating the dandelion greens. And, of course, picking the mushrooms. Mostly the morels. Chuck is the mushroom hunter.

Now this year, he and my brother went up, and they found just a few. 'Course he's been so busy, and it's hard to get into the places that we used to hunt 'em. There's somebody there. And they have so many commercial people buying them. And they pay such a price for them!

Like one of the gals up at Preston Store said that these people that don't want to work the rest of the year, they go out during mushrooming season and gather all these pounds and pounds of mushrooms, and sell them, and then the rest of the year they just live on welfare and whatnot. You see the ads in the papers, and up at Preston, during the morel season there, sometimes there will be two buyers buying morels.

B. B. Do you have any thoughts on the environmentalists and the spotted owl?

Vera Well, I don't know. Seems like lots of times there are a lot of people involved in that that aren't even from this area. People come in from another area and get involved in what should be our business! And just keep it stirred up all the time. And they can't get it settled. I read in the paper where there's a woodpecker of some kind that's now in the Southeast in the woodlands that's going to be about the same thing as the spotted owl is in the Northwest. So now everybody will probably be moving down there. [*Laughs*]

And who's right? I don't think any of them are completely right, and they're not completely wrong, but where do we meet, you know? To get a happy medium, so to speak. [*Chuck comes back in.*] We're discussing spotted owls.

Chuck I'd rather not even discuss it. And I believe in preserving the wildlife. Don't get me wrong. But I don't think one owl needs six thousand acres to live on. And then you've got like your BLM, they'll say, "Oh, we did a study on this, and it takes so and so and so." And your environmentalists come along, your dyed-in-the-wool hard environmentalists come along and say, "No, we say it takes six thousand acres." So. Who's right? I don't know.

There's something to whether that's the question, too. That's like that logger who was over on the coast, logging over there, and the game warden come along, he's shooting seagulls. And the game warden says, "I'm going to have to give you a ticket for this. This is illegal to do."

And the guy said, "All I'm trying to do is feed my family! You know how the logging business is and all that, don't you?"

And the game warden said, "Well, that being the case, I'm going to let you go this time. But don't let me catch you again." And he started to walk away. He stopped, and he turned around, and he said, "By the way, what do those seagulls taste like?"

The logger said, "Aw, somewhere between a spotted owl and a bald eagle."

So there you are.

I was working up in Webber, Oregon. Used to be a town there. Now it's a big pulp mill. Was a lumber town, and Weyerhaeuser bought it out. We got a Texan working up there, and he's telling us about the big piney woods in Texas. And I said, "How big are these piney woods in Texas?"

And he said, "They're fifteen miles wide, and about forty-five miles long."

And I said, "Take a look. Any direction you want to look. For thousands of miles there's nothing but piney woods! You tell me about the big piney woods in Texas!" [*Laughs*] Standing right in the middle of the biggest forest in the world, telling me about this big piney woods in Texas. I said, "Get out of my face!"

Vera We've had at various times, we've had several other sons that weren't getting along at their home. And so they moved in here for a while. If Chuck would bring home somebody for dinner, or the boys would bring somebody home . . .

Chuck That's probably one of the biggest changes in the valley. Years back, when it come hay time, we'd all be at my folks' house haying. And then when we got done, you went down here and you all hayed.

They don't do that anymore. They could care less. It's a community, but it's not as tight as it used to be. I mean that, like some guy's farming down there, and it's raining, and all this hay or whatever is out. The people look down and say, "Hey, you've got a problem." Where years back, everybody'd be down there trying to help him get his hay in before it gets wet. But that's not only here — I think that's all over the United States. Same way. Too much "I don't care what happens to you, as long as I get by." I think it's the way the kids are raised anymore. We didn't just all of a sudden, just like turning on a light, everybody's different. This came along gradually.

Of course, I think a lot of people are come to the country from the city, and down there you can live in a city next door to some guy for nine years and never know what his name is. The people out there that've lived here all the time, they still associate with each other. And there's still kind of an inner community or something. But it's — population. I mean, the people that's moved in, they're just not the same. They're different. And that's not saying they're bad — don't get me wrong. But they're different. They don't live like we've lived here for years.

GARY CARTER (age 38) Gary has the lean, wiry look of someone who could plant a thousand trees a day. His story of Latino tree planters, although ten years old, could be told today. Latinos, many at the mercy of unscrupulous contractors, now represent between 60 and 90 percent of the tree-planting workforce.

I was born in 1950 in Medford, Oregon. From about two until about six we did a little bit down in southern California while my dad was getting in the electricians' trade. What I can remember about that was going to kindergarten, and show-and-tell was telling everybody we were moving back to Oregon.

Here, you pretty much knew everybody, and you could really just run anyplace you wanted to go. If you ran out across somebody's field, or were down in the creeks, or down by the river, they'd look down there and go, "Oh, there's the Carter kids." Or the Smiths', or the Raymonds', or whoever.

We rode the bus to high school. Twenty miles in, twenty miles back. We were the hicks from the sticks. Got up in the morning, catch the bus just as the sun was coming up, and ride into school. Get home just about the time the sun's going down. Of course we'd feed and water and shovel manure and all that good stuff. Weed the garden. Feed the dogs. All the normal chores. Get firewood.

I graduated in sixty-eight. While I was in high school, you know, sixty-five, sixty-eight, that was when the heavy stuff was in Vietnam. That was probably partially a factor of my going to college. Besides, that was just the thing to do. That was what was expected from family.

I had friends that finished high school, and friends that were borderline, and friends that didn't. 'Course, where I grew up, you knew everybody. Because there wasn't that many. So you pretty much learned to get along with everybody. 'Cause you grew up with them and you were around them and you did everything with them. Then when we went to ninth grade and then on in to Grants Pass High School, the diversity there was a lot wider-ranged. You got your jocks and the Socs and the hoods.

I learned at a twenty-year reunion that there are a lot more people that I went to school with actually stayed around the area than I thought. I talked to a lot of people that I didn't even realize were still in Grants Pass. One guy working with his brother at a radiator shop. And a guy doing sheet metal work. Guy that installs heat pumps. Surprising how many of them actually stayed in Oregon.

I just never had any desire to go anyplace else. I went to Southern

Oregon College. Well, Southern Oregon State. It's still SOC to me. During that time was when I met Theresa. She got pregnant, and we got married. And then I decided, you know—better really get serious about this. And pretty much was keeping my schoolwork together.

The summer that I graduated from high school, I was bucking hay, picking rocks out of fields. I'm thinking, "Ohhh, God." Well, halfway though the summer my cousin called that worked for the forests and said, "One of my guys just got drafted. If you want a job, get in here right now." And I went straight to town.

So I worked summers there while I went to college. And it made a great summer job because they started hiring for the fire season just about the time spring term was over. They were just starting to lay everybody off about the time fall term would start.

About the first six years I worked there, I worked on a hand-trailing crew. It's a crew of nine people. And you've got your forest officer. We'd load up in a crummie, with all the tools and the shovels and axes and pulaskies, hazel hoes. And they'd roll you out to a fire. They would send you to the area where they couldn't get the pumper trucks into. Or the direction that the fire was headed.

You'd line out. The fire warden starts out with a chainsaw. And he brushes everything out of the way—opens up an area. And then the guy following him carries the pack with the saw gas and the oil and the extra chain and the tools. And he throws the brush out away from the fire. And then the hand-trailing crew comes along. And you've got the lead-off man, and he sets the pace. And he scouts eighteen inches wide down to mineral soil. The guy in the back calls the shots. And he's back there with a shovel. The guy leading out, he starts digging, and then the guy in the back yells, "Move!"

Well, this guy—the lead-out man—he has to assess the ground and assess how fast you can move and how much you're going to be able to dig in the people between him and the shovel man. And then he moves up, paces out, and moves up to another spot and starts digging. And then the next man moves up to where he left off.

So by the time the guy with the shovel gets there, it's a progressive trail. When he gets there, it's cleared, and all's he has to do is just kind of kick the stuff off. Or maybe finish up a little bit. If you're trying to get to a place and pinch something off, he might move you a little faster, and then he kind of finishes stuff up. So you're right on the fire line. I mean, it's as close as you can get to it.

I didn't graduate from college. I found out from working fighting fires—and it's funny, some people will come out there, boy, and it's, you really have to have a feel for it. It's hot, hard, scary work. It can be real scary at times. And people come and go, some people stay. And I — it was just something about fighting fire, it made me feel like I was accomplishing something. Not only for me, but for the area.

And one summer I worked doing that, I was trying to decide what I was going to do. I had went to school for four years and one term. And at that point I couldn't decide if that was really what I wanted to do. So I worked that winter at Harry and David's. And at a grape-stake mill. They make all kinds of stuff there. They make box cleats and I don't know what all. But the main thing that they shipped out was grape stakes. You know, the stakes they drive in the ground. And then they make the little cross arms that go out across.

What they do is buy all this cull stuff from the mills. Like cull-grade two-by-fours and two-by-sixes. And then they either split it in half or into thirds. They've got another area that they buy the stuff that's already that size. One-and-a-half by one-and-a-half. Then they have a guy down there with a swing-arm saw. He cuts it into lengths, and then he hands it over to the guy that sticks it in this machine that's like a giant pencil-sharpener. And it just goes EEEEEEeeee! [*Laughs, while imitating vibrations through his entire body*] That's not the machine you want to work on. [*Laughs*] When I worked there it was minimum wage.

I got to working places like that, and here I started running into these people that I'd went to college with, that were like a year or two ahead of me, that had degrees — Biology, Secondary Education — driving hyster at Harry and David's. Or out working cutting grape stakes.

And I thought, "Gol'! Now what?" So I'd went back to the forest for the summer, and they offered me this other position about the time the fire season was over. Well, it turned out they [a CETA program] were going to give them money for twenty positions through the winter. But they told them, "We'll let you put on half the people that you want to put on. And then we're going to send half the people down from the Employment Division.

As it turned out, there was just ten people that wanted to stay. So I worked during the winter. We did maintenance. Went out and cut sugar pines and bolted them up. I learned how to make shakes. We built nature trails.

It was real interesting working with some of the guys that they sent from the Employment Division. What they were trying to do was get people off the welfare system. And so most of these guys that they sent down there had been on welfare. Some of them, you know, like seven, ten, twelve years. Probably half of the ten they sent there had been in jail at one time or another.

One guy they sent there — Ol' Frank. They sent them out to the forest, and he shows up in his creased pants, you know, and his patent leather shoes, and his shirt with this sweater. They told us how much we were going to make working there. So the first thing he does is, sets down and figures out how much he's going to make a month. Well, he finds out he's going to be making twenty dollars less than he was making on welfare! So he was pretty upset. [*Laughs*]

So, he thought he was going to not have to work there. 'Cause he went back and told them at the Employment Office, he said, "I don't have boots, I don't have the pants, I don't have the shirts." So they took him down and bought him the stuff and sent him back out there and said, "You're going to work there, because if you quit, you're not getting back on welfare."

So that pretty much settled all the rest of them. He stayed. Everyone lasted. And once they got into it, they just loved it. Just getting out and doing stuff. Some of them had never done anything like that ever before in their life. Being out in the woods was scary to them. You know — way out! [*Laughs*]

And I enjoyed it. It was like I felt I was accomplishing something. I had a lot of friends that worked in mills, and boy, I heard them bitch and complain. You know. The same thing every day. The noise, the sawdust. At that time there was no problem with being laid off or anything. It was pretty much steady but, boy! The same job day after day after day. Which this was something different. Maybe you'd go out and thin for a month. And maybe you'd be over building nature trails for a month.

Then when the next summer came along, the guy that was doing the forest work over in Timbers, his dad got him a job in one of the mills. And they asked me, "Would you be interested in moving to Timbers?" And I said, "When can I go?" [*Laughs*]

So we packed everything up and moved up to Timbers. Lived up there for three years. It was seasonal. 'Course, being that they'd start you a little sooner, and then you'd work a little longer. During the season they paid the electric bill. The water was free. Then in the winter, you just had to pay the phone bill, the electric bill, and they charged you fifteen dollars a month rent. So we just got to live there year-round.

See, about the time I moved up there, they were changing people at Headquarters. They replaced them with guys that came right out of college. And then, when it got right down to it, a lot of people, particularly the firefighting crews, didn't think much of it when these other guys came in. At first they thought, All right. Because things kind of slacked up a bit. But then they got into paperwork, and everything was by the book. Everything. That's another reason I went to Timbers. I thought, Seventy-five miles away from Headquarters, I'll get away from all that stuff.

Well, they'd send you little memorandums in the mail. You know: "You will wear your uniform. You will wear your badge. You will wear a white tee shirt. You will not wear blue jeans." You know, here they see you coming for years with just a regular truck. All of a sudden they go to these big rigs. Here you are getting out with your uniform and your badge and your nametag with your ticket book in your hand. And people just go — . [*Mimics aversion*]

The first summer I just went about normal procedure. If the lookout calls in and says, "I've got a smoke spotted just down the road," you go down there. Well, they don't have a permit. So you tell them, "Well, listen. It's fire season. Permits are required." You look, and maybe they've got it cleared around the pile they're burning. Maybe they're out there with their hose and their tools and everything. You'd have issued them a permit anyway.

So you say, "Well, you're doing everything like you're 'sposed to. I live at the station right up the road. Give me a call, you know." And go ahead and write them a permit. You know — no problem, permits are free.

When you fill out a permit, you kept a copy, they get a copy, then a copy goes into Headquarters. So when they get a call from a lookout that says, "OK, I've got a smoke at such-and-such." And then they call you and say, "Do you have a permit at . . . ?" And you look on the map.

Well, then they started this thing, "The first time you will issue them a citation." Or at least a warning. Then the second time is to appear in court. Before, they left it up to your discretion. Well, then all of a sudden they're trying to tell you how to do everything. That just seemed to rub people the wrong way.

I quit because they were cutting my time back. I worked at the grape-stake mill again. I planted trees one winter, worked with a contracting crew. I got to know a lot of the people that worked for the Forest Service. These guys talked about, you know, they'd go out and plant two, three hundred trees a day, and I thought, "Oh, gol'! Two or three hundred trees!"

So this guy said, "Well, if you're looking for a job, the contractors are looking for tree planters." 'Cause of course all these people that were loggers and everything, they didn't want to go out and tree-plant. 'Cause they could set in the bar and collect their unemployment and wait till logging started back up again. It's hard work. It's back-breaking. Some of the younger guys did, but most of the older guys, they'd just as soon hang out and wait till logging started back up.

I got out there to plant for these contractors. I went out with this other guy, we were both new for the day. They lined the regular crew out and sent them off up the hill. And they said, "Well, we'll have you plant this corner out. We'll pay you according to planting. What we shoot for is a thousand trees per man a day." And I just went — . [*Mimics collapse*]

So me and this guy thought, Oh, gol'! You know, we're just really going to have to get after this. So we went over there, and I think we planted four hundred, four hundred fifty trees in the day. And we were just dragging, you know.

And it worked out that we got hired on a Friday. And they weren't working weekends at that time. So we actually got the weekend off, which was good. I laid at home for two days. And I — my hands were like, you know, claws. [*Laughs*] I couldn't hardly move. And I thought, Oh, I'm not going to be able to go back and do that! No way!

But I went back and stuck it out. And a lot of these guys, that's all they do. They just travel around. We had guys that had just come from planting in Montana. And were planting here. And then they were going to the coast. And then they were going to Washington.

They got to a point where they were hurting for people, they just couldn't find anybody that wanted to plant trees. They put signs up all over town and everything. Well, as it turned out, this guy that was like the right hand man to the big boss for this outfit, one day he shows up with a pickup load of Chicanos in the back of his truck. The thing is, this being winter, there they are sitting in the pouring rain, and they're just soaked. They're anywhere from about twenty years old to — there was a couple of guys, fifty-eight, sixty.

And they crawled out, and the only thing they had was the clothes on their backs and like a bedroll. And they put them up in this trailer that didn't have anything in it, no heat, no nothing. And, of course, once we got to planting, and eating lunch and hanging out, and got to talking with them, come to find out that most of them had come from Mexico and were trying to make enough money and then go back, because all their families were back in Mexico, at least half of them. But they'd been down in L.A. splitting oak firewood for five dollars a day. So they had this opportunity. In the back of a pickup — open — clear up from there in the pouring rain.

These guys, that's the kind of work that they'd always done. They lined them right up with the crew. It took them one day to get the drift of what was going on, and off they went. And they planted as fast or faster than anybody else on the crew.

What we found out was, they got paid the same wages as we did. But they had to pay like half their wages back to this guy that brought them up. They called him "Tricky-Dicky." [Laughs] We'd get the checks and we'd stop in town on the way back and go in to cash them. And we couldn't figure out why this "Tricky-Dicky" was there every time. And he'd go in with these guys. And come to find out, you know, after we got to talking with them, was that they were having to cough up part of what they were getting paid. And I don't know just what was going on there, to tell you the truth.

But they said they were still making enough money, if they could just go for three or four months, they could go back and live the rest of the year in Mexico. And live better than if they'd stayed down there and worked.

I started driving truck, making deliveries. While we were still in Timbers, Theresa's dad decided that we needed a piece of property. So every time we were down visiting or whatever, he'd yard us over to see this piece or yard us over to see that piece. And we went anywhere from Williams to Grants Pass to Rogue River. Wherever. I think we still were in Timbers when we bought the piece where we're living now. While we were in Timbers it was just too far away to ever try and get over here and do anything. So when we got moved down and moved into the valley, we thought, All right. We'll be able to go over and do stuff. We'll have the time, we'll have the money.

Well, you either got the time or you got the money. You never have both. So several years we sat over there and didn't get really much of anything done. And we finally said, "The only way we're going to do it is to be there." So we hooked on to an old sixteen-foot travel trailer. [Laughs] And drug it up on the hill. And moved in. [Laughs]

While I was driving truck, some friends we have got a call from some people out-of-state about getting seedling trees to plant on some property they had up here. They had ordered five thousand Douglas fir and three thousand incense cedar seedlings. And they said, "Well, do you happen to know anybody that knows how to plant trees?" And Theresa happened to be standing there at the time and said, "Well, Gary does!"

In the meantime they'd found out that through the State Forestry, they have what they call a cost-sharing program. And they got on this because, of course, then they get reimbursed a certain amount that they put into it.

So the State guy comes out and assesses the situation and says, "Ponderosa pine!" And has them order ten thousand ponderosa pine. Well, they've already got, you know, five thousand Douglas firs, three thousand incense cedar ordered. So here comes eighteen thousand trees.

So I got ahold of a friend of mine that wasn't working, and we got out and planted all these trees. Well, I got a letter from the people, and they said, "Would you be interested in keeping the place up?" Now it's worked into a thing where they've got all the rest of this four-hundred-plus acres classed as a tree farm. It's a tax write-off, a tax break, and I'm sure he's got an accountant that handles all that. And I'm sure there's a break-off point there somewhere. And through my working there, I got the drift of how many hours I could put in. It's worked out to be such a great job.

B. B.   What kind of changes have you seen in the area, in the forest?

Gary   Well, working around the Forest Service and seeing the stuff that goes on out there — it doesn't make me happy. Take in Timbers. We got to where there were a lot of places we used to go out and hike down into the river. You'd turn off on this road, and it was just like two ruts down through. I mean, I've got a truck, and it would just barely go. 'Cause some of these big old trees were right on the edge of the road.

Well, we drove out there and got to where we thought the road was, and I mean, it was — *pfft!* Clearcut. Nothing. We thought, this can't be, this isn't it. So you drive off down, you know — and then we came back. 'Course now the road is — *whoosth!* So we drive down, and not until we get down to where the actual parking area was there any trees again.

And then you go out, you think, Well, gol', here's someplace that they're actually doing a good job. They came in and made a partial cut. When I was planting trees up there, and they'd actually made them clean all the old buckskin and logs out of the woods. Had them decked on the road for firewood cutters. And they said, "OK. Go in there and plant the skidroad, plant everything."

So we planted all this area, then—same thing. We happened to be going past there, up to one of my favorite fishing places up there, and we went right by this road that went up to where we planted this area. And I thought I'd like to go up and see what kind of survival rate, you know. See what they're doing.

Went up there, and they had logged it again, and logged almost everything, the rest of the merchantable stuff. And of course logged and drug everything over all the trees that we'd planted in there not three or four years before.

B. B.   What kind of survival rate did you see?

Gary   [*Laughs*] About zip! I mean, it was so sickening I couldn't hardly even get out and look at it.

They sent us up to another place to plant, where they'd helicopter logged, because it was such steep rocky ground. And there was only a road at the bottom and a road at the top. That was the only way they could really go about it. And they did a real nice job of it.

Well, then they decided they'd come in there and burn the slash out. Well, when they burnt the slash, they probably killed—everything at least thirty feet and shorter was scorched. Because once it got going, it went up the ridge and down over the other side. They ended up burning twice the area that they had logged. I saw that a lot when I worked fighting fires. I went out to a lot of out-of-control control burns. [*Laughs*]

You can only go out there for so long and drag stuff out of there. And they've drug and drug and drug stuff out of there. To it's—you know, they're kicking up this fuss now because they've put a halt to all this. But if you look at it, and the way things have been going, it was going to happen sooner or later anyway.

B. B.   Why do you think so many guys are so upset?

Gary   Ahhh—a lot of it is because that's the only work there is around here. And that's the way it's been for so long.

I have lots of friends that are looking for work. I've got friends that I went to school with that have tried and tried to live here. One that just moved not too long ago, up to Seattle. He said, "I give up. I just can't make a living here."

B. B.   Do you know folks who have been hurt in the woods?

Gary   Yeah. Logging. I went to school with a lot of people, and that's what they did. Log or go to the mill. I know people with missing fingers. And a guy I got to know pretty well up in Timbers, he got killed.

I think that was another reason that I stayed away from it. You hear all those stories. People that's got scars all over their legs from chainsaws. Or people that've got fingers crushed off in the chain drive stuff at the mill.

B. B.   What other kinds of changes have you seen?

Gary   The growth in Medford, for one thing. I just don't go to town unless I absolutely have to. But then again, you know, you've got all these people that are moving in, and they've got to work someplace. When there isn't work, then you've just got that many more angry people.

I grew up hearing, "Those damn Californians coming up." You know. And for years and years and years. Me, myself, I've seen both. I've got friends that are from California, and they're no different than I am. But I've also run into people that have moved up, and they move up to get away from all that down there in the city. And then they move up here expecting to have the same conveniences that they had down there.

I saw a real good example of that over where my uncle lives. These people that moved up and bought the store up there, they weren't there probably four, six months, and they just were ready to tell anybody and everybody how they should be living their lives. And that didn't go over very well at all. [Laughs]

There was another little store, and everybody started going to the other store. But some stuff you couldn't get there. So you had to go to the store there. It was a general store that'd been there forever and ever and ever. And it burnt down in the night one night. And nothing was ever really proved, but, you know, of course the rumors circulated that they got what they deserved. So. You know, who knows?

You know, when I was growing up in Blaketon, we could run anywhere. You know. Fish. Hunt. Do just about anything short of serious mischief. Which we did some of that, too. [Laughs] Not real serious, but, you know, kid stuff. Go out at night and gather cans up along the road and set them up in the road and wait for the drunks to come home at night. [Laughs] You know.

But everybody knew everybody. And everybody seemed to get along real well, other than just minor spats about this and that. But, boy, anymore you try and go back to some of the places where we used to go and fish, or we used to go and swim. Somebody's down there and they're calling the cops. They're siccing the dog on you, they're pulling a gun on you.

Go out to a place to pick mushrooms where you picked mushrooms forever. Morels. Have somebody out there going to shoot you. And now, with the influx of people here, and the demand for morel mushrooms, they're buying them everywhere. And people are out there combing the brush. It is unbelievable.

I just don't have a desire to go anyplace else. 'Cause there's a lot of stuff around that I personally enjoy doing. I can go right out here and fish and hike. It's just being so determined to be someplace that you'll do anything to stay there, I think is what a lot of it is. Because this area has always been semi-depressed. As far as work. But the people that stay, they're going to stay no matter what.

But now, you know, with everything building up, I don't know. I see it and I hear about it a lot. You know, lot of people coming here to retire. And of course that's what builds the service industry in the towns. And it's like a different mindset that those people have. It's just hard to explain.

One thing is, it's like I say, the Californians moving up. It solidifies the people that are here, too. It's something to do with, as soon as something's different or as soon as something, you know, starts to change a little bit . . .

And then when this was the Job Corps center, the big kick was the Blacks. Boy, they just gave them such a bad time that they finally had to close it down. I think that was a lot of it. They were having problems downtown. They were trying to let the guys from the Job Corps center come down—they can't hang out there all the time. Come down and do stuff in town. Go down to the Rollerdrome. I was there when they were there a couple of times. And, boy, I mean, it was just like, you know, a wall of ice. I know they had some serious fights down there. About the time they were kicking around the notion that it probably wasn't a good idea to have the Job Corps center here.

Of course this was about the time I was in high school. So a lot of what I was hearing and the input I was getting was that age. But of course a lot of their attitudes is what they got from their parents. It's still around. You see more Blacks. You see more Latinos. But you still hear some bad stuff.

I just always—I never had a problem with it. I guess my most serious attitude change was when I went to college. There was a lot of Blacks. Lot of Latinos. Coming from California. And other countries. And one thing that opened my eyes when I was going to school there was when I started taking history classes, and got into some upper-division history classes. One in particular really stuck with me was "History of Black America." And to learn what actually went on. What's been eliminated. What's been cut out of high school history is almost unbelievable. I got a real good idea then as to why attitudes here were like they were, too.

When they brought those guys in to plant trees? There they looked and looked, put posters up and everything, to try and get somebody to come plant trees. And nobody wanted to. But as soon as they brought the guys up from California, they started raising a big stink in town. 'Bout all these Mexicans coming up and taking our jobs. When they didn't even want it in the first place.

B. B.   What would you like to see happen in the woods now?

Gary   You know, we're back to this thing where you've got the environmentalists over here, and you've got the industry over here. And for some reason you've got the extreme right and the extreme left. And, boy, they're locked in. And I'd like to see something happen where they couldn't reach middle ground on some things. I mean, they get so locked in on something that they're just almost unwilling to negotiate at all.

Not working for the government anymore, I'm not around the Forest Service guys and whatnot, so that I know a lot of what's going on. But the stuff that I hear, if they're going to cut something back, it's they're cutting back on reforestation.

And I see that commercial, and that almost killed me. Where the music comes on and they say, "Hundreds of millions of trees," or whatever. You know, working planting trees, and knowing what the survival rate is — they're planting all these trees. But they don't tell you how many of them survive. The estimates I hear are thirty percent.

They're working on that. When I worked planting, the object was to get the most trees in the ground. In the shortest amount of time that you could. 'Course the Forest Service sends an inspector out there. But when you've got ten, twelve guys out there planting an average of a thousand trees per man a day, you know — how many trees can he actually check? So you see things go on. They go behind the tree there and here's this stump and — *whwwt!* There goes a bundle of trees there.

But what they're doing now is — I heard a lot of the contracts now, they hold back part of the pay. Until after it cycles through one season or whatever. And then they go out and take a count on the survival rate. And then they get paid the rest of the money according to the survival rate.

The survival rate may be up from that thirty percent. This was back ten years ago.

THERESA CARTER (age 36) Theresa is a quiet, generous woman. Her comments on methamphetamine producers will resonate with most citizens of southwest Oregon. The Rogue Valley region attracted the entrepreneurs involved in the relatively simple but extremely toxic process of manufacturing "meth" (or "crank"), in part because of its geographic position (remote, but close to I-5), in part because of the ineffectiveness of Oregon drug-sentencing laws and the budgetary constraints on the state's frustrated sheriffs. Raids on meth producers often uncover arsenals of automatic weapons.

I was born in Germany in 1953. My father was in the service, so we moved several places, and ended up in Oklahoma. Then he retired. And he wanted to come up to the trees, so we came to Oregon. That was in 1964.

His folks came from Kansas. They were farmers. My mother's family is from South Dakota. And they're big farmers. She has brothers that have big farms.

I was in the third grade when I moved up. The first place we came when we came here, we packed everything up that we had accumulated in a forty-foot trailer. And we drug it up here to Oregon. They were going to go up to the Willamette Valley. But they got here and the truck broke down. And this is where we stayed. [*Laughs*] So we ended up first thing in Medford in a little tiny trailer park. My mom had never worked all her life, and all of a sudden from being a housewife she had to go and find a job. My dad hated living in a trailer. His main objective was to get us out of the trailer. And he had been looking for some property to buy anyway.

When we came to Josephine County I was about fourteen years old. I thought moving way out in the country was going to be the worst thing in the world. Medford was, you know, not big-city life, but still, we could walk to the Rollerdrome. And there was gobs of people around. And I thought, Oh, my father, how could he take me to the sticks? Nothing is going to be there. Hillbilly people. I just thought that that was the worst thing he could ever do to us. He just didn't listen — went in one ear and out the other.

It worked out great! It was completely opposite of what I thought it was. The only thing is, I had to leave a boyfriend that I really liked. We had a big trailer, and then we had a little camper trailer — and I just spent the whole summer in the camper, just totally depressed.

People are different in Oklahoma than they are here — they're a lot friendlier than here. Oregon, going in, seemed to be pretty standoffish. The church that my mother belonged to in Oklahoma, everybody was really close. Then to come up here and go to the same church and people were just really cold. You'd go to church, and they'd never ask you where you were if you didn't come or anything. So she's off and on. My dad never went to church. Occasionally. They're not really social people. Just real work-oriented.

In high school I was pretty quiet. Small social circle. Like in between the popular kids and the hoods. All the smokers and the hoods hung out on Smokey's Corner over by Hodges. And you didn't hang around by there if you were a nice girl. I was always trying to get to the popular group, but I just couldn't quite make it. Because I wasn't this cute thing.

And then, of course, I thought that girls, they had to be secretaries. I never even dreamt that you could do anything else at that time. You took business classes if you were a girl.

When I was a senior I got pregnant, but I still finished high school. I found out that I was pregnant when senior year started. I only had like a couple of classes to graduate. So I got them done before I got real pregnant. Like for six months I just denied even being pregnant. I didn't think about anything. Sort of in a blur, I think. Not really wanting to face reality and all.

B. B. Is this the child you live with now?

Theresa Yeah! That's my son. Fifteen. And I'm still married to the same man. He was really a changing point in my life. He was the first person in my life that said I was great the way that I was. I was always trying to, you know, be somebody else, and it wasn't OK just to be Theresa.

I met him at an after-game dance. I couldn't quite figure him out. It was like the new thing in this area — the hippie generation was just coming in. He had, you know, real short hair — maybe just barely over his ears a little bit. And he wore dark horned-rimmed glasses to finally the wire rims came in. Shades that were like real dark ones, but he'd wear them at night. Because that was cool. And he just started talking to me. And I thought, Oh, gol', why does this — . And all my friends said, "Theresa, how could you like somebody like that? That hippie!"

So one day he came — it was after school. He probably rushed — he was going to SOC at the time. He rushed over, and he asked if he could take me home. And I thought, Well, heck, I didn't want to ride the bus. But what in the world would he have? You know, I had all these illusions — probably this hippie bus, you know.

But he had just a really nice car, and he was really nice and really together. I sort of had to fight all my friends about it. My dad liked him immediately. Because he was in college. And had to have some perspective on life.

B. B.   In your family was there an expectation of going to college?

Theresa   No. None at all. When I told my parents that I was pregnant, they were just wonderful. And that was a real fear. You know: "If you'd ever do anything, we're going to send you away to some girls' home." But, in actualization, they wouldn't ever do that.

Right about then, that's when people were starting to get loaded. A lot. You know, when the pot thing was really coming in. I was a young mother. I had illusions that life—you had a house on the block. Then things didn't work that way.

My husband went to college for four years. All of his friends that had graduated, there was no jobs for them, so he never finished. That's probably not too good a foresight. I can tell that now. But that's what we did at the time. He was working at like maintenance stuff. Then he got a job working in the forest. So he just didn't go back to school.

We worked at various jobs in the woods for twelve years. What happened is, we rented the place that we were living when my son was a baby from some friends, and then they sold it, and things changed drastically. We went from renting for next to nothing, to people buying it from California and thinking they were going to get the same amount for rent [as in California].

So we had an opportunity to go to Timbers. So we just went up there and had a magical life. My ambitions had changed. Drastically. From being with my husband. And his expectations were far from the typical house on the block. He was sort of the hippie generation. And he's real artistic. He's just sort of an individualist, to say the least. Where I'm more of a go-along-with-the-crowd kind of person. Or I used to be.

I'd go, "Oh, I'd like to live in one of those houses." And he'd go, "No way!" So I sort of started readjusting. You readjust to what you have to do, I think, in life. If you think that you need to be someplace where you're not, you're not happy. And no one likes to be miserable. I certainly didn't.

And it was fun being up at Timbers. The little houses we lived in—we were poor—pretty much you had to fix up to be nice and clean. All of our furniture was always just given to us. We never bought anything. We'd go camping. Every weekend we'd head out to someplace. I didn't work at all until my son was eight years old.

We never have thought or would want to move out of this area.

One point, they kept cutting back Gary's position, so it was getting to be more and more of a struggle in the winter. From being, like, in the winter, when you could collect unemployment, and life being so easy, after like the big gas war? We were up there then. The price doubled. It was big jumps. All of a sudden the unemployment wasn't making it as far as to make the bills. Where before it was like this magical life. You could get unemployment and go do whatever and have money left over. Those days were gone.

That's the first time I ever went to work. It was for a vineyard. My parents knew the people out there. They had came from back East, lived in a tent for the winter, trying to start this vineyard. I got a job out there. Then worked there for several years.

Then he got another job where he's still working now. For an independent person. The Chinese mined in the area. And my husband finds stuff all the time. Gary replants, he thins, he does whatever there. He loves it.

We have a really strong family network. Plus then friends. Nothing is above friendship. Our network is friends. Places I've worked were really an important network for friends. I pretty much gave all my high school friends up. Everybody went off. Gary's network of friends stayed closer.

We live out on sixty acres. And we've been building a house. When we did the foundation, there's about twenty-five friends that came over. When we framed up the house, we had about thirty friends there that came to frame the house with us. We go and do stuff for friends, too. We have a lot of friends from everywhere — raised in this area, from back East.

B. B.   You've seen changes over the years, I'll bet.

Theresa   Yeah — oh, yeah. Lots of changes. You know, all the people moving in. From it being fields to being houses in the fields.

It really hasn't affected me at all. I think that we really adjust. Think back about how it used to be, then relate it to what is now. It's like the ultimate goal is to make your life work here and be happy. Ultimate goal is not to have to worry about money and such all the time. Ultimate goal is not to want stuff constantly in your life.

B. B.   The economy here gets real shaky at various times.

Theresa   Yeah. And we've adjusted to it every time. I've seen so many people come into the area from other places and be so unhappy, and felt they can't understand why they can't make as much money. They just don't understand the trade-off that they have. My husband and I accept the trade-off gladly.

I want to stay in the area. I don't need to make a lot of money. Our income has been like around fifteen thousand a year. We used to make six thousand a year when we first got married. It's went up to fifteen thousand. We could use a little bit more money. But things just keep going up. Seems like every time I go in the grocery store, stuff is up another five cents. I'm starting to realize what an effect that is through the years. I remember when things were easier.

B. B. When you and your friends get together, is there anything that's coming up a lot these days?

Theresa Oh, probably the unemployment situation in the area comes up a lot. A lot of friends have moved. We just had a friend that moved to Seattle. Because he couldn't find work here. He was a mill-worker. And then he hurt his hip and got out of the mill.

Unemployment in general — that's a basic one. We had another friend that — a mill just shut down. They shut down and opened up, but they wanted to give them a cut in the pay, and he was just tired of it. He plans to go to school. It's the mill down here that they do like molding and stuff like that.

B. B. What was the sense of why the mill was closing?

Theresa Well, the people that work there, I don't know if they would even say that it was a timber supply thing. It was really mismanagement. He never even thought about the timber supply — he never commented on it. We didn't ask.

Friends of ours that are in logging and stuff, they don't, you know — realization that the time was coming. And people just have to adjust. Because of all the trees that were being cut down. Where we live, the log trucks just bustle down there. Constantly. Take a drive out in the forest and see how many old stands of timber there are. There's not very many.

B. B. The industry says the environmentalists are messing things up.

Theresa I don't agree. They have to blame somebody. So they're just blaming the environmentalists. We were talking this morning: Hood River had all the log trucks coming through and that. Had the owls hanging by the yellow ribbons. And Gary and I were just going, "Oh, God!" We would rather save an owl. [*Laughs*]

You know, it's sort of — sometimes environmentalists have to be radical to make any kind of a change. You have to see that point, because a lot of times, you're real radical, and then you just gain an inch with things. It's really so sad that they can't meet in the middle. But, unfortunately, they just can't.

B. B. Why do you think people are so upset about what's going on among the environmentalists and industry and the spotted owl and all?

Theresa Look at how many people work in the mill. That's been people's whole life. In this area. But then, they know people have to survive, and that's their lifestyle. It's going to take people a while to adjust to what's happening. And it's hard to find new things to do. We could say it's almost impossible around here — the mills shutting compared to the jobs that there are for people.

The friends that I have, the ones that are involved in the mill are single. They've been divorced. And the rest of them aren't involved in the mills. Probably people like that aren't attracted to us as friends, actually. The ones that were involved in the mills, a lot of them have already left. Because of closures. And just sick of the lifestyle. Wanting something better.

The mill work, you know, you're a dime-a-dozen type of thing. "We can always find somebody to replace you." And it's back-breaking. When you get to thirty-eight years old, you're looking at forty, you're getting pretty tired of pulling boards through.

B. B. There's been a large influx of folks from California here.

Theresa Uh-huh. Was I adverse to that at all? I started to be. 'Cause I labeled them. As "Those people from California." But I know that's not right to do, so I stopped doing that. It's like, you try not to be prejudiced.

I really started seeing what I thought prejudiced people were really, really about. There's a lot of them moving in here, 'cause they talk about, you know — the low-life Oregonians. And sort of cruelly. Like we're all backwards. You know, people that had lived in the area for a long time. That they're just a bunch of dumb people. Because they've been back in Oregon where nothing's happening like in the Bay Area. Really cruel things.

I think it's a real prejudiced thing to think that somebody that didn't come from a big city wouldn't have anything to offer. That they weren't intelligent. They probably knew just as much or different kinds of things than them.

B. B. Do you think a sense of community has changed any?

Theresa It really hasn't changed in my experience. I'm mad that the logs are going to Japan. The whole logs! They're not even sending lumber over there. That's pretty ridiculous.

We vote. We're avid voters. We have always voted. We didn't vote one time. One day, when Jason was a baby, we were in town and we just didn't make it out to vote. And they lost the vote like by one vote. Like our two votes. The whole family was pretty mad. So like I say, we are avid voters. That's pretty community-oriented. Feel like you're part of a community.

I feel like I'm part of a family—it's more a real family-oriented type thing, instead of community. And really work-oriented. Because we've been building the house for years. We didn't get a loan or anything because that's the way we do things.

B. B.   In the past the county was ninety-nine percent white people. That's changed.

Theresa   I think it's wonderful. Like the generation that we came out of was really non-prejudicial. Because you didn't have to be.

I remember going to California. And you know, we'd try to be nice to Black people. And they would just call us really dirty names and stuff. It was sort of a reverse discrimination. I don't know if that's the word. But that was really weird to me. I thought, Who's really prejudiced around here?

We were bound and determined to have this child that wasn't prejudiced. Because part of my family was real racist. My son, he has lots of colored friends here at school—not a lot, there's probably three in the whole school. My son has all kinds of friends. Like he has friends that are skinheads. We try to tell him what two kinds of skinheads are about. Are they prejudiced? You know, maybe you could kind of bait them and find out where they're coming from.

B. B.   Has any part of your life been touched by the drug culture here?

Theresa   We had friends that were involved in growing. Everybody that was half-way smart always was really careful anyway. It wasn't a real blatant thing. It's a big money-maker in this area. It all goes around. Buys new trucks. Buys this and that.

But the only thing is, what happens is people get into greed. And then you have to be careful going out in the woods. And when it came to that point, that people were afraid to go out back in BLM land, forest land, because of people growing marijuana, then it wasn't worth it.

I would think that you should turn methamphetamine manufacturers all in. Just because of what they're doing. You know—burying chemicals. Finding bells of chemicals floating down the river. I think it's real frightening. But, what the reason is, is because of the economy. And you get people up here that—they have nothing to lose. They've scared all the poor little people that, you know, have a supplement income on growing a few marijuana plants.

You have these people that have nothing to lose that come up here. If they're growing marijuana out in the forest lands, it's boobytrapped. They have the methamphetamine labs. A real subculture that have a lot of, probably, felons behind them.

I don't—you know, the whole thing, the drug thing—I think they try to make it more significant than it is, because I think they try to skirt the main issues. You know, the problems as far as the change from the logging economy to trying to figure something else out for the area. It's all "the big drug problem." It's not because the whole area's falling apart. The teenage problem, you know: Is it drugs? Or is it that the families, everybody's had to go to work? And everybody's really unhappy because they're losing their jobs? You know, and the kids get into things.

It is hard to get to those main issues. Most people probably don't want to see it. Because they don't really want to make changes in their lives. That's the hardest thing to do. People are afraid. I see people that are scared to death. I see people that are afraid, or just so oblivious to it all that they don't see the forest for the trees.

It sort of relates back to the environmental issue. Generations are changing. From my parents' "Just do whatever you want," to knowing that you can't do whatever you want. And families have controversies all the time. Our family is real controversial, even within the family. I argue with my husband about things, and then I argue on with my parents. But my husband and I are joined forces in argument with parents, you know!

WAYNE DOUGLAS (age 47) Wayne Douglas tells it straight as he sees it: the real estate manipulations transferring property from locals to developers, the business deals behind Wild and Scenic River designation, and the local dynamics of race relations.

Wayne knew what he wanted early on and planned his life to continue a tradition of hunting and fishing. The interview took place while Wayne filleted two sixteen-pound spring Chinook salmon he'd caught earlier in the day.

My dad was born here. My son, my grandson. My grandmother was born in the Illinois Valley. My grandfather was born on a wagon train coming north. They were married in 1900. They came from the Missouri wagons up the Emigrant Trail into the Applegate Valley. Originally my grandmother was Pennsylvania Dutch. And my grandfather was a Welsh-English type. What they did back then was mine, log, whatever they could make a dollar at. They would homestead, clear the land, sell it, homestead another place someplace else, clear the land, farm it. The homestead laws ran out on them so where they couldn't just keep doing that.

I grew up right here in town. Got out of high school, I worked in the bulbs. Which was an industry here that's gone. I worked in a grocery store, delivered this biased newspaper that we now subscribe to around town. My friends were pretty much the same group of kids most of the way through. Lot of them are still here.

My dad had a civil service job. His last job was as a custodian. He left home at sixteen — was valedictorian of his high school class. Went to California for four or five years, worked on farms. Came back, went into the Navy in forty-two. Came out in fifty.

My mom grew up on Hurdy-Gurdy Creek. Her dad died of malaria when she was six or seven. Left a widow with five kids. My grandmother married a trapper-miner-fisherman type guy. Between him and her brother, they were my basic role models. It was fishing and hunting and the outdoors. So that's where I got my love for that.

I went to church until I was fifteen, and finally said, "Hey. You can't whup me no more. I ain't goin' no more." And I haven't been much since. But my family, they're all real religious folk. I came to a point where I believe in the concepts but have problems with some of the biases and Dudley Do-Rights. So I pretty much give it a wide berth. I think church was probably the center of their life.

We had a cabin up in the mountains that we got in the fifties on a veteran's deal. Supposedly a ninety-nine-year lease. This was before

BLM. When it was under the Department of the Interior. And it was real loose and it wasn't so managed and organized? When you could go out in the woods and camp and have a bonfire and go hunting and stuff? Then we had it for about thirty years. And then he sold it. Didn't leave it in the family heirloom. I wasn't happy with Pop.

I had it all planned out what I was going to do. I was ready to leave town. I had made my mind up. I would go in the service, do my twenty years, come back, and hunt and fish and have fun. It was a means to an end. It was a quick way to get what I wanted out of life.

When my grandma married this miner-logger-whatever during the Depression, they kind of lived off the land. Had a cow and chickens, and they got by. He panned gold and semi-precious stone out of the Rogue River. He was a pocket miner; he'd go up in the hills and look for gold and pockets of salable stuff. Ran trap line, and however they could make a buck. Raised all their own crops and did it all the old way.

I spent time there at Granny's. Like my dad's side of the family wasn't close. I never could really figure that out. My mom's side of the family was real close.

B. B. What do you think kept all those folks in the area?

Wayne Roots. I think it was basically their attachment to the roots. The land, because everybody had some at one time. To the going through the hard times, which makes you appreciate the good times. And I think the general beauty of the area.

For me, the reason I came back—I've been everywhere. Florida to New Jersey to Maine to Iceland to the Panama Canal. Been to the Caribbean and been to Asia—parts I didn't want to be in and other parts I was looking around in. You know, Hong Kong and Japan and Taiwan. Driven both ways cross-country and kind of had a good look, and I didn't see anything I liked any better.

I'm a country boy, basically. You get more peace. Feel better about your life. And it's not as hectic and pressured, it's kind of laid-back and easy-going. And people let you be. I've got a three-piece business suit, pin-striped, and I've done some things in that. I feel just a lot more comfortable in a ball cap, scroungy Levis.

What I did when I got out of the service was go to community college for as many years as I could without transferring. Which was about three.

When you're young, you're not really concerned about business. And about the ways things are done—as far as who owns what and how it all gets done. But there were five or six people that controlled business. Like they didn't want big business in Grants Pass. They didn't want any non-whites spending a night in Grants Pass. I can remember my mother being threatened because she served some Black people.

The people that more or less controlled the town didn't want new business. Who was what? County commissioner? Good ol' boy? People got really fat round here as far as bucks-up — realtors and developers. My personal view is leap-frog development is a way that you castrate a community. And it's the way it happens. The old farmers that live out there, they built these subdivisions out around them, and then all these people that move in complain about his cows and the smell and this and that. And they do ordinances. And petitions. And pretty soon he's got to sell. It's like what happened in L.A.

In this area, especially, people come from a long way to fish. You bet. And it's good fishing. If you know how. If you're proficient. There's people that are proficient that sell their services.

I'm not a guide. Because the bureaucracy wants to do too much managing of our time. And I had twenty years of strict managing of my time. You know, when they tell you when you can go to the bathroom, and which line to get in to get your shot — you know. Pretty soon you just say, "I don't want no more of that stuff." And so you rock your own boat.

That's where I'm kind of at, personally: Do it my way. And what I was hearing was that BLM and the Forest Service and basically the government was saying, "No, you'll do it our way." And you'll tell us who you're doing it with and how much he or she paid you, and how much they tipped you. And then you'll give us a hundred dollars a year to use the service of the river.

The river belongs to the State of Oregon. And the Watermaster will tell you whether you can take water out of it. The Marine Board will tell you whether or not you can take gravel out of it, because State of Oregon Marine Board controls the waterways in Oregon. But the federal government controls the surface of the water that a commercial boat driver operates on in the Wild and Scenic or Rogue Recreational Area.

And they come up with this shit and dropped it on our laps. That's seventy-nine or eighty when they started doing that.

See, there was a group of good ol' boys — old-timers — as soon as that Wild and Scenic River bill passed, there was control on the lower river. You know, to go down the canyon. And a lot of people wanted to do it, and it's a gorgeous place to go and see.

So these guys, not the original river guides, but second-generation river guides, got together and says, "Hey, if we can get this through legislation, we can control the means and manner by which people make their living on the river. And they'll have to work for us. All the independents will have to work for an outfitter, rather than by themselves." And they used the Wild and Scenic bill to feather their cap.

So then they could control charges, who stays in what lodges. There's a whole lot more than meets the eye, than just a bunch of nice guys going down the river. There's a lot of competition. There's a lot of scullduggery goes on, too. Like putting acetone in a guy's worm box, for instance. Because they want him to fish with flies.

The guy with the nightcrawlers catches a whole lot more fish. Then the people get in the lodges and they're all paying six, eight, nine hundred dollars to go on this trip. And here's these guys with a whole bunch of fish, and there's these guys have only a few fish. And they get together drinking whiskey and say, "Hey! Man, I've turned loose thirty-seven steelhead today. How many did you get?" "I got four. Who's the guy you're with?" You know what I'm saying? That's the way that works.

I got back before the migration, you know. Before Proposition 13, really. People couldn't afford to live in California anymore. And a lot of them seized their opportunity to get out of there, and moved up here, because they could — their property values were going up.

When I was a kid growing up here, the local folk laughed at the tourists. They thought they were crazy. "These guys will spend money like crazy!" You know. "Hey, look here, I got this house down there. If I can sell that sucker for four times what I paid for it, I'm going to sell it."

We lived right on a main street. Everybody on the block put a "For Sale" sign out. Everyplace you looked was a "For Sale" sign all summer. Then, boy, come September, school starts, and all the signs go back into the house.

There were some people that really took advantage of that, like some of your realtors and developers. *Really* took advantage of that.

About the same time, a group of southern Oregon businessmen calling themselves "Oregon Farms" went out, and all up these creeks and hollows and where all the old homesteaders lived. Like my grandpa, you know. He would've sold to Oregon Farms, but they didn't come along quick enough for him. I mean, he was out before that. Sold one hundred sixty acres for eight thousand bucks, with a house and everything else.

Anyway, these guys went around. Oregon Farms built a big retirement home over in Medford. And they went out to all these old folks whose kids wanted to go to California and elsewhere and make their bucks, and didn't want to farm no more.

And so they came to these old people who didn't have much. They were rich beyond belief in aesthetics, but didn't have no bucks. They didn't have no Social Security to speak of, because they're independent. These are great folks, grand people. And these guys went out with their salesmen and their high-pitched bullshit and said, "Hey. We'll give you fifty bucks an acre for this property. Think of it! Think of it! I mean, you got five hundred acres here. That's a lot of money." Or, "We'll give you five hundred . . ." Or whatever. They stole their land.

And they sold them this beautiful retirement concept. To go live in this mansion. "We got doctors and nurses and shuffleboard." They conned them! And taking all the money that these old folks would have realized from their land, and charging it back to them with this retirement center. And basically just getting that land for nothing. And getting rich off of it, you know?

I think the biggest scam was mobile homes and five-acre lots. Oh, they could get you on that for fifty thousand bucks. Maybe get eight or ten thousand down. And they'd sell those things over and over and over. Same ones. Because people couldn't make it. They'd come up here with the country-life ideal. And could not make it. Wages are depressed, the jobs are not here.

I remember the day I got out of the service and I went down to Unemployment to sign up, you know? My unemployment counselor was really a bitter lady. I think she had a masters in something, and she was an unemployment counselor, you know?

And I said, "Well, I just got out of the service, and I think I'd like to go to college out here and then transfer over and get a psych degree."

And she just kind of, "Oh, not another one! Not another one! Uhhhh." You know?

She says, "Just go out and get a job." She says, "This area has so many people that are underemployed, overqualified."

And I know lots of folks that have lots of background training, experience, that could make big salaries if they want to live in Hell. Or New York City. Whichever comes first . . . [*Moves remains of fish from the countertop*]

Bartering to me is the only way to go. I tie fishing flies. I trade that for fishing poles and reels and equipment. I don't like cash money too much. It ruins people. It ruins their perceptions of who they are. How they fit in. It's the root of all evil.

I take my dentist fishing. He fixes my teeth. Works good. Take my mechanic fishing. He fixes my car. Works good. [*Hefts another fish up*]

Ohhh. I think it's probably sixteen pounds. Something like that. They'll range anywhere from about twelve pounds to twenty. [*Removes hook from deep inside the fish's gullet*]

Deep. See all these hooks laying up here? [*Points to about seven hooks*] These all came this week out of throats. Then at the end of the week I clean them all up and then I re-do them. These are very expensive for a fish hook. Feel that point. Surgical carbon steel. High tech.

B. B. What did you catch these on?

Wayne [*Pulls roe out of fish*] With this. Roe. I've never eaten it. I eat the roe out of shad, but I don't eat this.

But being well traveled, I've eaten stuff that most people would puke if I told them what it was. But you go to different cultures, you eat what they eat. I didn't want to go have a hamburger in Japan. I say, "I want what you're having for dinner. I'll pay you whatever it's worth." And then pretty soon they'll talk to you, like a person instead of a patron. Because you've shown that you want to do a little leveling.

You know, I don't think I ever forgot people threatening my mom for giving food to people that were Black. I couldn't understand that.

Sam and Melinda were the people that owned the Yellow Cafe. It was a little drive-in restaurant. It had a square counter, with stools. She made the best homemade food. Cheap! Two bits for a hamburger with a little side of fries. Somebody was traveling and they stopped to get something to eat. And Sam and Melinda were nice people. And they wouldn't turn anyone away that was hungry. And they were threatened, and so was my mom.

I didn't understand it at all. I was brought up that people's people. My mother is a very caring person. A religious person. A racist person, but she doesn't know it. If you told her she was a racist, she would say, "Why, those darkies? They're just like we are." No exposure to anything.

To this day, I don't know who it was that threatened her. But I remember she was frightened. And she came home and told me about it. That was probably about 1947. And Dad was gone. No man around, you know. It scared her.

And I didn't understand sundown laws, and I didn't realize Grants

Pass was like that till I left. Got to rapping with some Black guys that was my age or older. They said, "Hey, man. We heard about that place."

And I says, "What about it?"

"Hey. People like us ain't welcome there."

And I says, "Well, you can stay at the Redwood Hotel. They let the basketball players stay there."

They says, "Yeah. But us . . . ? No."

And I finally understood. That's what it's all about! It's very insidious. Very low-key, very quiet. You know, no Klan, no nothing. There was just no people of color. There was some families. You know, the Chinese restaurant. They've always got a couple Asians. Maybe some Mexicans. But the folks were all assimilated. Totally. I mean, the value sets, lifestyles — same, same. There was no concept of ethnicity.

But that's what happened. She just got threatened about it. And that's about the end of that. But I never forgot it. And I think that may have had some bearing on why, when they wanted volunteers for race-relations training after I went to a seminar in the service, I may have raised my hand. Because I still had that "Boy, that really pisses me off" feeling, you know?

I met guys back in training that were exactly like me. Liked to do exactly the same things, same values, and you know, here I was always under the assumption, hooked into the stereotypes, like everybody else does until they're exposed to something different. And get their level of awareness raised.

I think it's changing a little bit here. Mostly because there are a lot of people in the community that are not old-core. The old-timers ain't changing. But most of the new folks, it's no problem. There's no inner city, there's no ghetto. There's no groups, nothing threatening about non-white people because they're such a small minority. However, I think attitudes would show themselves were the numbers bigger.

I think among young people, that's where you got to do it. Younger people are much more tolerant, and they learn quicker. They're not so stubborn and set in their ways.

B. B. What about how the long-time locals deal with the newcomers?

Wayne Well, one of the things I saw a lot of was, folks who didn't like it, left. And went over to places like Madras and Prineville and John Day. Looking for same way it used to be here.

B. B. What about the timber situation here?

Wayne   Oh, a lot of people are hurting. Financially. Emotionally. They're seeing their way of life change. I think that's hurting them probably more than cutting down trees. There's somebody telling them, "*You* can no longer be what you desire to be. Or what you have skills to be. You have to be something else." And resistance to change is a tough issue. The less aware people are, the stronger that will to resist is.

And those folks by-and-large are operating from a low educational base. The loggers. The loggers are a lot more dangerous to the quote–unquote yuppies than the yuppies are to the loggers. Physically. Not economic — economically only on the short haul. It's just like getting even type of deal. Somebody that's low on education, they look at getting even in different ways. Physical ways, you know? I listen to them guys talk, and it's kind of scary.

B. B.   What do you hear?

Wayne   Oooh, like the tree climbers? I know the guy that undercut the tree the tree climber was in. He was born and raised here. And I don't know why he stopped cutting the tree. Must have a little conscience someplace. Well, his mama's a good Christian lady.

B. B.   What about environmental groups like Headwaters?

Wayne   It's a very vocal minority. And the silent majority's sitting back and getting pissed. That's what I'm hearing. From a lot of people.

You know what this local old boys' culture is all about? It's about hunting and fishing. Well, I reckon I kind of joke about it, you know. [*Mimicking*] Pickup truck, cowboy hat, Budweiser beer, get drunk and fight. And that's kind of like what it is a little bit. There's an awful lot of pickups around. And a lot of ball caps and a lot of beer drinkers. Rowdy. Lot of rowdy activity. It's a kind of a lifestyle.

The threat from the people that are well intended, and — you know, well intended . . . [*pauses*]. I hate to see them build a dam. At Elk Creek. I hate that. I mean, it's an asinine way to spend my money. Plus it's going to silt up the river I love. Maybe screw up the fish run. They've already screwed up the spawning beds for miles up there. Where they used to spawn, there ain't nothing to spawn in except boulders.

'Cause I want these guys [*gestures at fish*] to keep coming back. I love to catch these things. I like to eat them and share them with people. This is kind of my mini-culture. My little niche, place in life.

One of the things — I guess it may be a little bone stuck in my craw, being a local and having grown up here — was that I had access to just about anyplace I wanted to go. I mean, not in people's yards and shoot their pets. But I could hunt anywhere I wanted to hunt. Fish anywhere I wanted to fish. And people didn't put up fences that say, "No Trespassing." "Keep Out." Or, like it is right now on the Applegate, "Riverbank Closed." There's a big sign. "No Trespassing. Riverbank Private Next Mile and a Half."

There's another law says you cannot fish out of a drift boat in the Applegate River. You can float through that part, but you can't get out and fish, because this guy says, "No. It's my land." And then the state says you can't fish out of a boat because you might catch a fish. So where are you at? Catch-22.

It's like the river right now. There's a problem with operating the big jet boats? There's going to be a public hearing. Well, what's going to happen is going to cause a big row, and people overlook some of the basic realities. That those big boats bring big dollars. Big enjoyment to a whole lot of tourists. They see the fishermen hold these salmon up. They want to go catch one. They stay in town three days more. Three more motel bills. Twelve more meals. Some fishing tackle, license. Everybody makes money off of it.

And the timber is damn near gone. When I was a kid, there wasn't no roads up in the mountains. It was all timber. Now it's cut down. I don't like that. I hate to see that happen. But it's happened.

They've overharvested. But they cut old growth, they're not getting very much good wood. Because a lot of the old growth is rotten. It needs to be harvested before it rots. I think that's a given. If it's going to be a valuable crop. Which, I look at trees as a crop. A renewable resource. With lots of information to bear that out.

The Tillamook Burn was thousands and thousands and thousands of acres of trees burned to nothing. Now they're able to log it again. And that happened in my lifetime. Here's proof in the pudding. The stuff comes back. I go out in the field where as a kid there wasn't no trees, and now there's, shit, trees thirty, forty feet high. And I say, "I don't remember them trees being there." Well, they weren't there. They grew.

I don't understand what the other side wants. It sure isn't the owl. The owl thing is stupid. Because the owl will go wherever the food is. He doesn't have to have a big tree to sit in. He goes to the big trees because the big owls can't catch him as easy. He's prey for the big owls. Great horned owls eat spotted owls. The great horned owls have a wide wingspan. Great horned owls have a hard time flying in old-growth timber. They're much better adapted to hardwood and along rivers and things where they can spread their wings.

I think one of my fears after watching what happened down south — I watched San Jose go from fifty-four thousand people to eight hundred seventy-eight thousand. The orchards become asphalt. Everything disappeared. And became parking lots and high rises and condos and walls. Little walled cities.

One of the field trips I did in the service was in a high-rent district. Lot of real rich homes and these little walled cities. In this affluent neighborhood you never saw any people. Nobody talked to anybody. Nobody was on the street.

As we got into the buffer zone, where there were people of lower socio-economic status, you started to see a few people. Not many, but a few. And they were willing to talk a little.

When you got into the really mixed neighborhood, there were a lot more people. People sitting out on their steps. People talked to each other. "Sit down. Want a beer?"

It was amazing to me. How as you go down the ladder of success, you go up the ladder of life. Of quality of life, as far as interacting with other humans.

I understand this place. I can survive here. But I do understand what Governor McCall said when he said, "Don't Californicate Oregon." And if it was up to me, I'd be a State of Jefferson supporter. Make California start about halfway between Red Bluff and Redding. Make Oregon start about halfway between Salem and Eugene. And we'd be the State of Jefferson, and they'd be them and leave us alone.

And somebody's actually said things like that, and I stupidly agree with that idea. I don't know — I was in Monterey County [California] a lot of years, and Monterey County is a cow county. Lots of cows. Lot of farms. Lot of ranches. And a little bay. A little group of people control a huge big chunk of land. And the same thing here. All of the people live in Portland and Salem, and a few in Eugene. Basically they all live in the metropolitan area. And they make all the rules and laws for everybody all over the rest of the state. It's crazy.

You know, it's a matter of: What are you willing to live with to live the way you want to live? And you find that this is still a damn good place to live. Not a whole lot of alternatives for the lifestyle I want.

In our lives

RHONDA MARSHALL (age 39) Rhonda Marshall's words epitomize the intersection of public and private dilemmas: an abusive ex-husband who was himself working in a body-abusive job typical of lumber and plywood mills. Rhonda's intelligence and initiative pulled her through. Her multi-sided appreciation of the strain on all members of the family brings this interview full-circle.

We spoke in her office during two long breaks. She is a determined woman who speaks with a quiet thoughtfulness and modesty. Even though it is obvious that she is prone to workaholism, and we were talking in the middle of a busy day, she set a relaxed pace for the taping and answered each of many outside interruptions with grace.

I was born in Utah in 1950. My mother was a homemaker. My father was a road mechanic for an automotive franchise chain. Until I was nine, we were everywhere. By the time I had gotten to the third grade, I had been in five different schools in three different states. We started out in Utah, we moved to New Mexico, Washington, back to New Mexico, to Colorado, and then to Oregon.

I don't remember a lot before we came to Oregon. I'm sure it was because my family is an alcoholic family. On both sides. So you don't remember a lot of your childhood. I can remember the strict rules.

When we moved to Oregon, it was scary. It was real hardship times for us, but really good times, too. Hardship-wise, no money. We had to learn that beans are OK three or four times a week. But I think it drew our family very close together.

Most families split when things get real hard. But I can remember my folks would take things and make them wonderful. There wasn't any money. Once a month they would go downtown and buy hamburgers. Ten for a dollar hamburgers. The whole family would sit down and everybody would have to set the day. And it'd be like two weeks from now. So all this anticipation, like Christmas every month, you know? We'd go get the hamburgers and we'd bring them home and we'd talk about everything that had happened, and how we anticipated this particular day.

Mom started out working in the pears. Working in the canneries and doing that kind of thing. Then she went to night school and correspondence school. And worked in legal for about fourteen years.

Basically I was a loner. I really didn't have lots of friends, because of being raised in this adult atmosphere. I spent more time doing things like keeping this family together. And reading books.

Ah, dreams when I was in high school, I think were other people's dreams. I don't think they were ever my own. At that time it was kind of a norm that women get married, they have kids. They become homemakers. So I was always on this intent that this was my lifestyle I was going for.

Education was more my preference. School was a big, important thing to me. I had perfect attendance all four years of high school. I like the idea of knowledge. And that was a continuation into college, was more knowledge. And then I met my husband and got married, so that was the end of that for a while.

In my ancestors, up until my generation, no one graduated from high school. My father graduated the eighth grade. My mother was into the eleventh grade when she quit. My grandparents — fourth-grade levels. In our immediate family, I'm the first to go to college. All of the grandkids at my age have graduated from high school — none have continued from there. I'm kind of the pioneer, have to build the enthusiasm. [Laughs]

I lived at home until I got married. I worked as a nurse's aide. I started out in a convalescent home when I was sixteen. When I was thirteen, I started picking wild blackberries. I became an entrepreneur. Pick blackberries and sell them door to door. You pick blackberries, you put them in flats, you clean them, you go to stores, get contracts. I sold to grocery stores for three years straight. When I was sixteen, I was able to purchase my first car, paid cash with blackberry money. You had dreams of these humongous blackberries hitting you! Trying to get away from them.

I worked for the next eight years, and at that point I started going through medical problems. And the medical problems kind of pulled me away from people. Plus my husband was an abusive person. So I kind of withdrew from other people even more. I withdrew more and more. I needed something to draw me out of the house, and people could tell it. So I was invited by a friend to go to a tailor shop and do design and sewing as a business. I went in and did that, and the entrepreneur came out again. Just jumps right out there! [*Laughs*]

My husband's great-grandfather and grandfather were both green-chain pullers in the mill. My father-in-law was a tallyman for thirty-eight years. And my husband was a greenchain puller when we met, and up until the last seven or eight years of the marriage. And he worked at Southwestern for seventeen years. He worked at Trentville for nine. It was moved from Susanville to Trentville. It's not there anymore because it was sold out, when my father-in-law was forced to retire, due to the sale of the mill. And it was sold and moved out of Trentville. All that's there now is like one little store. Nothing there. It had this big productive mill, and my mother-in-law and father-in-law and my ex-husband used to live there in town. There was a big school. Everything was moved.

The design business was my main focus for a long time. But in the process, due to inexperience of maintaining a business that grew that fast, you don't want to let go of bits and pieces of your business to other people to do for you. So I worked the business for fourteen years basically eighteen hours a day, six days a week.

I closed my business the day that I left my husband. I had two children. My oldest one was thirteen and my youngest one was seven. And they couldn't afford to have Mom gone eighteen hours a day to maintain this business. And in any type of business, there's no guarantee that every single month you're going to be able to provide for your family. And so I closed it.

When we left, my husband did not pay child support, and hasn't since. He, in fact, quit his job at Southwestern to run away from the responsibility. Which he had done before, so I knew that was happening. And he has not even tried to contact the children, and it's been over two years.

From there the kids and I moved to a shelter home for victims of abuse. We lived there and kind of got ourselves situated and straightened out what we were doing. Rented our place, and two weeks later I went into the FSA [Family Service Act] program and started back into my education mode. And all of a sudden found out that I was a totally different person than I had ever been in my life.

It was like I went to college before because I wasn't married. You know? But this time I wanted to go to college for me. As each paper came back, more self-assertiveness came. My self-esteem, I could feel it picking up and moving.

After the first term I thought I was going to die. [*Laughs*] Because I was carrying twenty-one credits that term. *And* being a mother and having to deal with welfare and all these things.

But after the second term I was a fleeting victim of circumstance. A business person I knew a little bit had an employee that was sloughing off at the job. And I was being a perfectionist in my computer courses — helping out other students, teaching them how to do computers. And when the employee really messed up and didn't show up for a week, I was asked by this business to walk in and help out for a while. And I did. At the end of that one week, my employer asked me if I would be interested in becoming a regular employee at a very responsible position.

So now my goals are, to get my four-year and my bachelor's. When I was in high school, I took all the business classes. I got A's in business classes. English, Basic Math, the things that are required in high school, D's. And it was because there was no encouragement. I could do the work, but I didn't do it. I liked the business part, so I did the business part, but that was my own encouragement to myself.

B. B.   What kind of changes have you seen in the valley?

Rhonda   Within Medford, lots of changes. For many, many years I feel that Medford was almost like a retirement community. It was ran by older people who really didn't want change within the valley. They didn't want new industrial type things. Everything was stagnating. I think a prime example was the Mall — the plans for the Rogue Valley Mall were started, and seven years later they finally made it through the Planning Commission.

Computers went from a backdoor type business right into multimillion dollars overnight. We went to not so much the working force, but into mental force. And now our whole resource of the United States is just the people.

Lumber is a good example — a timber family. It's good enough for Dad, and it's good enough for the kids, and all the way down the line. But Dad doesn't remember that his father died at age forty-two, because he just actually tore himself to pieces working in the mill.

I think this is the one war that I have with my [ex-]husband. He has no idea what he's missed in his life. He's happy-go-lucky, and he's still just a timber boy. He doesn't realize there is fine art. He doesn't realize there is fine music. He's worked so long in timber, but he's never taken an actual sit-down-and-look type walk in the forest. You know? So it's kind of like the saying that "The timber's too high, you can't see the sky."

People have come out of high school, they've gone right into the lumber industry. They're making ten, twelve, fourteen dollars an hour. Just as nineteen-year-old kids. They are receiving good medical plans. Good pension plans.

Well, with the coming from generations of timber workers, they don't have the fields available to them. They only know timber. So it's a panic, because if that job is no longer there, then the jobs that are available are four- or five-dollar-an-hour jobs.

My father-in-law was, what? He must have been sixty-one or sixty-two years old when they closed the mill at Trentville. OK — no job available to him for his age. The only jobs that were available to him, due to his knowledge abilities, were dishwashers in restaurants and this type of thing. A very devastating blow. He was a tallyman, walked like fifty miles a day. All of a sudden he's home? Big controversy, change in the household.

My husband, as soon as he found out they were going to close, he converted to Southwestern. When he originally started at Southwestern, he was working forty hours a week. Sometimes he would work fifty, sixty, seventy hours a week. Lots of overtime. Lots of free money.

But as the timber industry started coming down, the overtime was cut back and cut back, until probably two years ago, overtime was almost unforeseen. Then at that time they started devaluing insurance policies.

I see lots and lots of people, all the people that were associated with my husband, and his family, trying to move into other careers. My husband's best friend worked in the mills for nineteen years, and after nineteen years invests in a maintenance business and quits his job at the mill, and he goes to work cleaning buildings! Because he can foresee that the timber's going down. It's not as accessible. They can't bring out as many trees. They're not working the trees as well.

They're not being safeguarding — cutting the trees so that it leaves trees in that area growing. Instead, they're more clearcutting. Clearcutting causes the industry to die, because you can't replant twenty seedling trees in the place of a hundred-year-old tree and expect in twenty-five or fifty years to have another tree to cut. So it's decreasing our woods products that are available.

My sons, they definitely don't want wood. This was a controversy throughout my marriage, because my husband was always, "Oh, you need to go into the mills. It's good money." And I'm going, "No!" My own personal beliefs are that people shouldn't have to work their bodies so hard. They should work their minds. And their father was a good example of it. He was forty years old when we divorced, and this man walked like he was seventy.

When you first start in a mill, you're quick, you're fast, you're strong. So they put you into the harder-labor jobs. My husband started out as a greenchain puller, which is pulling raw lumber off the chain. Back in 1971 he was making five dollars an hour, but he was making so much per board foot that went across the chain. He was bringing home almost a thousand every two weeks. In seventy-one.

But he injured his back, so then it was lighter-duty jobs. That was at Trentville. When he went into Southwestern he went into pulling greenchain, but it's a lighter cut. The wood isn't as thick when they cut it and slice it to put across. At Trentville they pulled between a hundred to a hundred twenty thousand board foot a day in an eight-hour shift. And there were five men on the chain. At Southwestern there were eight men on the chain, and they pulled eighty thousand board foot in a twenty-four-hour period. So lots of difference in work.

Then, in seventy-three, whenever all of the mills in the valley went down, my husband was laid off five and a half months. Which was a total devastating process for us. And all of our friends. Everybody would go from one person's house to another house to another house, every night of the week to keep these guys busy. If you didn't do this, there was more anger within the men. They had shorter fuses.

Just as an example, he was laid off day before Thanksgiving. And he was off work till the first part of May. Someone walked right in front of the car, and my husband proceeds to get out and beat the guy up for doing this. Because everything was short-fused.

We're back to this excessive amounts of income, and then all of a sudden you're on unemployment at eighty-eight dollars a week. My husband took great pride that he took care of his family. And all of a sudden we're on food stamps. And he can't cope with this.

What we would do is, like our friends would come to our house tonight, play cards, do something to keep the guys active. Then tomorrow night we went to someone else's house. And we just kept doing this for five and a half months. I mean, you get really burnt out at that point. I had a one-and-a-half-year-old baby, you know?

The women worked together. It's like, "No, I don't want everybody here every night!" And when you're on food stamps, you can't afford to feed four couples every night. But each couple could afford to take care of it one night a week.

It was hard! But it was just survival. But you have to realize that it's almost like a different type of world compared to what most people are aware of. In the valley, this is what I see: All the millworkers is one kind of a community, as far as their survival techniques. Then you have managerial people — their survival techniques would be totally different.

I think the timber industry is pulling out because they're there for the profit. They purchased a hundred thousand acres of land that has timber on it, OK? They have abused this land for many years by their cutting processes and this kind of thing. All of a sudden, compared to when they first purchased the land, they almost have a barren land. So now they have to go somewhere where the timber is.

One of the really sad parts is watching so much of our timber being shipped out of the States. And you have guys here that are depending on these jobs to take care of these families, and timber's going overseas to be worked, because it can be worked cheaper.

Southwestern is pulling in more and more automation. The automation that's being pulled in is cutting back jobs, manpower jobs. But Medford hasn't even gotten to the point that they're offering the technology education to their employees to upgrade their employees.

Southwestern comes in and puts in new systems, and it's a pushbutton system. And they're hiring, or taking one or two of their people per shift, put them on this job. But they have depleted fifteen or twenty jobs. But in the process they're not taking and incorporating the other things. They could put these workers working in a more technical area. But these workers are out. So then these workers are being faced with these five-dollar-an-hour jobs.

Southwestern also has educational plans that are available to employees' children. But this is a new thing for the valley. Because Southwestern is not created in Oregon. Southwestern's from another state. It takes and picks up a lot of trends from all over the United States. But like a locally owned mill, for instance — these types of things I don't see there.

I have a really hard time understanding how, for instance my husband, at forty years old, can have a third-grade reading level. Actually go through school and education in the valley, and have a third-grade reading level. He did graduate from high school.

He works in a mill. He makes thirty thousand a year at age forty. There's very low education levels existing for a lot of the guys. I have a real hard time dealing with it, because the millworkers proceed to tear up their bodies very fast, because of these injuries to their bodies from the work. Lots of back injuries. Getting hands run through saws, and this kind of thing. The mills work very hard to keep their safety, because Workman's Comp is high. But you just spend just so much time with so much weight on your body. Their backs are wearing out. Their shoulders are wearing out. The necks are wearing out, hips — from the twists and swivels.

Basically I don't know very many women that their husbands work at the mills and have lower education levels that are not physically or verbally abused by these men. In my instance, it was this as a part, but not the whole. It's like summertimes are the worst. Because if it's a hundred degrees outside, it's a hundred and forty in the mill. The men come home from work, they're tired. They're hot. They've lost a lot of salt to the perspiration, to the point most of the men take salt tablets in order to revive that salt in their systems.

In the process, they come home in angry moods. They're angry with the timber, period. But it's the only thing to do. So it's like a frustration in their life. And then their other frustration is no education to get out of that life. It's almost like a constant circle, and they're always in the circle. It's almost like a walking timebomb sometimes.

Most of the women spend more time catering to these men. Trying to keep them as comfortable as possible. Trying to keep children quiet. So you're almost taking and putting a disability into your family.

And so it's like a war within the family at that point. So the self-esteem of the kids starts going downhill in the process. If their self-esteem goes down, their ability to assimilate the information goes down. They're not able to comprehend knowledge at that point. And when they have a problem with comprehending the knowledge, then when they are nineteen or seventeen or whatever, to go out to go to work, they're instantly back into the mill. Which they're going right back into that whole round-the-bush syndrome again.

I feel like the spotted owl controversy all has to do with the mills pulling out of the valley. All of a sudden there's this big "threat." Because the mills don't want to just take and pull out. So this controversy is a good way to slowly wean back the woods from being invaded by the logging trucks and this type of thing. I just think that it's a political thing to help the corporations bow out gracefully.

You're talking about this — I don't know how many — less than a hundred owls. And they're taking and saving hundreds upon hundreds of acres of land for this less than a hundred owls. They're not allowing any logging in those areas. They're trying to make it a reserve for these owls.

These owls could be moved. To a more virginal forest that does not have thousands of people's lives relying on it. You know, as far as, "How do I feed my family?"

So you hear more and more of the timber workers are angry, because if this is an excuse to keep the forest closed, then next week we're going to be saving something else. And we're going to slowly start cutting back more and more of the forest land that's going to be able to be cut.

By doing that, it becomes a very apparent point to these men that they do not have the knowledge. Their egos and their self-esteem start going downhill. Because they've been hit in the face with a brick that says, "You may not be able to take care of your family." And yet this was their biggest pride.

I just feel like — that it's a political thing. A way for corporations to go to the other timber lands that they own that they're going to take and start cutting.

Right now, at this point, I would say what has me tied here is my job. Because I need more knowledge to be able to do my job at the same level in other areas. But right now I'm going to school to develop that knowledge so that I can move forward. If I'm going to live in Oregon, then I might as well live in Oregon where I have a support system of childcare. I have a support system of family.

And if your family's lived here for three or four or five generations, it's almost like committing a crime towards your family to move away from. And it's just because, well, nobody's ever known anywhere but here.

One of the things that keeps me drawn to Oregon is the fact that I love the weather. I love the greenery. Up until ten years ago I probably liked Oregon because of it being slower-paced than other places. But if Oregon doesn't start picking up some pace, especially the valley, they're going to be in an antique mode.

Before I came into the welfare training program, I had a totally different outlook on it. It was like: You stay in your own little house. You do your own little thing. Where I lived before, I had the same neighbors for almost twelve years. And out of all the neighbors, I had two that I associated with.

The neighborhood that I live in right now, I know every neighbor. That's because we had the Medford police come out and set up a neighborhood watch. One of the main things that was brought to mind through this meeting was, it used to be where people would get home from work, go out and sit on the front lawn in their lawn chairs, and visit with all the neighbors. Now they go home, sit down in front of the

TV, and watch TV. Then they have even gone further to put family rooms on the back ends of their houses, so they don't have to deal with the road noise to watch the TV. So they're getting farther away from their street. Farther away from their people. Farther away from the community. I mean, my kids know everybody, because kids know everybody. But as far as an adult, it's like you don't want to be involved in their problems. You don't want to know what goes on in their household. Even down to when I left my husband. I had neighbors come over that day. My husband was at work when we went in and got our personal belongings. I had two and a half hours to do this. During that period of time, I had five of these neighbors that I didn't know come over and say, "Well, I should have called when your kids were being abused by this man. And, you know, I never did." And, "I don't know how you stayed here this long. I don't know how you dealt with this."

And especially, most of the millworkers that are working here in the valley that I have seen are between the age range of thirty-five to forty-seven, forty-eight. OK. You have all this anger and hostility that's dealing there. You are having this twenty-year lag of Vietnam crisis. Which is more anger within these people, more issues they're having to deal with.

And you see all of the people here in the valley going through this withdrawal; they're holding the anger in their houses. They're trying to hold everything in their homes, rather than branching off into technology, branching off into the funner things. Or the faster-paced things. The things that make it part of the world.

Through the FSA program, one thing I picked up is that I guarantee you that over fifty percent have never read a book completely through since high school. And we're talking about thirty-five to forty-seven-year-old women? Thirty-five to forty-seven year old Vietnam vets. They don't read. Because reading breaks them out of the isolation; they're being exposed to what's outside, they're not in this nice little culture of Medford, Oregon.

See, this is the thing: Whenever someone comes into the area, what they're seeing is low technology. So in the process, the people here have to be backwards. They don't have this knowledge, so instantly a lot of people assume that no knowledge means illiteracy. See? Rather than working with it a little bit and seeing that no knowledge can also mean not having the introduction to it.

But as far as mental capacities, I feel like there's a lot of smart people that just don't know how to use it. I can take myself as an example. When I entered the FSA program, my own personal point of view was that I would never maintain a job. I would never be able to walk into a job situation. And it was because of these environmental things that go on within the home.

And of course you take that and compound it by the fact that I was married to this man that was an abuser with a third-grade reading ability. And his way of power was to tell me how I did everything wrong. Until I left the situation, I didn't realize that this meant that I wasn't doing things wrong. It was he was changing all the rules all the time on how it was supposed to be done.

But then when I went into my course of study, the first term I came back with a 3.73 GPA. And it was like, Wow! I got my certificate. At that point, one of the choices which was given me was this company owner that recognized I had an ability with computers and business. When I was approached with that, I didn't believe that either. I'm the person that for probably five years prior to leaving my husband, I bought groceries at midnight in order to not run into people. Not to have to talk to people. Not to have to deal with looks.

And then all of a sudden I had this business owner walk up to me and says, "Oh, you'd be wonderful!" And I went, "No way!" But in the year and a half since then, I've gone from one extreme to almost the other extreme.

SUE CLEARY   (age 38) Lesbian and gay people are invisible as a community and ignored as individuals in virtually every study of the rural United States. Lesbian and gay youths leave rural areas at a higher rate than their heterosexual counterparts because regional prejudice and lack of internal community support systems make it dangerous to stay—physically, emotionally, or both. Even so, a good proportion of locally born lesbians and gays either choose to remain or eventually return because they love the area and want to be close to friends and family.

Like other local citizens, lesbians and gays are concerned about the issues of timber, the economy, and the community. This interview took place in Sue's small, well-tended home. She was nervous about talking but made me comfortable in an overstuffed chair and dived in.

I was born in Roseburg, Oregon, in 1949. I was raised in a small town. My dad owned a little store there, and my mom also worked there on and off.

My dad was raised in southern Oregon. My mom grew up in Arizona — I believe she was born in Colorado. They traveled around, because my grandfather was in the service. Then there was parts of the family that lived in Oregon, so that's how Mom and Dad got together. I couldn't tell you what my dad's parents were doing. I don't know if he worked in mills or what he did. I know he had a lot of tools. I've just never asked.

We were like half a mile out of town — it was within walking distance of school. The town, I don't think it ever got much over a thousand. But it was probably nine hundred most of the time.

I had woods on three sides. I played a lot by myself. And my horse was very important to me. Being down at the creek where I wasn't supposed to be was very important to me. I did what I wanted to do — and got caught. But most of the time I went off by myself and played by myself, rode my horse, occupied my time until my parents got home.

I was never afraid. I mean, I was never afraid of somebody getting me or getting in trouble or anything like that. Like I would be frightened to death to do it nowdays, go off by myself like that into the woods — you just never know. But I was really fearless, I guess.

My dad, I remember that he had this box of cards, where all these people owed him all this money. The miners would come down, and they hadn't hit anything for months, and he would just say, "OK. Take what you need." So he'd have a bigger box of those kind of people, the loggers and stuff who just weren't getting it. Or really down-and-out people, you know. I think that he didn't make as much money as he could have. [*Laughs*] But I always was real proud that he did that for everybody. Because there was another store down the street who didn't do it quite as much. Dad didn't want them to go without, 'cause they had lots of kids. It seems like there was always little rug-rats running around, hanging out the trucks. How could you go and not feed them?

Mom and Dad were real active in the community. It seemed like all of our games at school—I mean, the town closed down if we had a football game. My dad closed the store. It was just a real tight community back then. I couldn't imagine not having that be. It's consolidated now, and the high school isn't the same.

But the kids, you could ride your horses right downtown. No restrictions, like there are now. No drugs. The biggest thing that I know of anybody did was maybe have a beer or smoke cigarettes. Or if they wore their hair slicked back with grease and a leather jacket. That was about as bad as it got. Somebody might get pregnant. I had no idea what drugs was.

At one point—I think it was in the early sixties, maybe fifty-nine. My dad had come home and said that our sheriff had—the bus had come through, and some Black men, I guess, were going to get off. And he says, "We don't want any trouble here. You get back on the bus and you stay there!"

And I just got really upset. I was only ten or something. But I was real angry that we were having this kind of a social problem, and I couldn't believe it! Don't know even if I'd seen a Black person. You know? But panic! "Stay on the bus." And I was real disappointed, because I always thought we were so OK with everything.

So maybe we were really redneck, and I didn't know it. I really didn't know what the situation was anywhere else outside of there. [*Laughs*]

One of my friend's father was in an accident. He was dying, which at that point I didn't know. But they had set off the fire alarm, that there was an emergency in town. And everybody leaves everything and goes to the department. And they were all taken to the hospital to give blood and stuff, and try to save him. And right at that point, it was like a town grouping for me. It was like they were all involved, and it was instantaneous. As soon as that alarm went off, it was "What's happening?" And word spread like wildfire. And those kinds of things is what I grew up with. As far as being together and all basically thinking the same way—I thought. So that was a real powerful way for me to be.

And then my mom and dad got a divorce, we moved to Arizona, and my world fell apart. I was fifteen. I was active in sports, in the band, and popular. And went to a huge city where there was over eight hundred people in my graduating class? Which was as big as my town! I didn't know anybody. I couldn't get into any groups. I tried the band, and, "You're not good enough." My self-esteem went down to zero.

I tried out for track, and here are these great big Black women! I'm competing against them, and it was like I was standing still! So it was like, Where do I belong? And I cried and cried and cried.

I had gotten there the year after all the civil rights stuff. They had locked up the schoolyard and fenced it in and chained everybody in. And there was knife fights and people being hurt and stuff. So the Blacks were there, and they were against the whites. And the whites were against . . .

And I'm going, "I don't understand any of this!" And so I spent most of my time in the head with the Black women. I never really became real close, but I felt like they were kind of outcasts, and so was I. So we just kind of hung out together there. But never out in the open.

And it was really unfortunate. There was one gay man, or boy—he was a junior. They picked on him something fierce. I didn't understand what being gay was, really. I would just watch them pick on him in the locker room, and tease him, and he'd cry. And I'd just be going, "Why is all this going on?"

I felt real sorry for him, but not ever being involved in anything like that, I didn't know what to do. I didn't join in, but I didn't try to stop them, either. I knew what he felt like. It was a real ugly time for me. I went two years there and graduated. Then I came back here to go to SOC, because there was no way I was staying there. The clouds would go over and I would just wait for it to rain. I wanted trees and rain.

That's when I had my first relationship with a woman. Had no idea of what I was doing. I thought I was the only one in the whole world. We didn't really get into heavy-duty stuff. Her parents found out. It was kind of an ugly overall scene.

Then I moved to Portland. I was rude. I was angry. I didn't get into trouble or anything, really. I was just angry that things weren't working out. And I didn't care.

In Portland I couldn't find any work, didn't know how to look for work. My dad was supporting me, my mom was sending me money. I mean, we were living on chips and mayonnaise and ketchup. And if guys came over, they'd bring over food. Because we didn't have any. And of course we were into drugs—not heavy-duty, just smoking dope.

My dad came. And he says, "I want you to go to secretarial school. The offer's there. You don't have to pay anything." So I said, "What else is there for me to do?" So I moved back here. I went through school. A friend of mine was working in a small mill that's gone now. And I said, "OK. I'll work there through the summer until I get a job." Well, I started working there, and it was good money. More money than I could make doing office work. I started out at a dollar seventy-five an hour, I think. And went up to two dollars an hour. So I was making big bucks and real happy with it. It was a real nice place to work and I enjoyed it. I was tailing off of a saw. He'd cut the parts and I would stack them and put them on a pallet. It was a furniture mill. Then we'd send them down to California—they'd make couches and chairs and stuff out of them. We have so many different mills that do unique little things.

I had my first real relationship. And not knowing anything about lesbian relationships, I got my big watch and my wallet in my pants and I got my big boots and I started storming around and cut my hair off, and my dad practically disowned me. But that's what I thought I was supposed to do. And there was more trouble in my life. Because I was out to prove to the world that I was OK.

In one way it was fine. Because those were the clothes I was wearing anyway in the mill. So I just continued wearing them all day! Go out at night and wear them at night! I'm glad I went through it. But I'm glad I'm out of it now, too. I finally realized there's other ways to be a lesbian. [*Laughs*]

It made a hard time for my family in this area. Because my brother, he drank and he would go to the bars, and of course I went to the bars. He knocked a guy off a barstool once because, "Don't you know your sister is a queer?" It just broke his heart. I don't really think he knew at the time.

What was really funny is that some of my brother's really best friends that he drank with a lot said, "Hey, if you need any help or you need somebody to talk to, just come to us, and we'll help you." And my own family wasn't saying that. So they were kind of being supportive. I'm sure they talked about me also, but they were at least being supportive of me because they knew he wasn't. He was flipping out.

I started finding more lesbians in the area. Being aware of them, being friends more with them. Then hearing that they didn't want me to be around them because I was so butch. It drew attention to them, and they didn't need to have some butchy person drawing attention to their lifestyle. So that's when I started changing.

Then I got another job. I said I was going to work at this one mill, and I wasn't going to work anywhere else. They had good benefits, and they were a good place to work. So I waited two months and got on. And that's where I've stayed. I knew one person who was working there, and she kind of got me in the door. Then I just did it on my own from there.

It was one of the lowest-paying jobs. And my boss had said, "This is the worst job in the whole plant." And it's like, I don't care. And it is a bad job, but it's not that bad! And for somebody that doesn't have one, it's wonderful. [*Laughs*]

I've basically stayed in that mill. My big bosses, they all know that I'm a lesbian. I'd say probably half the other people do. It's not talked about, I don't do anything. My workplace is my workplace.

When the yellow ribbon stuff came, I tied a yellow ribbon on — with the Silver Fire thing. 'Cause in part I realized there's a lot of timber up there, and why let it go just to rot down? You know? And I thought, Well, the roads, they'll all grow over and be gone. *If* they did it the right way, you know? And so then I tied the ribbon on. It was a real good feeling to be one — there was a lot of ribbon people. And so I'm thinking, Yeah, this is neat, everybody's fighting for the same thing.

Then I started talking to different people. Well, they're not going to do it the right way. They're not going to be careful, they're just going to go in and leave trash and oil, and the roads, they're going to be there forever.

And then I started thinking about it in another direction. If they're not going to do it right, I don't want them to do it. There's too much of a chance of really them going in there and ruining it. They're not supposed to be in there in the first place, but I was going to let them in! But if they're not going to do it right, I don't want to let them in.

I had a real turmoil with that. Because my friends were all "anti." They don't want the loggers in there. So we didn't discuss it amongst ourselves. Because I got angry.

Then I took my ribbon off in about a week. Because it started evolving into something more than what I could handle emotionally. If everybody could guarantee that they were all going to do it the right way, then I wouldn't have a problem with it. But there's too much of a chance of it being done incorrectly. And having to pay for it.

The Silver Fire was a step, and the owl is a step, into making us realize we have some resources we need to start taking care of. If it hadn't've been for these issues, I don't think we would have paid any attention.

And I think our export situation is now in everybody's view. Like I didn't know anything about the magnitude of what we're exporting to

Japan. I had no idea. Now that's an issue for me. It never was before. Somebody knew it, obviously, because somebody was making money off of it. We could feed everyone in Oregon for the rest of our lives on the stuff that we're sending to Japan. There's no excuse for that. Why have Oregon at war with each other — the people here — when we could solve it just by somehow changing that system? We're all hating each other for no reason. There's plenty here if we keep it here.

I think it's great that this community has pulled together. I think it's unfortunate that they're all pulling together in a direction that I don't consider a real positive one. I just know not to say anything.

The market that I do my business with, the little market, I know that I can't say anything — and here we're good friends. I've lived here for ten years, and we've talked about everything. And this is one issue I can't talk to them about.

They have their petitions on the counter, and, "Sign this! Sign this!" And I said, "Oh, what is this?" Knowing that if I read it I'm going to be in a position where I'm going to have to make a stand. And I'm going, "Oh, boy. Let me think about it. I just don't know about this for sure."

I don't want to piss them off and have a confrontation. Yet it's an opinion, and I have a right to my opinion. And afraid to say anything. So those are the kind of things that make me uncomfortable. Because everybody's so adamant about it. But it takes both kinds for all of us to see what's going on.

I want to have the timber here. I like the trees, I like to see them. I like to live in a wood house, too! [*Laughs*] But maybe there's an alternative. Maybe there's some other way we need to start looking at things.

I have two friends that were born and raised in this area. And the rest of them are from Virginia and California and Missouri and Ohio and Washington. Very few of them are from here. But they've moved here because it is a small town, and trees and river. Most all of my friends are lesbians. I really don't socialize much with the straight people. I don't have a desire to. I mean, I work with them everyday. [*Laughs*] We really don't have anything in common. I'm not really "out" as far as talking to them about my personal life or anything, and so I just choose not to. I have a lot of friends, so I don't have that need to really have any straight friends.

What I like about the small-town area is being able to go out to the woods that's just out your door. Fishing. You don't have to travel fifty or a hundred miles to go fishing. Everything's here, as far as the

land opportunities. And my dog. I can take him where I want to. I
don't have to keep him chained up. I can't imagine living in a city and
being that confined. I wouldn't mind living in a city for a couple of
months out of the year! Maybe that would be the ideal thing, if I had
the money.

I have real double standards where the Californians are concerned.
I don't want anybody coming here from California and boosting up the
price of everything because they've got the money to buy it. On the
other hand, I don't want it to remain so backwoodsy that it never
grows, either.

I would love to buy some more property, but I was looking in the
paper today. [*Laughs*] Property with nothing on it is how much I paid
for this house. How do just middle-of-the-road people ever buy any
property or homes or anything? They can't afford to. And even the rent
here is astronomical. You can't exist. It's no wonder so many people
are on welfare. I'm real fortunate that I bought my house when I did. I
got it in seventy-eight. So it was just before my work went way down. It
wasn't a good time to buy, but at least I'm in. I wouldn't be able to do
it now.

Like my uncle. He's got a house up for sale that he's just waiting
for a Californian to come up here and pay this outrageously high price.
And he bitches when he's not selling it. And that's my own uncle. I
mean, if he's doing it, everybody's doing it. He's out to make as much
as he can. And that's really sad. Why not sell it to somebody who's
here?

I don't get involved with the community that much. I just go to
work and come home and just socialize with my friends. I'm just a
middle-of-the-road lesbian is what I call myself. I'm not really the
upper class and I'm not really the lower class. I'm just kind of in the
middle, and I get along with everybody. Or try to. I know some older
lesbians that don't socialize with many people at all. It makes me angry
when I read articles that they want to get all the gays and lesbians out
of this area. I mean, how do you do that? Why would you want to do
that? You can't do that! Come on. It's just these narrow-minded people
who — some of their beliefs are just too weird. They want this to be a
"perfect" community. Well, it would never be perfect if that was the
case.

As for the economy, I really don't know. On one hand I think that
we're going to have to open up our system a little bit more and loosen
some of the restrictions that we have in the area, because there isn't
companies coming in here and building. Because it's so hard.

I think welfare is one of our biggest problems. I'm glad we have it, but I think that it's easily abused. We pay people not to work, basically. The more kids you have, the more money you get, and you can always find some reason why not to work. I think the elderly suffers more than their share. They get the brunt end of it. Welfare's abused, and I think those kinds of services for the elderly get cut.

And the logging—I feel that it's going to take people, whether they're right or wrong, on both ends of the scale to do what they're doing for attention to be drawn where the problem is with the environment. If they're drawing people from somewhere else and they're just getting in here and getting involved in the fight because it's just an area to where they kind of believe in and they don't know any facts or anything—at least they're doing something. To be on record.

I don't know. Like the tree spiking. That made me angry. So I can be angry at both groups, but we need both groups, the extremists or whatever, just to make us listen. I think it's unfortunate. But without them, we would have destroyed us.

And like I said, I don't think the owl is really the issue, or the lizard, or the salamander, or whatever. It's just—the point that they're trying to make is that we need to stop and look. It's obvious that people are out of work. That's something that's in our face. But the owl's not in our face. So it's real easy to turn our back on it—and it won't be there if we don't pay any attention to it. We just have to meet in the middle somewhere.

B. B. Has the level of safety you feel in the community changed over time?

Sue I still feel fairly safe—not as safe as I did, but still fairly safe. I have a belief that most people are basically good. I would be aware and cautious. Probably more so than I would have ten years ago. Not that I feel like there's going to be any gay-bashing. But, then again, I might be oblivious to what's going on. There's always articles in Medford, how bad it's getting. I've never experienced it.

I went down to the park for the Memorial Day thing and sat there and was just watching the kids walking around. Some of them had shaved heads and purple hair and funny clothes on that had their group names on them, or whatever they're called. And I just wondered, are these the people that we're hearing about on the news? How would I know? They're walking around, free! [*Laughs*] Should we be concerned?

It was a real confusing thing. I know that people are just dressing that way, too. But then I know that people with shaved heads and who wear the clothes that they were wearing and their chains and everything are people I don't want to get involved with. But how do you know?

That's where my prejudice comes in. I am pretty prejudiced when it come to skinheads. I think we ought to run them all out of town. Get a big bazooka out. It just makes me angry when they start forcing their rights on people. Anytime that happens I'm against it. I don't care who you are. I mean the ones that really harm people, that have this weird white-supremacy or whatever it's called attitude. That scares me. They're my neighbors, you know? But then again, I haven't experienced anything. I've just heard horror stories. That we have a whole group of Nazi people from Eugene all the way down here. Older people. They're unfortunately categorized as the "logger" type of redneck people. They have their meetings, they've got some support. At least that's what I've heard rumored and heard people say that they've talked to — and obviously couldn't say anything back to them. Just kind of had to bite their tongue, because they're in a position not to say anything.

KATHY DODGE (age 27) Kathy Dodge is a survivor and has maintained her cheerful demeanor despite hardships. Her whirlwind young life dropped her in the netherworld of the Rogue Valley, where drugs and dealing and physical abuse trap many young people. The combination of lack of basic education, lack of vocational training, lack of work, and lack of transportation is an old story to many lower-income women of the area. All these deficiencies serve to deepen the problems caused by the massive timber and electronic-industry layoffs in the area.

We spoke one weekend morning at her kitchen table.

I was born in Medford in 1964. My parents and grandparents were all raised in southern Oregon.

I was ill on and off throughout early elementary school. My world was very small. So then when I got better, and then got into high school, it was a real different ballgame. Because I had been out of the social scene for so long, I went overboard into trying to fit in. Which was real difficult for me.

So in high school I guess I became a real rebel. Just to prove to the other kids that I wasn't a goody two-shoes. And I started hanging around with the real "bad" crowd of people — although a lot of them turned out to be good people. It was what we called "hoods." And although I still got along with all the "sociable" people, I chose to hang around them. They were the type of kids that would stand out at the gate and smoke cigarettes on break, because it was "terrible." [*Laughs*] And it progressed into other things. We'd skip school. I got invited to parties and they were smoking pot. That was the big thing. We weren't talking about crank and crack and all this stuff. It was a different scene then. Pot was the real bad, bad thing. So things change. *Now* if that's all we had to worry about, we would be lucky. [*Laughs*]

When I was younger, I guess I kind of lived in a dream world. Everybody just took care of me. My brother and sister lived at home. My sister moved out when I was five. She was pregnant at seventeen, and got married when she was eight months pregnant, was married for about eight years.

I spent a lot of time with her from five to eight. She would babysit me. I kind of feel like she raised me, because my mother worked all day, and when she came home at five o'clock, her energy was pretty well drained. And she still had to cook dinner and clean up. My parents would go out a lot because they had to go to meetings, et cetera, et cetera. So I spent a great deal of time with my sister.

Then my brother moved out also. Him and my dad didn't get along. I remember them getting into it quite a lot. He did get married when he was twenty, and they were married for fifteen years. They just divorced a couple years ago, and that to me was real earthshaking, because they had the picturesque situation. I thought they'd be together forever.

My mother comes from a long line of alcoholics. And today, my brother drinks a lot. I feel like it had a lot to do with my brother's divorce. But it scares me because he hasn't reached his bottom yet. He worked in the woods for years and years and years, and hurt his neck, and then is unable to do that. So he's working at a mill in Grants Pass.

And I think growing up in a small town like that in my early years, I did have a sense of community with everybody. Not just my family, but the whole community as a whole. Everybody knew everybody. And then this big change went on. It grew, of course, and just *changed.* I don't know what the cause of that was. A lot of new people came in. Particularly in high school. Because we had not only the local kids coming in, but we had kids that were bussed from other areas, too. All of a sudden there was all these new faces. The school expanded. And the community at that time, they didn't want to support the schools. A lot of my friends moved. So not only did it affect our personal friends, but the school spirit as a whole. There was no sense of togetherness.

I had a real hard time in school, and it wasn't that I wasn't smart enough. What happened, I dropped out of school when I was a freshman, and again when I was a sophomore. And it was, like, "Well, if you don't want to be in school, then fine. We don't want you." They don't have the time to mess around with it.

I got pregnant at sixteen, just like my sister did, although I was a little younger. We got married, and I was married for two and a half years. It was fine with me. I loved him. On the rebound, I got involved in a real bad situation. Very abusive partner.

I was just trying to make a life for myself and my son. I got on welfare. And tried to move to Medford so that I could work. I didn't have any transportation. What can you do? You can't work, 'cause you can't get there. It is a real Catch-22. Plus my self-esteem, you know, was completely zero. And you can't go out and sell yourself and get a job when you feel like that. One of my nieces is going through that right now, and it just, it's déjà vu for me, and I just wish there was some way we could break this cycle that has gone on in this last three generations of my family. I'm real paranoid about my children going through that also.

I learned everything from the streets. From my friends and all that sort of thing. Including my period. Sex. All that. I didn't know what I wanted. All I knew, I wanted something. I didn't conform to any of the things that society wanted me to be. So I just went out and partied. And got pregnant. And started from zero.

So, I had my name on a waiting list for a low-income apartment in Medford. I got a car. I finally got the apartment, and was ready to move in there, just me and my son. My abusive partner didn't want me to do that, of course. And he just kind of moved in there, too.

And then things were really bad. He had friends over all the time. He was a real heavy pot smoker, so that's pretty much what I did, too. I wasn't allowed to go out of the house without him with me. I wasn't allowed to drive my own car that I was paying for. I didn't have a phone, so I had to use a phone booth, and I wasn't allowed to use the phone unless he was with me.

And he would get mad and beat me up. And was a terrible verbal abuser. Although he was great to my son. He thought he was his daddy. And although I wasn't real crazy about that, he didn't have anybody else around, either.

So I lost contact with my family at that time. And of course they didn't care for him at all anyway. I was still young enough that I was a real rebel toward my family, and that didn't bother me at that time. Until I realized I was in a situation that I was going to die. If I didn't get out. I was too afraid to hurt him. But I would either have killed him or have him kill me. And that's a really strange situation. That I've seen programs on TV and heard about it. And it's so much the same. When they talk about it, or see it—I'm there!

I lost my identity. I didn't have me anymore. I wanted to do better for myself. I wanted to do something. I had him arrested.

And the police don't want to get involved. There were several instances where he was going to kill me. And I, you know, passed these people and, "Hey! Help me! Help me!" And they don't want to get involved. I called the police several times in bad situations. It's a civil matter: They can't do anything.

Well, this was a matter when finally they could kick him out. Because he wasn't supposed to be there in the apartments. And I had word from the manager that he wasn't supposed to be there.

All of a sudden I was free. I had this freedom that I hadn't had for a year and a half. I met this girl at this job seminar that I went to, and her and I became friends. We were trying to piece our lives back together, but when we were together, we could just raise hell. I hadn't had any fun in a long time. She had a real hard life and had done some real bad things. Anyway, we were introduced to a big coke dealer in Medford.

Now, at that time my son pretty much stayed with my folks. I still worked. Then I ended up getting a DUII [driving under the influence of intoxicants]. I lost my license.

So I moved to Medford so that I could walk to work. I was doing a lot of coke and crank at that time. My son moved in with me. I moved into this house that was just the cutest little house, but the landlord, unfortunately, was also a coke freak. I didn't know that at the time.

Anyway, I was real close with this coke dealer, and I would deliver drugs for him. He would also pay my rent — or he would pay my landlord in coke, so that I could live there.

I'm not sure what his intentions were. It was more than what actually happened. I was so naive. I didn't know *anything* at that point, except that I was getting high and I was working and having a good time. And when you get into drugs, there's a whole circle of friends. Or — they're not friends. Let me clarify that. This was a group of people that were very scary.

But I was working through this whole time — working ten-hour days. Then this abusive partner of mine showed up in town, and I ran into him. And I always had this righteous anger since we had been apart. That some day, if I ever saw him, I was going to kick his butt. I wanted somebody to hold him and I was just going to pummel him.

But it wasn't that way when I saw him. I had feelings for him. One thing led to another, and I ended up just staying with him. Which I think to this day was the biggest mistake I'd ever made. I ended up pregnant with my daughter. And that's when my mom got sick, and I came back home because she was ill.

So. There I was. When I came back, I didn't have any circle of friends or anything, because I didn't want to be part of the drug scene. And those were the only friends that I had had in the last few years.

I moved back into another low-income apartment. The day that I came back home was the day I ran into this person that I used to drive his car, and he was real supportive. So we ended up dating. That's when I started going to school. This is what led me to be where I am today, I guess. Things are different for me now. Each little step along the way had taught me something valuable. I was exposed to recovery work and all that sort of thing. I really did go through a transition.

I like it where I live now. I like the sense of community here in this neighborhood. 'Course my kids are in school now, so I have gone to the PTA and have been involved in some of that. The parents have a real sense of caring about their kids. My son's always going to things. They do a lot of things at school. They have skating parties. He's involved in Boy Scouts.

We have—I call them organic people. [*Laughs*] But there's also a lot of farmers. Which we had where I grew up, too. We called them rednecks. Lot of cowboys and ranchers there. So we have some of those people here, too. And then we just have a lot of people that commute to Medford. There's a lot of Californians. This is a retirement neighborhood, lot of older people. I don't have any problem with that at all. It's just nice.

Community college has been the best. I like the atmosphere, the learning atmosphere. I got into school when I was living by myself and cleaning up my act. This girl living there in the apartments had been going to school—she got her accounting degree at RCC. And she told me what was available. So my boyfriend and I moved over here together. Then I went to RCC. So now I'm in my second year of school. I'm working close to forty hours a week and going to school half-time.

But you see, if I had my choice, all I ever really wanted to do was be married and have children. Raise my children and be home.

When I was in school, the majority of kids were real hellions. Really. That was fashionable then. Whereas now I think it's fashionable to be straight. I don't know if that's true or not, but I kind of feel that way. That I see as a change. Although I know there's a tremendous problem in some of the larger cities. And racial problems, all that sort of thing in the schools.

The biggest racial problem I see now is between Californians and Oregonians. And being a native Oregonian, it does bother me, I must admit. Just because I feel like they're going to price us out of our home. If they want to move up here and be part of Oregon, they want to be Oregonians, I say, "Go for it. That's fine. You're welcome to move wherever you want to be."

But if they come up here with the attitude that they want to make Oregon into California, because California is already too populated and this is a nice place, but they want all the benefits of California lifestyle in the Oregon area—then that bothers me.

For instance, they want to build this big huge resort over there in Rogue River. They're really serious about it. But of course they don't want to say who their people are backing them up. So I'm not sure that there's any validity of people backing them up at all.

B. B.   Do you think local people would have any say in whether that would happen?

Kathy   I don't. Because it's money. Money. And the people in power want growth if it means money to them. Some of our representatives don't really have the true Oregonian spirit, of what this area means.

What it means? I get choked up when I think about it. The Rogue River. Trees, the forest. Which are stumps. But we have the best of everything right here. We're close to the coast if we want to go to the coast. We're close to the mountains if you want the mountains. We have big, wide-open spaces in the valley.

We have country life and farming, but we have also a developing community in Medford that is a growing city. If that's what we choose to be part of.

Fishing, hunting. All these things that a lot of these people — that's all they've ever known. Logging, hunting, fishing. Which to me is a true native of this area. Is a true sense of survival. And so, is that what it means? Is that the spirit? Using what resources were put on this earth for us to survive. And I feel like California, or big cities, are an example of how that can be consumed and overtaken. Where it's not there anymore. So they come up here to enjoy some of that. Which is fine.

I feel like I wish that there were enough of us people that we could say, "No, we don't want this." You know. "We are the people, we . . ." You know. That's what it's supposed to be about. That we voice our opinion. That if we choose that we want this to stay the way it is, then it should be that way. But then at the same time, we also need to grow, too. We can't stay stagnant. So I don't know what the equation is.

This is an incident of a neighborhood that we just moved from — a very wonderful neighborhood. My daughter would go to this lady's house for a Brownie meeting, and then she would walk to the babysitter's, who also lived in the neighborhood, which is not even a block away. And she will not allow my daughter to walk over there, although it is my consent to let her do that, because she knows everybody in the area. She won't let her do that because she is from southern California, and she doesn't want to feel responsible if anything happens to her walking from there to the other lady's house. And that's the kind of attitude I don't want my children exposed to. It hasn't been my experience that that is that way here, and I want to keep it that way.

And these big resort ideas — if all those ever went through, we'd have traffic problems. We'd have a tourist community. Which we have some of that now, anyway, but it's mostly for the river. And these are tourists that come here to enjoy the nature we have to offer. These people are not a threat to us.

It's the people that come here and move here and want to take over that stuff. Not enjoy those resources that we have, but just live here because it's pretty. But want Bloomingdale's at their feet. That bothers me. And that would be a real misfortune for this town.

And, yeah, they have more dollars coming in from other places. See, they can price things higher for those people. Because those people can afford to pay it. But the people that live here can't, because we don't make enough, a higher wage. This is a very depressed area as far as wage earning compared to other areas. But then there's a trade-off. You have all the natural resources that I personally love. Which is worth more to me than the money.

The ideal situation for me would be to work thirty hours a week, be able to be home when my kids get home from school. I think that has a big effect on the kids today, is that they have to have double-income families for people to survive. And so therefore the kids are left to take care of themselves. Or if they're not taking care of themselves, there are people that maybe don't take care of them the way you would. That's a real scary thing, to have your kids raised by somebody that you really don't know.

That has changed, all over — women entering the workforce because they have to. So I guess maybe I live in a dream world. I guess I have been kind of old-fashioned, that the woman stays home and she can sew — I like to use what resources are available to me at a very small amount of money, and grow your own fruit and vegetables and that sort of thing. Without robbing things. I mean, without killing all the deer off so that we don't have any. Just use what we need.

B. B. Any thoughts on the controversy about logging and the environment and the mills?

Kathy The logging versus the spotted owl is a real controversial issue. It has been for a long time now. I have real mixed feelings about it, I guess. On one hand, of course, I don't want to see nature destroyed. But then it's been my understanding that they can — at least what I've been told is that they can live somewhere else.

But I have a real problem with logging. Although I know that it's a livelihood of a lot of people, and I'm all for that. I know they plant trees now that supposedly grow faster than they used to. And they are trying to beautify them.

I have a real problem with clearcut logging. I don't think that should be an option in this area. Although I know it's dollars for them, and I know that we need the dollars. I think the education is important. We need to educate these people that were born and raised in Prospect and Butte Falls. And logging is all they've ever known. If they *choose* to do that, that's fine. But they should seek an education and know all their options in case logging isn't there anymore.

The people that log, sometimes I get a kick out of that, "Well, logging is all I've ever known. I want to do it because that's what my father did, and that's what my forefathers did." And so what if that's all your fathers ever did? If society changes, then we need to change with it. To a certain extent. Because this area is what it is, I think we do need to preserve a certain amount of that. Crater Lake, and the redwoods — you know.

I like to go camping a lot. That's what we do in the summertime. As a family unit. And the river — we'd go rafting a lot. Yeah, I spend a lot of time in nature. Probably not as much now, because I'm too busy. And on the weekends I have to study. I have to clean house and do laundry. And now with the house, doing all these thing that we're doing ourselves, I feel pretty consumed.

It's peaceful out at our new place. We have an acre. It's important for me, too, for my kids to be there, and not have blacktop for a front yard. Well, and then there's another side of that, too, that if you want to live someplace like that, you do have to make good money to pay for that. So that's a real trade-off.

I am not real prejudiced, I don't think. Maybe I am and I'm not aware of it. But, like, versus the Californians or whatever, that's fine. As long as they don't take away what is important to me, and what I think is important for everybody that has grown up here.

Same thing with the Mexicans. We don't have too many Blacks, really. I guess we have some Oriental people. At school I noticed a variety of races. If they want to come here and be part of our economic area, and produce money for the area and what is better for the area, then that's fine. I don't have a problem with that.

I would hate to see things that happen in the big cities. Where they have this race on this side of the street, this race on the other side of the street. Against each other. I don't feel like that is good for anybody involved.

And then the school issues. People that are poor should be allowed to have the same education as people that are richer. I don't know the answers. People here are tired of being taxed to support the schools.

Particularly in this community, which is real difficult, because there's a lot of retired people that don't have kids in the schools. And therefore they don't want to have their dollars taxed any more for the schools that they don't have children in.

I would say my largest social circle right now is where I work. And of course people in my community that deal directly with my children and my family. Sometimes I feel like I am a minority, because there is such a large amount of people that are from other areas that move in here. In a way that's kind of sad. I go to Medford now, sometimes it seems overwhelmingly large for me. Because I remember it as being so different. But then I don't choose to live there, either. I can live here and commute there if I want to. Which is kind of what happens in southern California, too. People commute long-range distances.

I guess to me a community means people that all care about the same things and all care for it as a whole. I think that when you have a real large one, it's real hard to do that. Because there's too many people.

And face it. We are the only country that I know of that says, "Yeah, no matter what you are, come on in! We're compatible." And generally, instinct for people of races isn't that way. Really. It's not like that. You don't do that in other countries. They have a lot of pride in who they are.

So we come from a weird mix. That's what America is, is all of these different people. That come in and try to have some values and pride in who they are and their heritage. We're such a Heinz 57— that's really hard to do. So what we are made up of is, in this area, is people who have earned a living on the resources here. The logging and all that sort of thing. And that's who we are.

But the racial problems are real scary for me. Because it's really not in our instinct as a race. Like Black people, it's not their instinct to accept white people for who they are, because they are different. And they look at them different. And they compare. And, "We want what you have." And to me that doesn't make any sense.

So. I don't know what the answer is, you know? Because as the city grows, you have to expect technical change and knowledge in Medford. So naturally more people move into the Medford area to work. They're going to move into the outlying areas to live. And so of course that's going to change that.

But I just wish that everybody that moved in here could feel the sense of pride that we have here in what we have here, and not destroy that. Although I know they have to cut down trees to build homes. I know that they have to cut down trees sometimes to burn wood for heat, and all that sort of thing. But I just don't want to see them abuse it. I don't want to see the Rogue River become some vast wasteland like Bear Creek in Medford. I don't want it to be some poison water that we can't use because they dumped toxic waste into it, and it can't be filtered out. Or whatever might happen.

Who my children may be eventually will be somebody totally different than me. Because of what they grew up with. Which is fine. But I'd like them to have some link in the pride that we have. And the other people who come up here, they just come from a different background. But they need to leave some of what we have intact. And admire and accept it for what it is. They can come up here with their money and their big motor homes. These are the people that go camping in their motor homes and think that that's really roughing it. If they wanted to do that, that's fine. But, to me, I have a little bit of a problem when I camp right next to somebody that has a generator running all night long and I have to listen to it. I don't want to hear a generator! I go up in the woods to hear the birds and to hear the wind whistle through the trees. And to just feel at peace with myself. But not hear some generator and see somebody watching TV because they have a satellite dish on their thing. They bring the city with them. And I'm saying, "Leave the city where it belongs!"

GEORGE THOMAS   (age 49) Rough-hewn, polite, used to outdoor work, George Thomas lives a life consistent with his small-farming background in a mountain valley. His story outlines the transitions over five decades in one neighborhood, from tiny back-lot sawmills to transnational timber corporations, from an intimate community to the overlapping lives of strangers.

His penchant for an independent life manifests the bedrock values of a century of in-migrants to this region. Clearcutting is adamantly opposed by many old-timers who themselves selectively logged the land in small outfits. With the advent of large corporate clearcuts, people could not help noticing the harm done to watersheds as creeks dried up early in the arid season and cut deeper into the banks during the rains.

Networks remain strong among residents who grew up here in earlier decades. The fact that George realized in adulthood that he was gay has not destroyed those connections; similarities of class and intertwining histories have proven to be strong bonds.

The interview took place on George's front porch one spring morning, as we looked out to thousands of acres of forested mountains.

I was born in Grants Pass in 1941. I've lived all my life in Garland. Actually in a little town that was a mining town during the 1800s and early 1900s. At one point it was supposed to be about two thousand people, complete with saloons and boardwalks and gaslights. Most of it burned down a long time ago. So it's just hardly anything left.

My parents bought this land in 1938, moved here in thirty-nine, and I was born in forty-one. They had gotten married in 1929 and had left the States after the crash. They went to Canada and homesteaded. They had lived in Medford. My father had worked on the Crater Lake Rim highway and had also done woodcutting and carpentry. His mother had come to the United States from Denmark, and his father from England.

My mother was born just across the California border from Ashland. Her family has been in southern Oregon for a long time — it's a long line of farmers and carpenters and schoolteachers and preachers.

My father was farming this place. He bought sixty acres, then he bought more parcels of land as land became available quite reasonably. At one point he cut poles on the land and sold them for power poles. He did horse logging; he peeled them, and would send out a truck every time he had a load. Later he worked in the sawmills. He worked for a two- or three-man operation. The owner and my father would run the sawmill, and somebody else would go out and bring in the logs — they were skidding them in. The man owned a hundred acres or something, and it was just self-contained.

That was the era of many, many small sawmills. We hadn't lost all the little schools, or all the little sawmills, or the little businesses. Things weren't as corporate — the little man hadn't been forced out yet.

The area took a big jump in population around forty-six and forty-seven, because they were replacing the highway that had been built in 1921 — the old highway that wound around every canyon of the hills. And so a lot of people were coming in due to the construction.

Up to the point when I started school, my growing up here was just real, real remote. I doubt that I even played with any neighbor kids. I don't remember any neighbor kids.

My mom was mostly a housewife — she was a long-suffering woman. She was quiet, introverted. She did the canning, all that work. There was always food on the table. They put lots of food away. They didn't believe in canned foods that you buy from the supermarket, or the frivolities that we consider normal in these days.

Mostly I stayed pretty close to home. I socialized with one family that lived across the road that had come to the valley in 1951 or so, as loggers, when logging was just going full blast. They were from central Oregon. He was a hard-core redneck logger. Come home after having a few beers in the woods and have a few more, and it would get pretty rowdy.

The woods to me was a safe place. I explored. I checked out the wildflowers. I'd bring home bouquets of wildflowers, or I'd dig up plants and bring them home and put them in the yard. Because ever since I was about eight or nine, when we went to visit a neighbor, I can remember going to her house and admiring her garden. And she gave me a viola plant, and a begonia or something. She got me started.

Oh, and in the summertime, of course, we were at the creek swimming. Every day. And I was also working a lot in the garden. Because my parents sold produce from the place. They had a little sign down at the road, and people would come and get corn and green beans and tomatoes. Big garden — two, three acres of garden. We'd pick forty pounds of beans for somebody or fifteen dozen corn or something. That was normal stuff.

There was lots of family orientation. And it was a real working-class community. People weren't afraid of their neighbors, they knew their neighbors — who they could trust, and who to look out for. There wasn't all this closed-door sort of attitude that there is now prevalent in our society.

Issues were very localized. Like the people that drove up and down the road and spotlighted at night and shot deer out of season. That was an issue to a lot of people that lived here and had cattle and had land.

Squatting, as an issue that it is now, wasn't an issue. People lived on mining claims back in the woods undisturbed. If people wanted to be hermits, they could be hermits. There were wonderful people living up canyons that my father knew. He reached out to a lot of people, and never had trouble. He had a self-created image that said, "Just don't mess with me."

By the time I was in high school, I was hanging out with other closet cases. [*Laughs*] Especially this friend, I was hanging out with him, and we just had this unspoken connection that neither of us recognized at that point in our lives.

High school was in Grants Pass — that was a vast change. I couldn't relate to the social scene. Because there were all these city kids, and there was this Soc clique, and there were the jocks, and there were the brains. I hung out with a few rural kids. There were about seven or eight of us that would meet in the library before school each day. We were probably, you know, the closet cases. The misfits by some order or other. Too smart. Too unusual. Not white. Et cetera. [*Laughs*]

There was one kid that was Native American. And he was incredibly talented in the music department. He wanted to apply for a music scholarship. And they told him, "Oh, there's no point. You're not white." That was the bottom line. Obviously he didn't get a scholarship, but he went on with his musical career.

I was always heavy into math, but I wanted to be a teacher. And that seemed to be remotely possible to me. So I guess my last year in high school I was planning on going to Southern Oregon College, and I did in fact go. I went to school for a year there. College — I think it meant what my parents wanted. It meant not doing what they had done. Not having to work in a sawmill or a factory. My father really looked down on the kind of work he did. He didn't accept it as something that I should have to do.

I think to a degree the farming is what my father really wanted to do, and he resented the fact that he had to work away from home. Farming was not a profitable thing, even in the nineteen-forties and fifties you couldn't make it on a small farm. Our culture had already progressed to the point where the small man was out, and it's even worsened now. But I think my father did a lot of what he wanted, because in his earlier years, he and a friend would hike into the wilderness and camp out for two or three weeks. They'd take a pack mule full of supplies and they'd go into the remote areas toward the coast, or they'd go into the mountains.

He was an adventurer. He was a workaholic. That's where I come by it. He always was just tough and rugged. I was never displeased with my father. We were pretty close.

I left college because of lack of money, and partly because I really did terrible in English Comp! [*Laughs*] Soon after, I got a job at a local store. So I went up through the ranks. I stayed there many years.

B. B. Did it ever occur to you to leave the area?

George No. A lot of my friends did. I'd say half the people that I closely grew up with, the Fivemile, Garland people, about half of them stayed in the area. In fact, maybe more than half of them. Only a few left the area. I don't think as many people left the area then as do now.

A lot of people coming in had happened during the forties and early fifties. The postwar boom. There was quite a growth in Garland, people coming in and buying land, and big ranches being divided up into smaller pieces. And that's happened steadily, but especially in the sixties and seventies. And that's overwhelming to me. I just like to remember the way it was. It's hard to see it change and become all little mobile-home sites.

It's a bedroom community — it's no longer a farm community. There was a passing of local-oriented things. Many of the local schools were closed up, schools were consolidated. When I was younger there were probably twelve sawmills in Garland and Cornish in a ten-mile radius of us. Maybe more than that. Every little gulch had a sawmill. And as the fifties drew to a close, more and more of those were gone.

There was still lots of timber. And logging was still going strong. But it was being trucked to mills farther away, where they employed forty people instead of ten. Or a hundred instead of fifteen.

One of our close neighbors, they were the first people in the area to have a television set. Mr. Tipton was a logger, and he was a faller and bucker in the woods up here. Apparently there had been a tree fallen, and some debris had hung up in an adjoining tree, and that was the one Harvey was working under. And this huge limb fell down and hit him on top of his hardhat and gave him a concussion. And he was never the same after that. And other people were killed. I didn't directly know anybody that was killed then. Later years, though, I've known several people that have been killed. It was always considered very dangerous work. Very hazardous. There'd be log truck crashes on Gold Road, about a mile up from here. There was a really heavy-duty steep downgrade and then a curve right at the bottom of it. And the trucks would sometimes not make the curve. [*Laughs*] They would just smash into the hill.

I never wanted to work there. Also, my father was very influential. The family attitude and, generally, the prevailing attitude of most of the people that lived here was that logging was really, really harsh. They weren't doing it properly even then. There was such a nearness to clearcutting that people in the area freaked out.

My parents really resented that. The *way* that the logging was happening. The fact that there was so much waste. My father always had high regard for the native flora and fauna. And it was like, you know, lots of stuff is gone.

These logging concerns were rich, powerful companies that could get away with it. The little sawmill guys weren't as heavy-duty in that rapist attitude as the big timber holders that hold hundreds of acres and had big mills in Danby or Grants Pass, and just raped and pillaged. Some logging, they would leave trees periodically for seed trees. And then it got to be that that was too much bother. And they didn't reforest. They didn't go in and plant trees. In the sixties I saw them start planting trees. Most of the trees that have come back were nature's doing.

[*Waves up at expansive mountainside*] Most of this was logged since after the war. And thank goodness most of it happened early enough that now it's somewhat recovered, because it used to be incredibly ugly. The whole end of the valley up there, the high mountains were just ravaged. They were just mud. Hundreds of acres.

And right consecutive with that, each year there was less and less water in the irrigation ditch. Trout Creek was lower and lower. It was obvious to us that the ecology was being messed with. The water was the place that they noticed it. And the availability of the game. Deer hunters noticed that there weren't as many deer as there used to be. There weren't as many fish in the streams. All of that changed because there wasn't as much water. It was real direct.

B. B.   How much of this is privately owned?

George   I don't know what kind of percentage is, but a lot. There's some BLM around us to the north here.

I think that people that lived here — it's sort of like that cliché song in *Oklahoma*, of the ranchers and the farmers should be friends? I think the ranchers and farmers here were sort of appalled at what was happening to the valley. I think what was happening was that people that were too near were moving someplace else. Very few people saw any political action that they could take to stop it. So they left or they accepted it.

After I left college and started working, I was living with my parents, right here on this land. Then I met Mary. And she was like me, in that she was sort of a quiet, withdrawn person, too. She was from southern California. We got married, and that seemed, at that point in my life, like the thing to do.

Years later I started reading everything I could find in the library on — I forget what the Dewey Decimal is for that — the gay section. And then I met somebody. A young man confronted me with everything I'd thought about, so that was a start of something new, but that wasn't the end of the marriage either.

That was when I was twenty-eight years old, and steadily working retail, and just doing a whiz job of that and loving it. Because in that job I found my realm. Doing that pressure stuff. Doing lots, and high demand, and all of that. And it was a real good job for me because I learned to relate to people, and reach out to people.

Mostly my connections were with a local rural organization. They were other married people. And then later they were gay people that I met. I've always been real adventurous about trying things — foods and friends and everything, and consequently, I've always had no trouble making friends with people. And not had a lot of judgment about the fact that they might have been different than me.

That was especially important when, in the seventies, I started meeting hippies and gay people and people that were new in the community. Like part of me was wanting to freak out about their long hair, but it really didn't need to be an issue.

I can remember at work, there was a lot of attitude about hair. About hippies. Looked down the nose. About, you know, "My taxes are going to pay for these low-life people that just let their hair grow and smoke dope," or whatever. [Laughs] And they were so naive at the store that when hippies would come in smelling of patchouli, the clerks thought that was marijuana. But it was the patchouli that was covering up the marijuana! [Laughs]

There were lots of communes in the county. And in fact I was good friends with a few of them, just on a fringe basis. Like there was some of the people from the Mystic Arts commune would come into the store. I'd write down their order, no problem. And then when those things came in, I'd set them aside and they always looked me up. And, you know, one of them had a name like "Acorn." And the other one was "Jackrabbit" or something.

Yeah, Grants Pass was growing. It was relatively prosperous. I think it was just sort of inevitable. The comment was, there has always been some southern Oregon resentment to those people from California coming in here.

I guess big-city ideas are a little more callous. Some of the things that I heard when I was growing up was that the people from California just sue at the drop of the hat. That they are very legal-conscious. If their neighbor does something they don't like, they sue. People from California come in, and they buy a nice place in the country and the first thing they do is go in and cut down seventeen trees, because they might fall on the house! Those kinds of ideas.

People resent change, and suddenly they've got neighbors that they're not getting along with as well. It's just all those things, all that growth. I mean, suddenly when there's more people per square mile, there's more problems. And people from the big cities deal with that differently than the people from the country.

And even though Grants Pass was town, it was still pretty country in its attitudes. It's pretty redneck. It's pretty white. Until the last fifteen years, it's been really white. When the Harlem Globetrotters would come to town, they couldn't stay overnight in Grants Pass. They would play their little game at the high school, and then they'd have to find a motel in Fivemile or something. Grants Pass, had, you know, the KKK. Even now.

I guess early on in Grants Pass, in the 1800s, somebody came to town with a sawmill and a bunch of Black men that were his laborers, and they built a sawmill and were running it, and it burned down. And they rebuilt it, and it burned down again. That sort of thing happened a lot.

Grants Pass was always real hesitant about change. They didn't want industry. The city fathers didn't want the old downtown to change. When big stores would approach them about coming into the area, it was very difficult. They lots of times wouldn't let them in. I guess they were afraid they'd be lost in the dust. It was their town.

I had two kids. We had ten acres. In seventy-eight Mary filed for a divorce. She served papers on me, and I found myself walking out the door with a paper bag with some things in it, and myself in shock. I wasn't expecting it. I was presumptuous. Naive. Unconscious. Obnoxious. [*Laughs quietly*]

After we split up, I was living in Grants Pass for three months in a little ten-by-twelve room that I could rent real cheap and pay off all my bills.

This was a hay barn when I was growing up. Windows and doors sort of got broken out. When Harold and his friends came from San Francisco, I just let them move in if they'd fix it up. Here were men that were certainly more "out" than I was — gay movement from San Francisco. And I was seeing them living here totally not coping with it. No country abilities to fix that thing up. And I thought, Well, what am I doing in town paying rent? I might as well move out there, too. And I did. And that was sort of how Harold and I got together.

And the other two men that were part of the group had been lovers. And they broke up, and all kinds of weird shit came down. One kid was Puerto Rican, and he moved in with someone else in the valley. And his ex-lover joined what we called the Mad-Maidens of Mercury. This was a commune that this man that ran the place told these other people what to do and who to have sex with and where to go and how to do everything. They posed as Jews for Jesus and ripped off the church in Corners. They did all these *trips*!

And so Terrence went and joined them. They got this whole racist thing going, and they burned a cross on this other guy's front lawn because Ricardo was staying there. And the KKK heard about it, and they were freaking out about this unsanctioned cross-burning. And they like sent people here to investigate it. And then reporters found out. And they were here. [*Laughs*] Nobody seemed to know for sure what was going on, except that we knew that there was all this behavior going on because these two men had broken up, and one was not letting it die quietly.

I'd never been around that kind of bickering and chaos. Here we were, living in this house, no electricity, no running water. Plastic on the windows. Right in the midst of all that, I quit my job. Couple of months later, Harold and I took a job at the plywood mill. We went there ten days straight until they hired us. You just go at shift change, and sooner or later you get a job if you're there with a lunch pail and your work clothes on. And we did. We both got hired the same morning. We worked for one week straight. The only reason I quit was that I'd wake up in the middle of the night and my whole left side would be paralyzed, like numb. We were doing all kinds of jobs. We were feeding dryer, we were offbearing, sorting the veneer as it comes out of the dryer. We were doing clean-up work. We worked seven days, and then we put the tin roof on the house, so we didn't have a leaky roof anymore. We were getting paid very well, like seven ninety-five or eight fifty or something. That was in seventy-seven. Non-union. If we had been there any time at all, we'd have been up to nine dollars an hour. There were good benefits, and there was more money for overtime and all that stuff.

And then we dealt with the Health Department. Someone who had a grudge against us turned us in to the Health Department. Which meant they came out and said, "You can't have an outhouse without a door. You don't have a permit for an outhouse. You can't have running water and have an outhouse." All these weird things. So they says, "You have thirty days to conform." And they sent us this document in the mail that says you have to conform. So I put a screen door on the outhouse.

Then they came out to inspect. And they were asking things like, "Well, how many bedrooms are there here?" And I said, "There's one." And he says, "Well, do you both sleep in the same bedroom?" And I said, "Yes!" And it was like, these were pompous windbag bureaucrats that were out here on their mission into the slums. And they were freaking out. They were asking all this stuff, and somehow they weren't winning. Because I had done my homework. I wasn't going to be railroaded because some yahoo wanted to turn me in, just because he was bitched out at us.

At one point one of the men was standing in one small flowerbed I had. I said, "You know, you're standing on my violets. I wish you'd move out of there." And he backed up, and then I said—I don't remember how it all went, but slowly I backed them out of the back yard, around the corner, and right over to their car. And they were happy to get in and slam the door and leave when I got through with them, because it was obvious we were gay, and that I pretty much told them, "You don't have any reason to be here." And I told them who had turned us in and that it was just bullshit between two people, and they really didn't have any part in it.

And it was like, I'm sure they had to stop at the nearest coffeeshop and say, "Whew! Aren't we glad we got out of there! Those crazy fucking fags!"

And, boy, was I relieved. I had never done anything like that before. I had never met officials and scooted them out of my yard so successfully. It showed me a whole lot about what could be done in an emergency. My home was being threatened.

My father was never big into supporting the bureaucracy. And I really go right along with that. He hated all that permit stuff. If you do it right, why do you need all that? I mean, we weren't creating a health hazard to anyone. The neighbors weren't complaining. The neighbors have similar situations — some of the neighbors. As the area grows, there's more expensive homes. There's a house up the road a couple miles from here that's probably costing the people a hundred and fifty thousand dollars to be built. It's grand on the tract-house scale.

The position that Harold and I have taken is one of being pretty withdrawn from the community — the straight community, the community that surrounds us. We don't hang out, and we don't know everything and everybody that goes on. We shop in Grants Pass. I'm not into mixing with the local layabouts, a lot of burn-outs, lot of alkies and drug casualties. That's just people that have come, that are living on the extreme edge of the community. Living up the gulches, squatting on public land or whatever.

I think most of the local people are pretty much the same way. Their connection is with Grants Pass. I have good rapport with people I grew up with. People I've known all my life, I don't have any problem with them. They know what my situation is now. That I live here with my lover.

The ones that judge, the ones that have a hard time, are the people that are new to the community. That they themselves are on trial. It doesn't matter whether you're straight or gay, when you come into an area, you have to establish your place in the pecking order. Certain people will try you. Certain people it doesn't matter. But other people that makes a big difference.

I mean, some of these straight boys — they've got nothing better to do than want to clock the local faggots? [*Laughs*] Oh! The stories I could tell on these local straight boys would not be publishable. They do have contradictions in their sexual orientation. And they just make sure that somehow it's somebody else's responsibility. You know, it's, "God, I was drunk last night!" "He seduced me!" "I don't know what happened, I don't remember a thing!" [*Laughs*]

B. B.   Have any opinions on what's going on with the economy?

George   Well, southern Oregon's always had a hard time with all of that stuff because we have less industry. They rely heavily on the timber industry. They're trying to rely on tourism, but they're not doing a very grand job of it. And I'm one who thinks they're just reaping their own harvest. What's happening now is our industrialist society has approached harvesting. They've been very wasteful, all for today and not thinking about tomorrow.

The forests are sort of a mess. It's going to be fifty years before there's even much to talk about as far as timber around here. The area's really needing to find some other things to rely on. I guess I'm with the spotted owl people, too.

It takes me back to when I was a kid. There was a spot right up on this mountain that I used to go to, because the calypso orchids were so wonderful there. There was a place where there were cream-colored ones and purple ones, and they had crossed, and there were all these little hybrids of them. And there was a place like that down by the creek where the fawn lilies, the purple and the yellow ones, they actually came together at one point and hybridized, and there were all these exotic mixed ones.

And those spots are gone now because of encroaching civilization and logging. It's sad, because I just really have a connection with the woods. I don't go back to those spots. 'Cause people live in some of those spots. And they're damaged. They're scarred now. It's hard to go back and be reminded of that. It's real horrible.

And I think a lot in our country, that people are kept so busy trying to keep their head above water that they don't have time to think of the political-social effect of a lot of this that's going on around us. I think they can barely pay their rent and keep food on the table and have a new car. And they're accustomed to living in a certain manner, and they're using plenty of escapes to keep from thinking about the things they don't want to think about, whether it be television, or a bottle, or some other abuse.

B. B. Do you think the public debate between industry and environmentalists accurately represents —

George I think it represents a portion of the population, but I think there's a great sleeping mass that's not saying diddley. Because they've given up. Because they feel powerless. Because they don't think they'd be heard.

[*Laughs*] I remember one person telling me that she didn't have any opinions on the stuff we're discussing. And I looked at her and I just wanted to say, "Did they do a lobotomy, honey?" But I didn't.

I think what I notice the most is that culture has gotten faster and colder — and less tradition. Tradition is being wiped out just as fast as forests are. People assimilate. They don't want to remember. I think Madison Avenue tells us that that doesn't matter, that what's important is to be young and blond and blue-eyed. I'm sorry that so many people buy into it and think it has such great meaning in their life. Because they're going to be sad when they hit fat, bald, and forty.

What's already lost of this area is that it was, before timber, a very remote mining community. While the mining did do some ecological damage, I certainly don't think it did anything akin to what the logging did. Most of the mining damage is already healed.

I hate seeing the simpler rural ways go. That's what I was trying to say, I guess. You know, I don't know my neighbors anymore. I don't know very many people around that live the way I do. I do have a small, valued network of people that live simply and live in the country and appreciate the country and love the woods that surround us. That's how I grew up, and that's what's special to me. I knew lots of people that were poor — they weren't white trash.

EarthFirst!'s cardboard bulldozer "Billy" blocks logging road construction in the Siskiyou National Forest

Latina/Latino workers in gladiolus field, Josephine County, Oregon

LEFT: **Successful reforestation site in the Siskiyou National Forest**

Timothy Bullard

Overview of Grants Pass, with new home construction in foreground

Jet boat with tourists cruises through prime fishing area on Rogue River

Timothy Bullard

Auction of equipment at dismantled mill site, Murphy, Oregon

Mill worker with his daughter on the day the mill where he had worked since high school announced an indefinite shutdown

On the last day before mill closure, husband and wife feed plywood veneer into dryer

DOROTHY HARRIS   (age 45)   After generations of relatives worked arduous years in sheep and cattle ranches, on mountainsides, in orchards and packing sheds, Dorothy Harris, along with her husband, has achieved a modest though sometimes precarious middle-income status, which is still dependent on hard labor.

Despite the deaths and injuries that are the hazards of timber occupations, an abiding, knowlegeable love of the forests is revealed in Dorothy's stories of her father. This interactive relationship with the mountains is manifestly different from the more passive aesthetic appreciation of many newcomers.

She is a quiet, gentle woman, with an impeccably clean house. She served me strong, rich coffee at the kitchen table.

I was born in 1944 in Medford. My dad was in the service during the war. He was in the Pacific, and my mother was living with my grand-parents in Medford. He didn't see me until I was eighteen months old.

My grandfather and step-grandmother lived in Medford. My great-grandparents lived in Idaho, but they moved in my early childhood to Medford. I'm not really too sure where they were born, but I know they weren't born in Oregon or Idaho. My father's parents were born in Idaho. They logged, they ranched. I had a great-uncle who boot-legged. They worked on other people's ranches — they never had their own. They worked out in sheep camps.

My step-grandmother that I grew up being pretty close to, she taught school for a while. She had only graduated from high school, but then you could teach school with just a high school graduation. And she was also a midwife. After she got married she didn't work outside her home. And my grandfather — the only job I can ever remember him having was at a mill in Medford. He stayed there until he retired.

On my dad's side, seems to me that my grandfather couldn't find work in Idaho, or work he thought paid enough. When they moved out here, my grandfather actually went to work for my mother's grand-parents. And so my parents really met as children. My great-grandfather managed some kind of orchard, and he went to work for him in the or-chard. But my father's mother died. My father was seven.

My father was kind of farmed out to various uncles and aunts. Quit school when he was fifteen, and just went to work on the ranch, in hayfields. Hired himself out as a regular "hand," for what was then considered men's wages. In Idaho. Then he came out to Oregon and stayed when he was probably sixteen. I'm not sure what he did for jobs until he married my mother. She was seventeen and my father was nineteen. I know she was pregnant when they married.

They moved to Portland and my dad worked in the shipyards just around the time the war broke out. And that's how he learned to weld. Then he was drafted there. So my mother came back to Medford. And then that's where I was born.

I spent a lot of time with my grandmother at her big old house. My mother worked at a drug store. At various times, living in that house, there would have been my mother and I, my grandmother and grandfather, her brother, and this man boarder. She also took care of her sister's grandson when his family kind of broke up.

We lived right next to the railroad tracks. It's a mill yard now. The earliest memories I have are of trains at night — it was very comforting to me to hear that whistle. I remember seeing the passenger train, seeing people in suits sitting reading the paper at night. I would wonder where they were going. They must have a fantastic job that they could ride the train and wear a suit, and be that relaxed that they could read a paper on such an exciting trip.

We lived in various little places around Medford. I started school out in the country. A lady had a big old house and had redone her garage into a little apartment. We lived in a one-bedroom apartment. Sleepy little towns! Not the tourist attractions that you see now.

My dad was logging — worked in the woods for a small logging outfit. He set chokers. Sometimes he'd fell timber. Sometimes he drove truck. He ran a cat. We didn't have a lot of money. The lady who lived next door gave my mother an old coat, and my mother made a blouse for me out of the lining, and a skirt out of the wool.

My mom stayed at home. She was reared by her grandparents, and they attended church regularly. That stopped pretty much after she and my dad were married. She would attend on and off, but not too much. My mother had a fondness for biscuits and gravy, and she could make light-bread and pies, and still does, very well. Biscuits and gravy was a breakfast or supper.

It's hard for me to remember what I did as a child. I'm sure I probably heard stories from my father about the woods. I remember that there was one incident that a man was killed on the job that my dad was working on. He was killed by what's called a "widow-maker." In those days you could have a cat that didn't have a cover on the top of it, and he was punching on a tree. A limb came tumbling down and hit him on top of the head and killed him.

During the time that my dad was driving truck, he went over a bridge one night. His lights went out, and he went down into the river. Rode the truck down — he didn't jump out until they got to the bottom, and he just kicked a window out and got out. Was in the hospital a few days, really didn't break any bones. He was just very lucky.

But he would be gone early in the morning and didn't get home until after dark. They would be on the job by dawn. I think it's important for someone who might hear my story — not being able to remember too much from my childhood — my father binge-drank when I was a child, so a lot of times he would just be gone from the home on the weekends.

My dad worked in the woods, and then for a while he went to work at a mill. He never liked working in the mill, probably because it was structured. It was noisy. Out in the woods he could be more free and away from people, more on his own. I would say he had a real fondness for the woods, and a respect for nature and animals in the woods. He was really careful on a cat. I have had people remark what a good catskinner my dad was. He did a neat, clean job.

He would relate to me if he had seen a bear in the woods, or a deer, or whatever. If they had gotten into a nest of yellow-jackets. I didn't think about it much. It was just what my dad did for a living, and I just took it for granted. I didn't have any other frame of reference.

My dad never hunted. When I was in the eighth grade, we lived out past Jacksonville. And my uncle hunted. And we were really broke this winter. There used to be deer that would come up into the pasture of this house that we were renting. And my uncle and my dad poached a deer. They shot it at night and left it lay, because it sounded like the boom carried forever. Then went back and cleaned it, and we had venison that time. But my dad just never liked to kill anything.

It was seasonal work, too. There were times that he would be laid off for months at a time. Money would be tight. When he would drink, he would also give money away. Loan it out. He made good money when he worked, and he worked real hard. But it was hard for them to manage their money.

In junior high I was just a real shy, quiet kid. I went to school on the east side of Medford, and a lot of the kids from wealthier families went to school there. We were not wealthy. It was a difficult time for me because I didn't feel I had good enough clothes to go to school. To be accepted.

Just before my senior year, my dad was working for a man who wanted him to go to work down in California — one of those long-term logging jobs that, if my dad would just take it and move, he could work all winter long. He worked the summer and got laid off in October, and didn't work again until spring. That was a real tight winter.

I did *not* like that part of California. It was too hot in the summer, and I missed the mountains. My dad had to go a long ways to work to get to the woods. A lot of times he would leave, like three or four o'clock in the morning; he wouldn't get home till nine o'clock at night.

I always knew I was going to finish high school. It never really occurred to me that I couldn't go to nursing school until I graduated from high school, and my grades weren't good enough to get a scholarship or grant money. And my parents didn't have the money to send me to nursing school. So basically I just went to work. I don't really remember thinking beyond that what I was going to do.

When I did go to college, I thought, if I could just get a job to get off my feet. College was good for me, I think, in that it expanded my horizons out from the tight-knit little family experience that I had had. I came in contact with people from different economic backgrounds, and different ethnic groups and social groups that I hadn't been exposed to. I became aware for the first time of how much I did not know.

I married in 1974. So I came back to the valley about February or March of 1974. My husband's from California, but just before he was drafted, his parents moved to Talent. He moved with them. The draft was hot after my husband at the time — this would be 1966.

The first home we had after we were married, we lived out towards Trail. My dad was still in the woods then, and my husband did that then for about a year. Then he went to work for my cousin and her husband, who had an emergency repair business in Medford.

In 1970, when I graduated from college and I took a job in Shasta County [far northern California], was about the time when a lot of people were hitchhiking. And the counter-culture, hippie type movement really was coming into vogue, and you would see these strangely clad people hitchhiking on the freeway. It was hard for some people to accept. I considered myself at the time a bleeding-heart liberal, and I was kind of interested in this new way of living. But not enough that I cared to go out and live off the land like that.

During the eight-one–eighty-two recession, I took my husband to the Medford airport. He took the seven o'clock flight out. I can remember a block or two of people standing at the unemployment office. That was the most people I had ever seen standing at an employment office ever, anywhere. Although our work slowed down, we were still able to work and keep our house. A lot of people lost their homes. Nobody got laid off real close to us. Friends and acquaintances I'm sure I heard, but no one in my immediate family.

I feel a loyalty to the community here in Grants Pass that people seem to have. When we first moved here, I was struck by the different kind of churches that you could pick from. I'm not a regular church attender, but I certainly had my choice if I wanted to.

B. B.   Any thoughts around the environmental, logging industry controversies?

Dorothy   I think it's good. Certainly I can remember when there were a lot more logging trucks that you would see hauling logs. I think management was needed. I think timber is a renewable resource, but we have to take care of it. For too many years it was overused. So I'm glad to see the environmental groups — it helps strike a balance, I think, between just going in and hauling out all the wood you can get, and leaving some for our children and our grandchildren. And the animals — there's not a lot of room left for them.

We have a finite planet, and I believe there is only so much room for so many people. So I think it's a good thing that we have environmentalists who are concerned about monitoring things like the logging industry.

And I think it's possible to go too far the other way. Well, for example, like some people got real excited when there was talk about harvesting the Silver Fire timber. It's my understanding that there's only so many months that that timber can be harvested or it will get buggy. And so a certain amount of that has to go. Those places should be replanted, for the renewable timber, for soil erosion. I don't think there should be any question about that — that should be a given.

The Silver Fire Roundup — I've never seen so many logging trucks in my life. I couldn't believe they managed to get that many logging trucks in one spot from different states. No matter what your opinion about it was, it was an impressive sight. A gathering of that many people from that many different states for a particular issue was amazing to see. I couldn't help but be really rather excited about it. We watched quite a few of them roll in.

From what I was able to tell, it seemed that people were pretty much in favor of this display. That was the impression that I had. I don't have any close personal friends that I'm aware of who are members of any of the environmentalists' groups, so I don't think I'm privy to viable information, maybe, from an environmentalist standpoint. I pretty much get my opinions from what I read in the newspaper, see on the news.

B. B.   Do you think that growing up in a logging and ranching family, that your relationship to the land was any different than if you hadn't?

Dorothy I suppose so. You know, I still like the smell of sawdust and diesel. [*Laughs*] I can remember that I really liked the smell of my dad when he would come home with dirt on him, and diesel. Well, there's nothing like that! I like the smell of a dairy barn, too. The smell of pine needles.

B. B. What would you like to see for the area?

Dorothy I suppose I would like to see people quit building houses and businesses. [*Laughs*] You know, I'd like the population to quit growing, all those things that just probably aren't realistic in my lifetime or in my children's lifetime.

I'd like to see places along the river that are still accessible to the public preserved. I'm glad that the Oregon coast — that there's still a lot of public land that we can see and have access to. [*Long pause*] I think probably what I would like to see is just not realistic. You know, for reality is we're probably just going to continue to have a lot more people move in.

There are things I would not care to go back to. For one thing — it still is not all that common to see a Black person in Medford or Grants Pass, but it hasn't been all that long ago that there were actually sundown laws for them. They just plain had to be out of town by dark.

My husband's parents were stationed at Camp White during the war, and they had a troop train come in with Black soldiers on it. And they actually had the curtains drawn, just so people wouldn't know that they came through town. I wouldn't care to go back to that.

I can remember when there would be the Mexican population come in that would work in the fruit, and still do — but there would be no migrant schools or anything like that. Which we probably don't have enough of, but we have some now. There's a need for migrant health care, schooling — should be more of that.

I always probably thought of my daughters as not having to do manual labor. I waited tables and worked in the fruit, too. But I always have had it in my mind that they would probably have some kind of higher education that they wouldn't have to do that kind of manual labor.

B. B. Do you know anyone who's been hurt or killed working in the woods or mills?

Dorothy Yes. It's a real dangerous occupation. When my husband went to work in the woods, he went to work setting chokers behind my dad. And I never worried about him setting chokers behind my dad, because I knew my dad was careful to a fault. Although he drank, he never drank on the job.

I worried about my husband working in the woods when he was setting chokers behind other people. And he did have a couple of real close calls. But I've heard my dad say more than one time that if somebody gets killed in the woods, somebody's been careless. You know, you were where you weren't supposed to be, or somebody didn't know where you were.

Clearcutting used to be real common. And it's not so much anymore, and I'm glad to see that. There's helicopter logging, which didn't used to be. I think it probably must be a lot more expensive and a lot more difficult. But I think it's good because it's less damaging in some ways to the environment. And some places, that's the way it's accessible, and it has to be done that way. So I don't necessarily see that as a bad thing.

My dad, I would respect his opinion. If you built a road in to log, along the road you couldn't leave it just a slashy mess; you had to clean it up and lop brush. You couldn't just leave it looking bad. And I think that's good. If people have the access like that to make a living, they shouldn't abuse it, and should clean it up.

I don't know that I think so much about the future for myself. I suppose that if I had a thought for the future, it would have to be not so much for me, but for my husband. Just that he works alone and he works hard and he does hard physical labor. And I would like to be able to see the time when he didn't have to work hard physical labor by himself. And that when he got to the point where it was just too difficult for him to do that anymore, that he would be able to retire. I don't ever aspire to being wealthy, but just that he would be comfortable.

HENRY DUBNIK   (age 22)   Henry Dubnik is young, confident, and sharp. Henry is one of the newcomers who came to the area young enough to be shaped by the culture and values of the Rogue Valley. His story tells of his transition from southern California suburban kid to one of southwest Oregon's own.

We sat on used equipment behind his father's shop one hot, sunny day, the microphone wire dangling across the weeds and debris.

I was born in 1967 in the Bay Area. My mom was waiting for Dad to get home from the Vietnam War. Living with her parents. I think my dad saw me when I was eight months old, when he was on leave.

My grandparents have been in the Bay Area forever. Their parents came over. My grandmother's side came over from Ireland. My grandfather's side were Italian. So I'm what? Third generation, I guess. Don't know quite as much about my dad's side of the family. My mom got a divorce when I was three years old. One grandfather worked for the telephone company, and my other grandfather, I guess he was a carpenter. My dad's now a carpenter, and I've had some of those skills, too.

I don't remember living with my father. My mom started seeing my stepfather when I was four. They were married by the time I was five, I guess.

My stepfather's eastern European and English. His family still lives in southern California. Real interesting people, hard-working people. My grandfather was real good with equipment. It kind of came at me from that side, too. I was raised in that type of an environment.

When I lived in Oakland, when I was in kindergarten and first grade, fun consisted of basically getting ourselves into mischief. You know, just setting things on fire and whatnot. Playing in the streets. Throwing rocks at cars. You know, all that kind of inner-city type stuff.

It was a neighborhood, but it was a real mixture of different cultures. The guy I hung around with the most was a Black kid. And then there was an Oriental family across the street, and we hung out with them. So it was kind of a mixed gang.

When we moved to southern California, it was into a kind of a subdivision type of a middle-class area. Basically an all-white area. There wasn't too many other cultures in that part of southern California at that time. About the only other people there were some Mexican folks that were working on the farms and the orchards and stuff. But I didn't really hang around with them.

Most of the kids I hung out with at that time were just strictly in the neighborhood. As a matter of fact, my circle, four or five of us, we were basically all on the same block of the same street. I mean, you go around the block and it was like a different country. There was a whole 'nother group of kids. You go down the street a couple blocks, and you didn't even know them. It was kind of strange. But since we all lived in real close proximity within a few houses of each other, we just had our little gang.

B. B. Was your family involved in any social organizations — church, anything like that?

Henry Churches mostly. They've never been like Kiwanis or anything like that. Never been big into sports. We spent a lot of time with grandparents and aunts and uncles and doing those types of things. Fairly tight-knit family, actually.

We came through here on vacation. One summer. And the place was just a lot more beautiful than southern California. Unless you're into beaches. But they liked the atmosphere, they liked the idea of getting out of the L.A. area. Probably the biggest factor was just it sounded neat, to move to Oregon.

We knew some people that had moved to the Medford area from L.A. shortly before that. But we didn't know anybody actually living in Grants Pass or surrounding areas. It was pretty much a cold-turkey thing.

Dad did whatever it took to make money. He built the house during that time. Worked a couple different jobs. I think he worked as a street cleaner, and as a mechanic, and clean-up crew at a mill. I don't remember everything he did.

Then he went to work for a fabricator. There he met another fellow in the church we were going to at the time. They were both kind of disillusioned about working for other people, and they both lived outside Grants Pass in the same area, and since there wasn't anybody doing that kind of thing out here, they thought it would be really neat to open a business, and they did. It wasn't a very well planned out opening of a business. But it worked out. That was his first partner.

When we moved here, I hated every minute of it. I was mad. I was really mad. If I thought I could have walked back, I would've. Boy, I voiced my opinion pretty strongly all the time. I was just generally upset. Everything that went wrong — if I had a hard day at school, or if I had problems with something — I blamed it on where I was at. My life down there, in the three years that we lived in southern California, had become pretty set. I had my friends, my turf, my school, and everything like that.

Up here it wasn't the same. You couldn't really get together with people after school. School, in southern California, wasn't a social center. You just went and got it over with so you could play afterwards. In this area school became more of the social center, because of how spread apart everybody is. That's where you made friends, was at school. My friends ended up being like ten miles away from me.

And so I started to have to rely on myself a little bit more. Become a little more self-sufficient. I slowly grew into enjoying it. I had my dog, and somewhere down the line I got my BB gun, and I'd go traipsing off through the woods and just explore and do that type of a thing. There was just huge tracts of land I could go cruise around. I started feeling like I had something over on the people that were still stuck in the cities. But it took a year or two before that started to happen.

Going into high school, I got interested in business, and that's pretty much where my interest has stayed since then. I realized that Grants Pass, Oregon, didn't hold a lot of opportunity for a young entrepreneur. By reason of lower population and economic situation, there's not a lot of opportunity to create something of your own without a lot of hard work. At that time I wasn't into the hard work. I was into the easy money or the excitement of doing it, but hard work was kind of— you know, my dad had to work hard, why should I? That's kind of the mind state I was in.

During the eighty-two recession there was an influx of people; some people left, some people came in. It was kind of a time of people moving. At that time we really weren't doing too bad. Dad's always been a wonderful money manager. Even in the tightest times there was always food. He's never been big on credit cards, so that when the tough times did come, it was the necessities that he was able to take care of. So when the recession did strike, I didn't have a real good understanding of why it was such a big deal. I had been working for a couple years during the summer. So I had taken over responsibility for choosing my own clothes, or spending my money.

The area was just so different from southern California, which is rather rich. Down there we had our paper and pencils and books provided. You just had to show up. When we lived up here, your parents had to buy all that stuff. Books were still handled by the school, but notebooks and paper and art supplies and things like that. Because of the school funding. They didn't have as many programs.

Then I didn't have much of an opinion on school funding. But these days it's a multifaceted thing. People like to have control over at least their own environment. And it's getting to the point in this area, in Oregon especially, where you can't do anything with your own property. You're starting to feel controlled in just about everything you do. And that probably factors into the school-funding thing. They still can vote "no." Or they still can vote "yes." And so you get a bunch of different factions who are all thinking different things, but the end result is that the schools are having trouble getting funded.

I wouldn't blame it on any socio-economic group. I myself have my own reasons for not wanting some of the funding. Going through local schools myself, with eyes open, I was able to see problems. There's changes that are necessary. Because it's not running right.

The drug problem was never anything I had to deal with. I went to parties. I drank a little. And later drank a lot. But because my parents had friends who had been involved in the drug culture — they had smoked marijuana and done even other things that they're not really willing to tell me about — I just had seen where it hadn't done them much good. They would relate some pretty bad times, actually. I just managed to stay away from it — never even try it, so I never had to kick any sort of problem like that.

I came really close to dropping out. About my junior year I really became aware of the crud that was going on in the schools. You know, you have teachers and administration who are playing their own politics trip. I was just more interested in what I did for myself at that point. I would only learn things that I was interested in. A lot of teachers didn't like that because they were very much into making you conform. 'Cause it made their job easier. If they didn't have to answer a question that they hadn't prepared for, then, you know, they could just sail right through, collect their check, and go home.

I got a job in September following when I graduated. I really didn't have any college plans. I didn't want to go to college because I was so freaked out about the educational system. I saw college as just another four years of unnecessary bending to other people's social pressures. People said I was rebellious; I'd like to say I was realistic.

B. B. Did you stay involved with the church?

Henry Yeah. Less through high school, mostly because I was rebelling from basically everything. Recently more so, just because some of the fundamental values kind of mesh with my own. I've basically settled down and consider it a personal thing. I think about other people making bad decisions, but basically I realize that it is their decision. As long as it doesn't affect me, they can go right along and do whatever they want.

I've spent some time and actually thought through some of society's common faults. The crime problem or the drug problem or, you know, welfare system, and tried to get to the actual root of what causes the problem. They all seem to point back to the same root problem. People are very reluctant to take on responsibility for themselves and their family. There's government agencies and social agencies that will take care of different problems. The poor no longer have to be taken care of by me, because there's a welfare system, or food stamps, that just automatically takes them money. Parents no longer even have to pay any attention to what their children are learning in the schools. All they have to do is pay for it.

B. B.   Why are people not taking responsibility?

Henry   Mostly because they don't have to. There's other people that will handle it. There's always someone else. If you get in trouble, there's the police you can call. If some kid's speeding down your road, you call the police, because, boy, that's their job to handle it. I think it weakens the community. Because you have people that no longer have to stand up for themselves or to help each other. And that's been removed by time and progress.

B. B.   What's "progress" mean then?

Henry   More involvement by government. People are more removed from their roots. They don't know how the soil and the rain and the air all work together. I mean, you can take the pollution problem. People just didn't know how it all interreacted, so now we've got a pollution problem. It's the same type of thing with the social problems. People removing themselves from each other, because they don't have to come in contact.

B. B.   Have you seen changes since you've come to this area?

Henry   I think it's gotten worse. We were probably part of the first wave of Californians: [*Laughs*] *The dreaded Californians.* And there was a bit more of a community spirit. There was more of a neighbor-oriented attitude, which was noticeable because it wasn't present in southern California. And that, I think, has disappeared.

People are less likely to just stop and talk to you. They have to know you. That was true to a certain extent even when we moved up here, just because it was a tight-knit community. But they were generally interested in the welfare of the people. I've met a lot of people that're fleeing to this area. They're seeing the problems and seeing the drugs and the crime that are going on in the cities or wherever, and they're actually fleeing to here. So they're seeing a dramatic difference in their lifestyles. They've brought in different ideas and different attitudes.

Especially I can see it, 'cause I have dealt with tourists. You'll see an attitude. You see mannerisms. More abrupt. Or, you know, when they come driving up, depending on what business I was working with, they have an air of superiority. And it's not necessarily where *you* think they're superior, but you think they think they're superior. [*Laughs*] It's an attitude problem, and most people get turned off by it. 'Cause they don't understand what creates it. And so it makes some hard feelings. Some of the old-timers that don't appreciate those kind of attitudes will just pretend that the newcomers don't even exist. Just try and shut them out so they don't have to deal with it. It's unfortunate.

I began my life in a area where Blacks and Chinese, Japanese and Indians and everybody, we were all together. But this area, it is kind of removed from reality in that there's not a lot of different racial groups represented. I lived in Portland for a couple years, which just has a mixture of different peoples. You could see the way the different societies lived, and it was a real good learning experience. Here you don't have that opportunity.

But at the same time, we don't have a lot of the pressures and hassles that go along with it. So much time and money is being spent for securing racial equality. Those things that in the cities you run headlong into once in a while.

I had trouble getting a particular job in Portland because I was white. That disturbed me. I guess I realized how a Black person felt, not getting a job because they were Black. I was qualified, but they had to meet their quota, because the local government had a program set up for making sure everybody hired across the board. In this area you just don't have anything like that.

There's a lot of extreme prejudice in this area. Which I find kind of sickening. I neither think any social or ethnic group is better or worse than anybody else. We all have our creeps. There's certain groups that, you know — in the opinion, might sound kind of extreme — but there are certain groups that because where they're at socially, where they live and how they're brought up, they don't have the performance intellectually that a lot of the upper-class or middle-class white people have. I mean health-wise. The way you're fed as a child makes a big difference on how you mature and how our brain develops and whatnot.

There's a lot of people in this area that see every Black person as some sort of a problem. I'm not sure they see it just because the Black himself causes the problems, but they see the problem of trying to mix races. Whether for the right reasons or the wrong reasons, a lot of the people just recognize that when you start mixing the races like that you get a certain amount of jealousy, you get a certain amount of pride. The haves and the have-nots. And all of a sudden it just becomes a big stressful situation.

The whole country is mixing up a little bit more. I mean, I come from backgrounds that all hated each other's guts. Irish and Scotch, German, Italian. I don't know. In Europe they're all battling it out all the time. And you do have a tendency to mix up. I think it'll happen, but a lot of the racial pressures are going to have to ease before this area starts having that happen.

After high school I worked at a department store for a few months. And just kind of got a wild hair. [*Laughs*] My real father lives in Portland. I moved out of my parents' house. Left a relationship with a girlfriend, left my best friends, left everybody I knew, and went to a totally foreign environment. I made it for a while, then a friend of mine moved up there with me, so that kind of made it easier. But there came a point where I was missing the family, and things were kind of going rough, and everybody wanted me to come back, and so I just kind of did. I didn't even make an honest decision to move back. I came back to visit, ended up going back to work for my dad—he had someone quit. A week's vacation turned into two weeks, a month, and pretty soon I was going back up there to get my stuff.

B. B.   What do you think about the lumber controversy here?

Henry   I am bright enough to watch the economic situation of the rest of the country. Housing is at an all-time low. They're not building houses. They're simply not using the lumber. I don't think the demand is there if all the trees were getting cut. So in some respects I kind of feel that maybe they're using the spotted owls as an excuse. Kind of like the oil companies used the oil spill in Alaska as an excuse to hike the prices up so suddenly.

That's all fine and dandy, but people take it very personally around here. They seem to see for some reason they deserve the job or they deserve the income. And that someone else is trying to take it away from them. They've reduced it down to a very simplistic viewpoint, pretty much black and white. "They're against us." For some reason. For whatever reason. Whether it be the owls or the lumber companies or the mills.

There was a real boom here for a while. A lot of money coming into the area from lumber sales. And as a country we're just getting away from it. We're using plastic bags in supermarkets instead of using paper ones. We're recycling paper. Building out of different materials.

Building more efficiently. Not building, for that matter, because of the finance rates and whatnot.

The people are just going to have to make the adjustment. They're going to have to face reality and do something else. Either that or they're going to have to go to another area that can employ their talents.

I'm not really looking to leave. I haven't had any place interest me enough to leave. I'm not anxious to live in a city anymore. I'm just going to do whatever it takes. Right now I'm spending a lot of time in the library learning how to grow food. It might be a necessary thing. As a matter of fact, I kind of think it's going to be.

B. B.   Do you know anyone that was hurt in the mills or logging?

Henry   I don't think any of my close personal friends, but I do know people that have been injured. As a matter of fact, I do know somebody who got killed in a logging accident. It just happens. That's life, I guess. I almost got killed myself a few times [*laughs*] working on equipment. It's just something that happens.

B. B.   Do people take sides on the environmental–industry debate?

Henry   People will back either–or, simply 'cause they think it's a football game where one side has got to win. Or only one side is going to be right in the end.

Any local media discussion you see on anything that goes on, whether it be the health of our forests or not, they'll have a logger and they'll have an ecologist — they'll have an EarthFirst!er or somebody they've managed to find on the other radical side, and they'll put them together. Because it makes for good newsprint. That doesn't do any of us any good, because it just splits everybody up. I mean, theoretically, since we're all humans, and all basically have brains in our head, we should be able to find something that works for all of us. I don't see any sense to be for two sides.

B. B.   What would you like to see for the area?

Henry   I'm kind of pessimistic for the area. I'm not real confident that the rest of America is going to wake up and make the necessary changes. The size of government, our defense spending, whatever. It's all getting out of hand. We've removed so much responsibility from the individual that they no longer pay attention, they won't get into the actual issue of what's going on.

I have a theory. Depending on what belief you subscribe to, whether we evolved or whether we were created, either way, we started at a much different point than we are. The human being survived at a different technological level for a long time, and as we've removed ourselves from that, it seems like a lot of these social problems and governmental problems and other things become the paramount thing to worry about.

You go back and look at the Romans and the Babylonians and the Syrians and whatnot. They started having social programs and governmental things, the people had more time just to do whatever they wanted to. They could waste time watching the lions eat the Christians. Whatever was going on. It's like people watch TV today. They have free time. And it just gives, you know, those old adages, "Idle hands do the devil's work" — or whatever. It's true to some extent. When people are concerned with providing for themselves, they don't have a lot of free time to get into mischief. They don't. [*Laughs*] There's certain things I'd like to see occur. I just don't have a lot of hope that it's going to. And I'm not going to let it affect me. If a certain law gets passed, then I'm going to have to adjust. If the economy goes a certain direction, I'm just going to have to live with it. I can't scream and use up a lot of oxygen trying to make everybody else know I'm displeased.

I haven't studied enough other cultures to be able to draw actual lines that would divide us from anywhere else. There's a kind of freedom attitude, a self-sufficient attitude. It's an area that's more results-oriented. Your nice car still gets you some recognition, but you've got to do a good job to survive. In L.A. you can be, say, a lousy equipment renovator, and replace used parts and call them new and charge people for repairs that don't get done, or do things like that. Just be a general crook and get away with it for a long time. There's people that have made a livelihood of it for a lifetime because there's so many people.

In this area, a couple little slip-ups and you've pretty much lost the entire town as far as a customer base. They won't come back. Whether right or wrong, whether you do it intentionally or not. It's a lot more close to the cuff.

Things could get bad, and even if they don't, I've found a lot more happiness with — I hate to use the expression "being one with nature," because it sounds so cliché — but just doing things. Producing something. Building a house, or farming — I get a lot of personal satisfaction out of it. That's where I'm heading. I do whatever it takes to survive. That's why I say there is a survivalist attitude here, too, because a lot of people think that way.

I mean, "Survivalist," whatever that group has become, they're around. But they're extreme. They're actually looking for something very horrible to happen. Some sort of a cataclysmic situation. I don't know — this country is too big for that to happen so quickly that they would be effective. I don't see much of a threat of us getting invaded from without. I see the problem as being invaded from within by our own people. Americans' greed and their own willingness to trample each other. . . . Geez. Five years ago I never would have said something like that.

There's just a whole bunch of different things that I enjoy about this area. I guess I don't experience the same problems that other people do — people that would come into the area and find it kind of tight-lipped. I walk down the street on Saturday and I feel like I'm in a parade or something. You know, I've got people honking and, "Oh, hi! How you doing?" The way you look at this area kind of changes with your perspective.

You know, Dad having his business in the area, I know a lot of the sheriff's deputies. I got in a really stupid car accident one time, that was totally my fault — single-car accident. The officer who was investigating it didn't recognize me, didn't recognize the name, but when my dad drove up, he recognized him and said, "Oh, is that your dad?"

"Yeah."

He basically was ready to prosecute me to the full extent of the law. And then Dad drives up and all that kind of went out the window. I don't think he said, "Well, gee, you know, maybe Jim'll do me a favor or maybe Jim will that or that." It was just: "Boy, he's probably in bigger trouble than I'll ever get him in. I better not make this kid commit suicide by giving him a fat ticket — Jim's already probably going to kill him."

Just things like that. Or they recognize my family. My mom's been in the area long enough to where I run into people that she knows and, "Oh, you're Barbara's son. Oh, OK." And they'll deal with you a little bit differently. When people think they know you, they handle you much more comfortably. They feel better about having you around. That's probably the biggest thing about small towns, is just that familiarity.

Like in Portland, I had forty people I knew at one job site, and probably thirty at the other. I didn't run into a single one of those people in any of my shopping. I'd wander around downtown. I'd go to theaters, concerts. I never once ran into somebody I knew. Never. As a matter of fact, the only person I ever bumped into was someone from here that I hadn't seen in four years. We were in a shopping mall, and we walked by each other. Two hundred miles away.

What kind of future?

MARGARET and STANLEY NORMAN   (ages 42 and 46) Before the explosion of environmental activism during the 1970s and 1980s, government and citizen intervention to stop timber harvesting was rare. One exceptional example was the closure of thousands of acres of redwood forest on the far northern California coast in order to create Redwood National Park. The repercussions of that closure are a theme in Margaret and Stanley's interview.

Like rural wage earners from depressed areas around the globe, Stan found work that took him away from home. In his case the job is trucking—short-haul when he can find such work, otherwise long-haul, which can keep him away from his family for six weeks at a time, with only an unpredictable handful of days off.

The interview began at Margaret's place of work, then moved to Margaret and Stanley's home. Their son, Zach, joined in the last part of the taping, providing one family's intergenerational perspective on the topic of logging.

Margaret   I was born in Eureka, California, in 1947. My mother's grandparents had immigrated to Del Norte County from Germany. Then Mom's parents were born in Del Norte County. My dad was originally from Washington. Then when his parents divorced, he came down to the Klamath River with his father's logging operation.

Mom's father worked in the lumber mill. My mom taught school. She had one sister that was a court reporter, one that was a librarian, and she and the other youngest one were teachers. I don't think they had a whole lot of choice, because their father died when Mom was seven. He was a foreman at the mill and fell off a conveyer belt that went up into the burner. Fell into the log pond. Grandma took in sewing, and the rest of them had to pretty much get out and get some kind of a career. Dad was a logger in the town where my mom taught school. After they got married, he operated a small business. He wasn't a very good businessman, 'cause he would extend credit to people and they wouldn't pay him. He finally ended up losing his shirt.

And then the rest of his life he worked in a plywood mill. He ran whatever the machine is that glues the veneer together. The mill closed down, it would have been the early sixties.

When my mom and dad got married, the family gave them a house that another relative had built. The husband had disappeared out in the woods. He was a miner, and on the way out to his mining claim, he just disappeared. Nobody ever heard from him again — supposedly. There were some stories that he was seen down in southern California and in Mexico years later. His widow — or whatever she was — gave the house back to the family, so they gave it to Mom and Dad when they got married. They lived there till the tidal wave took it out in sixty-four.

Me and my dog would go to the beach and spend all day. Or if we were up in the mountains, we would go up in the hills and prowl around all day. My parents never worried about me. I could take off and head down to the beach right after breakfast and not come home until dinnertime. Back then there was nothing to be concerned about, really. Every once in a while there'd be a weirdo around, but in general, people were good people.

Basically our sole social life as far as the whole family was pretty much church-oriented. You associated with the people from the church, and that's who you went to school with. The Catholic church is the biggest church in the area, probably because so many Irish and Germans settled there.

In high school I had a pretty strict curfew, but we'd go out and just cruise around town. Every once in a while there'd be a keg party going on somewhere. We'd go drink beer and throw up. You know. It was a pretty boring, quiet, small town. Go to school, go home. Then I got a job during the summers, worked for the local drug store.

I went to Portland to college, and it was fun to get out. But I didn't really do anything different than I did at home. Cruise around town. Go out and drink. Go to the show every once in a while. There was a lot of things I could have taken advantage of, but I didn't. And a bunch of us were caught drinking beer in the dorm shortly before the end of the term. And asked not to return. [Laughs]

So I went back home, I went back to work in the same drug store. I had dated my husband in high school one summer. He came home from the service. I guess he was home for thirty days, and then he went back to Vietnam for a year. When he came back the next year, we got married.

I had thought of being an English Lit teacher. And I was interested in veterinary medicine. But I was raised to where you grew up, you got married, you had babies. And you were a housewife and lived happily ever after. You know? [*Laughs*] And that was it.

My family was probably lower-middle-class. We didn't have anything extravagant. We didn't have new cars or expensive furniture. But we never went without, either. I don't remember really being expected to work. I wanted to. But I'd just blow all the money I made. Sometimes I'd buy clothes, but generally I'd just buy junk. Makeup. Girl stuff.

B. B.   What were the main kinds of work in town?

Margaret   Mining was pretty well gone. The few people that mined were always kind of, quote, strange, unquote. You know — hermits who lived out in the hills. Fishing and lumber were the main industries. That was just what it was. I couldn't imagine being someplace where there weren't those industries.

I don't remember a lot of logging accidents. That's something that surprised me when we moved here to Grants Pass. Because somebody getting killed in the woods happened over there, but there were probably more people killed in the woods the first couple years we lived here than I'd heard all my life on the coast. I don't know if it's just because there are more people here, or the safety practices weren't as strong or what.

The main thing I remember over there is fishing boats going down and people being lost. It's not unusual to have eighty-, ninety-mile-an-hour winds during a storm over there.

I had gotten away from church when I was in college. We have found a church where we're comfortable. But we definitely no longer believe one church is the only church.

I really didn't like working when my kids were little. So I worked a little bit here and there doing part-time things. Stan worked on a fishing boat. I wasn't really thrilled with it, because of the storms and the boats going down. And then my best friend in high school's husband taught Stan to drive a truck, and he's been driving truck ever since.

The economy got so bad in Del Norte County. He was working for a company that ran mostly freight up and down I-5, so he was only home every other weekend. We decided, that's ridiculous! He's not having any kind of home life at all. And as much as I loved where we lived—I didn't really want to leave—it was kind of exciting to move to a new area.

And I thought: I think I can drive truck. At that time you didn't even have to take a driving test. You just went down, took your written test, and if you had a company or somebody that owned the truck sign that you could drive, then they gave you your license.

Stan taught me to drive. [Laughs] The worst thing about it was the width. It was a cab-over truck—you're sitting in a different spot than you are in a car. You're sitting right over that left front wheel, so your perception's off. I was sure I was too close to the center line, and Stan would say, "You're going to get in the ditch! Get over!" And I'd say, "I'm going to be over in the other lane!" "No you're not! Look in your mirror!"

And you'd look in the side mirror, and you're a long ways from the center line. But when you're looking out the windshield, you're thinking that you're right on top of it. So he said, "When you get in that truck, put your left foot on the center line. Look out through the windshield, you see where that white line is—your left foot should be on top of it." At that point you're still about four feet inside the white line.

It was a lot of fun. I never did do city driving. Mainly up and down I-5. I'd only go every once in a while. Because the kids were still young then. The longest I was ever gone was three weeks. Stan's mom would come and stay with the kids.

My daughter actually went with Stan and learned how to drive truck, and had her chauffeur's license, too. She brought a truck over the Siskiyous in the snow at eighteen. [Laughs] She's a gutsy gal.

We've rented ever since we've been over here—didn't have any money to buy. [Laughs] We took a bath on our house. Because we had to get out because of the economy.

B. B. Why was the economy so bad at that time in the Crescent City area?

Margaret Government regulations. The Redwood National Park had taken up so much of the timber land. And the regulations on the fishing had cracked down.

They actually set up a program to retrain people who had been affected by the park's expansion. My best friend, he was one of the recipients, and he did real good. They paid for him to go to college, plus he and a couple other guys got lawyers. And filed a suit. He got seventy, eighty thousand dollars, plus his retraining.

It wasn't only the jobs. There was land taken when the park expanded. We had two friends that lost their homes because of it. And, in fact, the government caused my folks to lose their home, but that was as a result of the tidal wave, not the park expansion. The whole block was condemned. And at that time they were told it was going to be made a park. And today the whole block is covered with Teamster apartment housing. [*Laughs*] So.

If Stan hadn't been trucking, if he'd had a good stable job where we were making a comfortable income there, we would never have moved. The only people we knew in Grants Pass were my cousins, who had come over a year before. That's probably when I started going on the road a lot. [*Laughs*]*

Stanley   Crescent City area, the same thing happened as in Grants Pass. People started moving in and retiring there. And pretty soon took over the city governments and changed everything to the way they wanted it. Made a puppet out of the area. Everybody was a cookie cutter.

When all the retirement people come from the big cities, they bring high prices into the real estate. Everything just all of a sudden just mushrooms. It gets so far out of perspective that the normal people that were raised and lived there for years can't even afford to buy a little old two-bedroom house. And they bring all the garbage they were trying to get away from with them! Just like a dark cloud. You don't have that down-home atmosphere. You don't have the friendliness that used to be there.

Margaret   Because you usually knew who your neighbors were, and the people stayed in the same places pretty much all their lives. Now all of a sudden you've got a neighbor that you don't know. You try to be friendly with them—well, they're from a different environment than you are. And they're standoffish.

Stanley   Different planets!

Margaret   They've come up to retire. I say "come up"—like everybody comes up from California, but I think most of them do. They come up to retire, and maybe you're still working-class. Where it used to be pretty much the same social setting in the same neighborhood, anymore it's not.

B. B.   What's different about this wave of in-migration, compared with in-migration in the past?

Margaret   Lots more people with lots more money.

---

*At this point we moved to Margaret and Stanley's home across town. *B. B.*

Stanley I used to work from time to time with a contractor friend of ours. A lot of these homes — I mean, you're talking thirty-five hundred to four thousand square feet to a house. Absolutely beautiful. But what do you have there? And old guy and his wife. Moved up here and retired. To sink all of their millions into this big house. And they just rattle in the place, it's so huge. I ran into that time after time after time. I said, "Good Lord! What a waste!"

Margaret And you can't blame the people that are in the community, because they're just trying to make the money off of the people that are coming in. If I was in their shoes, I'd probably look at the same thing.

Stanley But the whole mentality has changed. When that starts happening, it changes just automatically. At first you get more money out of some — and sure, they're going to raise their price a little bit to make a little more profit for themselves. But then you see the money moving in, the prices go up. And then, the inflation's like — I don't know — it's just a reaction you can't stop. It just takes off, and there it goes.

Margaret I think a lot of it is, people aren't satisfied as easily as they used to be. What is it your cousin says? [*Laughs*] His philosophy is: Whoever has the most toys wins. I don't think when we were growing up we were that concerned with material things. We were more concerned with people.

Stanley The whole world is in a faster pace now. Anymore, unless you have electronic gadgets, or some big trip to the mountains or something like that, nobody is content to just sit back and enjoy people for what they are and who they are. And you'll find that people are more rude. And don't care about the next person. I mean, people don't have just the normal respect for a person because they're a person.

Margaret It's all "me first." "Look out for number one."

Stanley The people coming in now, they work their way into government. They'll run for some seat or something. They don't have nothing better to do — they're retired. And they'll probably see something that they don't like. And then there are other things that they think could be changed to their way of thinking.

Nine times out of ten, people that'll come out to retire in an area like this, they have a little bit of retirement money. They can sit down. They're not hurting, OK? And so there's two things that go together: There's money and politics. And that's it. They're bedpartners and they always will be. So you have somebody with all this time on their hands, and they've got money. And they would like to see things change. And eventually they get into city politics.

Or they know these people. They go golf with them. Or they do all these social things with them that normally the blue-collar worker doesn't do, OK? And they get their ideas. Start swinging people this way or that, if they don't actually get into office and do something themselves. And this starts changing the mold of what it used to be.

That's the way I see it. I've seen it happen to two towns I lived in in the last fifteen years. It took a little longer to happen there than I've seen it happen here.

Crescent City, that little town went through some physical crisis there, too. That was a little bit different. They would come in and the national park takes all these lands. Well, the only thing you had over there was commercial fishing and logging. That was it! Other than tourism, in the summer people coming through to fish salmon and all that.

And then Ladybird Johnson took a little tour and decided all this was going to be park. And suddenly everybody's out of work. Leading up to that was people in the Save the Redwoods League. And the Sierra Club.

I am not against—and I was a logger, and I was a fisherman over there, OK? And definitely I'm against going out and raping the land, or any of our resources, whatever it may be. They have good plans today to log areas, replant them and everything.

Anyway, the park knocked a lot of people out of jobs. Complete mills shut down. People were bitter. But the government finally came through and retrained some of them at the college. Gave them some cash payoffs and such as this—went back retroactive for so many years.

It ruined a lot of lives. The community died. Man, you couldn't even hardly give away a house when we moved from over there. When we sold our place, the market was really bad. We lost a lot of money on it.

And then we moved over here. It was a pretty nice little town, really. It was a little bigger, but still it was kind of a homey little place. But man, now it's—well, you have a big shopping mall down here, Fred Meyer's. Oh, sure, it's nice to go to Freddy's to get something, but you could have got probably the same thing downtown at one of the other stores if Freddy's'd never come in.

Margaret I don't think the schools were as good as California schools. They didn't have the resources. They didn't have the extracurricular activities and the sports. In California the teachers were better-paid. Didn't seem to have as high a teacher turnover as you do around here. And I don't remember programs being cut at all. Where here, it seems to happen a lot.

I can see where people are coming from around the taxes, because I was appalled at the property tax rates when we moved here. And I could see where people would get in that mindset where they would say, "No more, period!" Especially people on the fixed income and low income. But on the other hand, if you want to look at it logically, this generation that's coming up now is the one that's going to be taking care of us. And we'd better see that they've got a good education so they can at least know what they're doing. [*Laughs*]

As for the high dropout rate, I tend to go back to the family unit and say, "If you haven't got the values there, you're not going to have them anywhere." I think that's nationwide. The nuclear family just doesn't seem to hold a very high place anymore. People are not willing to tough things out, or make a commitment and work at it. It goes back to selfishness. You know: "If it's going to be inconvenient for me, I don't want to mess with it. I want to do my own thing."

And I think probably starting in the sixties, with the do-your-own-thing generation: "If it feels good, do it." I think it's on the backswing. I think things are turning around. But right now we're seeing the worst part of it.

B. B. This area's projected to grow to a hundred thousand people in the county pretty quickly.

Margaret I won't stay. My own choice. We've talked about maybe moving up into the Washington area. We both like the area, especially over on the Olympic Peninsula side. It's a lot of small towns, rural. I don't know what we'll end up doing. Who knows? I may end up going on the road with Stan. Most of the people we know drive truck.

Stanley Let's see, shutdown of mills. Of course there's been effects. Not only the people that directly work at that mill, but that mill, it needs a lot of support services. And that means raw materials being trucked in, finished materials being trucked out. So that means there's less work. You have to go looking somewhere else to try to fill the void on the few dollars you were making trucking something in to those guys.

I've logged a lot in the past. I've hauled logs in this area before — it's been about four or five years ago. I hauled logs over on the coast, too, sixteen and seventeen years ago. This summer, we were hauling off the Silver Fire up here. And, surprisingly, some of the best money that I've ever made hauling logs. Because the helicopter was logging it. It was such a highball operation, because it cost I forget how many thousands of dollars a day for that thing to operate. And logging this area, I mean, you could high-lead log it, but boy! It's just steep as an old goat's nose out there.

But I'd get up probably two- or three-thirty in the morning. Get up there loading at daybreak. Well, a lot of times we loaded at four o'clock in the morning. I'd get up at one o'clock in the morning to go get the truck, take off from the mill, be loading before daybreak. And you made two rounds a day from there into Roseburg. And that's about a sixteen-hour day in itself, right there. Sometimes I got home as late as eleven.

They paid the truck so much for how many thousand board feet were on it. They scale it out. And then I get a percentage of what that load gives. I was driving a light-weight truck, so I hauled a lot of wood, and I did real good. For a change.

For a driver out there hauling logs, your average day is going to be somewhere between a hundred to a hundred and thirty dollars a day. And even for the guys who are working hourly, they're probably around two hundred, two hundred and ten dollars a day.

B. B.   Seems like politics have been hitting the slopes pretty heavy.

Stanley   [*Sighs*] Oh, you mean like for the logging and what it's done with that? Here again you have an area like you have along the coast, your main income is from your natural resources. And your natural resources in this area is your timber.

Politics and money, right? They're bedpartners. A lot of these originate in like your Sierra Club. Originates, to my knowledge anyway, originates out of the San Francisco area, out of the Bay Area there. OK. You've got a lot of people down there with a lot of money. And a lot of clout. And like what they did on the coast, they dictated pretty much what we would and wouldn't do with our lands. So that *maybe* once every three or four years they could take a vacation and drive up through there and see those woods from the road, and that was it. It's not balanced at all.

But granted, there's been misuse of our resources. I'd be the first one to admit it. But we've learned by that, and a few ways that they can go out and raise it back.

Associated, Inc., came in and bought Conrad. And all they've bought them for was a write-off. OK? They came in and Conrad had a

lot of private holdings. They went in, they're still in the process of logging those all out, cleaning them out. And then they're going to shut it
down and call it a loss. But see, that's your big conglomerate, Associated. All right? Those are the real bad guys.

If you have a certain amount of mutual respect for people in general, you'll have respect for Mother Nature also. If you're not inclined
to be that way, then you won't have respect for anybody or anything.

B. B. What do you think about the strategies that are being followed by the environmentalists?

Stanley OK. If I was a general and had an army, and wanted to
go into another country, I would infiltrate that country with small
groups with small numbers of people that undermine it. OK? And I
think in your environmentalists, this is the same thing that's happening
to an extent. You have their main political nucleus somewhere — let's
say the Bay Area. Their money comes out of that area and supports
and is behind your, like, your 'First!ers and whatnot.

All right. They're not getting hurt. They're getting a point across.
They're creating problems. They're holding up production. They want
to throw a wrench in the gearworks, OK?

Margaret Get the public eye focused on them.

Stanley Right. If I wanted to get your attention, I'd set off a
bomb. OK, that's basically in essence what they've done to the woods.
Making a big deal out of something.

Logging the rest of that timber up there that was burnt in the Silver Fire, and still laying on the ground — millions and billions of board
feet of timber that we can't go in and get, because they finally found a
line and drew it. Stopped logging. That wouldn't've hurt anything. It
would have benefited people. There'd have been more lumber to build
buildings and everything else. But it was the point they were trying to
get across — that they want the loggers out of the woods.

Margaret Well, people who are from urban areas come to an
area like this and they can't believe that there are areas with trees for
miles and miles and miles and miles and miles. I think it blows them
away.

Stanley Tell you something I ran into when I was back East.
This one trip, I went on over to the border of Ontario and Quebec and
loaded up there, a load of hardwood veneer skins. I stopped and was
eating, and this guy got to talking to me. He was from the local area
there somewhere, and he was really against what the loggers had done.
Around there and in Canada. Because he said that there is one area
that has been logged off so clear that it will show up on the pictures

from satellites, a complete clearcut for miles and miles and miles. Now, to me, that is totally wrong.

When I was falling timber, had my cutting contract all over on the coast, I worked right hand-in-hand with the Forestry Department. I was up there looking at some timber with this guy one day, and he was telling me that they don't allow any clearcuts any larger than . . . seventy acres, I think? And they were cutting it down to smaller plots than that.* And therefore you can go in and you can replant that area. It's a small area, and you're not hurting it.

And what they do is, they'll go through and they'll clearcut. Basically they won't select-log it because there's so many hardwoods and everything intermingled in with it. Then they'll go through and they'll burn it. Then they go back in, and they plant it with young, healthy trees.

Between here and Klamath Falls, they do a lot of select-cutting. You don't have what you'd call "trash wood" in there. So they'll go through and they'll select-cut this to where it will reseed itself. And then you're not hurting the area.

You go back thirty years ago, they weren't doing that. They were going through and just taking prime everything. Back in those days, when they would fall redwoods over there—when you drop a redwood, it's brittle. Today they go in there with a cat and build a bed for it. They'll go about every twelve feet or so and they'll hump up some dirt. Right where you drop it, and save it. Back in those days, they'd go through there and they would take prime good fir and fall it back and forth across, and drop that big redwood on it.

It's just the practices they used in the past was really destroying our resources. It was raping it, literally. But today it's managed pretty well, I think. There's a certain amount of politics in it. And a certain amount of money, which goes with politics. That forces some things—but then again, you know, we're small, there isn't a heck of a lot we can do.

I think that's why you see people here radical sometimes, is because they feel helpless. And whether it's pro or con, or whatever the cause may be, is they feel small, and the only thing they know to do is go throw bricks and smash windows, because they're small and that gets a little attention. They're just frustrated.

---

*With a few exceptions, including salvage cuts, the Forest Service has limited clearcuts to 60 acres since 1984 (many are smaller). The BLM followed guidelines from the 1970s for a 40-acre limit, but, according to a BLM Medford District source (personal communication, 1994), most clearcuts in the late 1980s were 20 to 30 acres. President Clinton's forest plan put further restrictions on clearcutting in the mid-1990s. *B. B.*

Big companies are going into South America. And just wiping it out. They'll go into these hardwood rainforests and just take everything. And ruin it. None of that can ever come back. They can replant and reforest here, but they can't do those rainforests that way. And this Earth needs those rainforests.

Margaret Well, if we want to keep breathing, it would be nice. Like, who was it? When they were going to log up on the hill behind us there in Smith River. Our water came out of a spring up there. You couldn't even hardly find the creek because it was so thick and ferns and everything. And like our friend said, if they log that, the creek's going. It will dry up.

Zach [*Comes in*] But I think the logging industry's definitely on its way out of this area. Because Oregon is such a wildlife area. It's such a forested area. I've actually heard people talking about making a large portion of Oregon into national park. Like a really large portion, like Yellowstone type. I don't know if that's true or not.

Stanley That's fine. What do we all do? Become park rangers?

Zach You've got to start looking in different areas, because the trees have to stay. I mean, there's a certain amount of logging that must be done, but clearcutting is definitely on its way out.

Stanley Depending on the —

Zach It just can't be done.

Stanley Well, it just depends on where it's at. Some places you have clearcuts, some you have to select-cut.

Zach I don't agree.

Margaret I think it's kind of a cycle. It's not unusual to have people retire at forty, forty-five, anymore. And more younger people still have the energy and the time to get involved. They're going to be coming from urban areas. And they're going to be getting into politics. They're going to be the people who are deciding policy, making things happen.

They're going to see what's happened in areas they've come from, so they're going to fight for it not to happen here. Just like happened on the coast. The only industries were timber and fishing. Government regulations started cutting back on those. The town started dying. Now the prison's going in. And that's bringing the economy back up.

Stanley The day of the blue-collar worker is rapidly on its way out. The biggest majority of your population — and I'm looking, say, fifty years down the road — there's going to be a more educated person, somebody that will be able to do something other than just be a blue-collar worker out there working with their hands for a set wage for every hour, every day.

Because these areas and jobs that used to be here aren't going to be anymore. It wouldn't surprise me to come back here in fifty years and see no logging, no anything. You'd have your forest left. But it would be more like a park setting, and you'd have a lot of people living down here, and retired here. But you won't see any blue-collar work, so to speak. You'll always have your janitorial jobs and such as this. But not to get out and work in Mother Nature like it has been for so many years.

Do I want to stay here as it grows? It wouldn't greatly excite me to stay in a big population. Not at all. Probably the only reason I may stay around till it gets to that point is if my kids stay in this area. Other than that, far as I'm concerned, her and I aren't losing anything if we move on somewhere else.

I think these kinds of things we've been discussing here, I think fifty years ago, sixty years ago, you could've interviewed people up around Seattle area. And it was probably twenty percent of the size that it is now. And people would probably be saying basically the same things as they see people coming in.

I was born and raised in western Washington. In what wasn't a very large town at that time. I had to walk to school, a mile and a half down a long hill.

Zach Right, and barefoot in the snow.

Stanley It did snow! It was a lot of mills, it was lumber. It was like Grants Pass was ten or fifteen years ago. It's fairly good-sized now. Then we moved on to Oregon. I was in the sixth grade. Folks had just split up. We lived there until I was a senior in high school. My mom worked at a department store. I worked there during the summers.

She got remarried. And that's when we moved to Del Norte County. Spent summers with my dad and stepmom down in San Jose. It was beautiful back then. One o'clock in the morning, you went out and opened the front door, and you could smell the apricots. It just permeates the air. Ah! It's not there anymore. All the orchards, every-thing was wiped out. Nothing but buildings everywhere. And that's how that area went. And then slowly all these other areas are gonna go the same way.

AMY STURMAN (age 28) Amy Sturman's determined, get-to-it personality has sustained her through personal misfortunes. Stuck at the low end of the wage scale, she is aiming to change that by returning to school.

Amy describes some of the starkly differing perspectives that course through the community. Sorting through hyperbole and conflicting information is difficult for all residents. The one solid reality in the area is the fact that things are changing fast, and local working people are hurting, upset, and reactive.

We talked over plates of spaghetti in a popular fast-food hangout.

I was born in 1961. Originally I came from southern California. I moved here when I was ten. We started out on it alone. And there's a lot of resentment in this area for Californios, you know? They don't like newcomers. And they'll give you as hard of a time as you'll take. And usually, if you can't take it and run away, they're more than happy.

I've seen a lot of changes in the area. Back then, everybody cared about their kids going to school and getting a good education. And getting as much out of the schools as they could. You know — the physical activities, the cheerleading practices, and all the extras.

And now, reading the newspaper, how much they've whacked away at the schools. And that's one thing that really terrifies me about having kids nowdays. There's nothing for them here. Everybody is so bound and determined for Grants Pass not to take another penny out of their pocket that their kids are going to suffer for the rest of their lives. There are going to be so many illiterate people.

And I've always been real intent on getting an education. It's like — it's almost like some of these people are way older generations. Their fifties and sixties. They didn't get any education — why should the kids around here get an education? Why should we care?

I graduated early from high school because it was a joke. I didn't like school because I get bored real easy. I was always a quick study.

B. B. Was there any question in your mind whether you were going to stay in the area or not?

Amy No. There's a lot of drawbacks to this place, but my property is my life. My husband wants to go someplace else. "There's nothing here."

Well, there's nothing here, but I'm here, and it's mine. And nobody can take that away from me. When I'm at home, when I'm on the land, it's the only place where I really feel safe that there's nobody can hurt me. And nobody can destroy what I am up there. I walk out the door, I go down the road, and people can make me feel like I'm

totally worthless. But when I'm at home, in my house on my place —
that's mine. It's the only place where I feel really whole.

When you're looking out the window and you're going, "My gosh,
all the change!" The things that have changed, and there's a new store
right there, and there's a mall down the street that wasn't there two
years ago. There is a mill that is not there anymore. There are streets
here that never existed before.

I went down a street the other day, down there near Jerome Prairie, and there's tract houses down there! They're all blue! They're all
the same! They're little clones.

Things that are changing that make me real unhappy are the lumber problems, the mills going down. They affect me personally. My uncle works in a mill. Several people I know work with the mills and stuff.
It's hard for me to see people that I care about versus other people that I
care about that are about the forest being saved. I see the clearcuts and I
see the wildlife and see Mount Saint Helens and what it did.* There's
nothing there anymore. You don't have to worry about that — it's gone.

I see all these people fighting with each other. I see the schools
closing down. I see all the wars that went on with Fred Meyer's being
built. That went on for years. People that wanted it to be here, and the
people that didn't want new industry, new anything. And now the industry that we have is going down the tubes.

My friends who work in the mills, they're scared to death. They're
scared to death. You see them with violence, you know, anger, and,
"I'll be damned if my lifestyle is going to go down just because of a
stupid owl!" And you see a lot of resentment. That an animal is going
to take away their livelihood. Things that they've always known.

The people that are in the mills see the owl as an object. Something that is in their way, and something that's destroying them. They
don't see it as something that's endangered.

And I can see both sides. And it is sad. I have seen groups of super
people almost coming to blows fighting over it. I've seen people with
bumperstickers that say, "Save a millworker, shoot an owl."

I have a friend of mine was talking the other day. He says he
knows where there are ten of them. And he's going to go blow them all
away with his twenty-two. I don't think he's serious that there are actually ten of them where he says that there are. But I think if he ever saw
an owl, he would shoot it, just for the spite. And he's not old enough
to really know what this conflict is all about. He is looking at it like,

---

*The Mount Saint Helens volcano in Washington State erupted in 1980, demolishing
many thousands of acres of forests within minutes. B. B.

"Oh, my friends are loggers. And these owls are making my friends mad because they're losing their jobs." This kid doesn't work for the mills or anything, he's just a teenager—sixteen, seventeen. He wanted to do it just because his friends are upset.

B. B. What do you think the issue is about?

Amy Change. Way back when we started horse logging, nobody thought of the trees disappearing. That wasn't planned for. They weren't planted again when they were cut down. And the seedlings did grow, and that's second growth. But nobody thought to plant back then. That wasn't a concept. It was like gasoline—nobody ever thought there would be a shortage. No one thought cigarettes could cause cancer, or alcohol could cause traffic fatalities. It just all existed, and people cut the trees down. Nobody thought to plan ahead.

People are so angry because the trees have already been cut. And now we're going to lose another part of our lifestyle. The owls have always been in the trees. They've always lived in the old growth. Nobody knows whether they can live in the second growth, or in the third growth, or any other generation. They live in the old-growth trees. That's their habitat.

And I didn't know until almost a month ago that our logs were being exported! I didn't know that! What have these people got, brains? We cut down our trees, and we have no jobs, we have no mills, the mills are going under, and we're sending our logs overseas? Somebody's out of their ever-loving mind.

I think a lot of my friends who work in the mills don't see it as an industrial problem. They see it as the animal versus the trees. And the trees are for the mills. The trees are for the loggers. That's what God made them for. He didn't make them for animals to live in.

And that's what I'm hearing a lot. That's what I hear when my uncle comes home from work. "Them damn birds!" It's not: The government's trying to put restrictions on this. Or: So-and-so is trying to make more money. You'd get five minutes of conversation out of him. He is one of those people, he don't open up. He will tell you that he thinks that it's politics. That it's bureaucracy. All kinds of other big words.

We were arguing the other day, we were talking about the logs being exported. And he started talking about the politicians being paid under the table to export our logs to foreign countries. He's just from the old school, you know? Something that we don't know about that's taking all this away from us. Something that we don't understand, that's bigger than us, and it's gotta be communists.

I think it is sad, and it's a waste. And I know darn good and well that nature is going to win. The environmentalists are going to win. Because, OK: The loggers and the millworkers are industry. And the environmentalists and the trees and the animals are nature. They're the environment.

I'm not saying I'm for them, because I'm for industry, too. I can see a lot of things that we're going to be losing. I keep picturing when I drive through Grants Pass, I keep seeing a ghost town. Empty shops. And nobody except for bag people walking up and down the streets. There's not going to be anything here.

I mean, the doctors are taking their families and leaving, because there's nothing here for them. The kids can't go to school, and da-da-da.

But we've lost a lot. When there are people that believe so strongly in what they believe in that they will chain themselves to a tree, starve, risk being beaten and run over by tractors and stuff—that reminds me a lot of the early Christians. They fed them to the lions, for goodness' sake. They fed them in rings, you know. Colosseums. For entertainment! OK?

These people believe in what they believe in. They are willing to injure and kill by driving stakes into trees, so they won't be cut down. They're willing to play every dirty trick which they know how to do, which is not good. I can't say it's good, because, like I said, I'm for the industry. I'm for both of them. I can't really decide.

I think that the environmentalists will win. Nature has the public sympathy. The public will always worry about the animals and the underling. And that's what this is all about. The owls are animals. They're underlings. And they are going to be destroyed, because of man's past ignorance. The things that we didn't know, you know. Ignorance is no excuse for the law, they say.

But it happened. The trees were cut down, and we can't replace them. They're not going to come back, not in my lifetime. Not in a lot of my friends's lifetimes. We'll never see it come back.

And the mills have closed down. How many are left running in Grants Pass? Twenty years ago, how many mills did this town have? Mills every corner! And they're gone. And they're not going to come back. And I don't see that there's any way that they can.

They've cut the Forestry program at RCC! You know? Gone! This stuff is gone. And it's not going to come back. And the people have got to find another way to make their lives. There's got to be something else to live for here. That's why I'm becoming a social worker and not a logger. But it's sad.

And Oregonians are moving on to different places. They're moving up more towards the Washington areas, and towards Reno, and so on and so forth. But I think we're following the weather. This all sounds really *strange*. [*Laughs*] But I really believe that the people are migrating with what they're comfortable with.

B. B.   What kind of impact do you see that having in the area?

Amy   I see bulk food in grocery stores is not going to be around forever. That was great while it was here, and I think that's going under. In California you had skateboards and punk hairdos and stuff. I see that is moving more and more our way. Punk hairdos and guys with earrings and stuff like that is now commonplace. The only thing that I don't see a lot of is Negroes. That surprises me.

Because in California, when things started changing, there were a lot of Negroes that moved into California, and fought racism and everything else. But up here, you're beginning to see a lot more Asian-type people. And you're seeing some Hispanics. But there's so much prejudice in this town, they're still not here.

Earlier in our conversation, we were talking about the Oregonians versus the Californians, and the feelings when we first moved up here — of how we got the idea that they didn't want us here. You feel undercurrents. When you're talking to somebody and you see somebody walk by that's of a different culture, and the person you're talking to, their eyes narrow and they breathe real deep and their nose smashes down against their face? [*Laughs, demonstrates*] You know that they don't like it.

I've read books of the history of Oregon. Grants Pass in particular. There were people beaten here, for being of a different culture. There were indentured servants type thing. Prejudice here in this town has rung very strong.

Takilma. What does the word bring to mind? Right? And Little Valley — you picture these people in love beads and flowers and wearing their bare feet and their frayed pants and the headbands and the braids. People still, they say, "You're from *Little Valley*?" "Is that anywhere out near Takilma?"

Takilma has its flower-child and its hippie population. But Little Valley has this real heavy-duty drugs. That place is a real heavy-duty drug place. They're kind of growing up now. And having families, and they don't have a choice but to settle down. There were lots and lots of fights and lots of guns, and all kinds of weird things going on out there. Constantly. Drinking is very prevailing out there. There's a lot of the people out there are millworkers and landowners. But you do see a lot of changes out there. You know, the people are growing up and growing older. It's too hard to sit on a cinder block and drink Jack Daniels, you know? It doesn't feel so good when you fall off anymore, you know? It hurts. [*Laughs*] Some of them still do that! But it ain't Jack Daniels anymore, it's Burgie. Henry Weinharts.*

I mean, we're all getting old, really old. I'm twenty-eight and I feel real old.

My brother would be a real unusual person to talk to, because he's always been a mediator. He got into jail, got himself in some trouble. And they had four EarthFirst!ers and two or three millworkers, confined by law in the same building.

And my brother's going, "Now, you don't hurt this one, and you stay over there." And he sat there in the middle and tried to keep these people from killing each other. And these millworkers are just, you know, smoking cigarette after cigarette, ready to just tear somebody to shreds.

But there has always been an undercurrent in this town. If it's not one thing, it's another. And it was the bit with the kids not having anyplace to go. Then it was the Fred Meyer's stores. When they were changing zonings for lands and properties? There was that.

B. B. Why do you think the area's like that?

Amy I think this area has got such a mix of people, with the different cultures, and Californians and Oregonians. You've got Californians, you've got Oregonians. But you've got two different kinds of Californians — you've got the rich ones and you've got the poor ones. And you've got half-breeds. You're not officially a Californian, you're not officially an Oregonian. I've told people I've lived here for fifteen years, I was raised here, I have the beliefs of this place, I was spanked with the branches off the trees here. I am truly an Oregonian.

"Noooo! You're not! You're not an Oregonian. No matter what you do, you're not an Oregonian." But you're not a Californian, either.

Everybody's afraid of everybody else around here. The people here are willing to help you, but they're not willing to get involved with you. That's the whole problem with this town. They don't want to be emotionally involved, attached, nothing. They roll up the streets at nine o'clock. Everybody shuts off their front porch lights, because they're afraid somebody's going to come knock on the door!

B. B. Is it different than you remember?

Amy I think it's stronger now. There's a lot more unsurety. That may be why everybody's so afraid. There's changes going on, that no-

---

*Inexpensive regional beers. *B. B.*

body knows what's going to happen when these changes finish happening. With the mills going under, and the logs, and the money situation and everything.

I'm terrified. How am I going to pay my bills? What am I going to do? And there are no answers. There's nothing in this town to tell anybody what to do. The water situation has gotten really bad, and the welfare situation in this town. So many people are losing jobs, and going on disability or unemployment or welfare or food stamps or whatever. There's no certainty in this town, and everybody's frightened. It affects me a lot, because I'm frightened all the time. I don't know what's going to happen tomorrow.

I have this uncle, what's going to happen to him? He's almost sixty years old. He doesn't know anything but work. I mean, he's got busted bones and twisted tendons and scars and curled knuckles because he's worked all his life. For who he cares about, for the people that he loves. And they're pretty sure by fall that mill's going to be closed down, and what is he going to do? It's all he knows. There's nothing there left for him. So he's going to lash out at the hippies and these people that are taking this away from him and that away from him.

I look at my paycheck. You've got all these things going out, and what do you live on? You buy ramen noodles, nine for a buck. You buy a lot of bulk rice. A lot of bulk oatmeal. And you look at these people with — there's two numbers and a comma, and three more numbers, that's their paycheck! They're making three, four, and five thousand dollars a month? To stand there and tell me what to do? No.

And I know so many people, "Why should I work around here? All's they've got is scrounge-the-floor jobs. There's nothing in this town to work for." And they're all on welfare. And I know so many people that are so much better off on welfare than I will ever be in my lifetime. There's one gal that I know for a fact, she says, "Why should I work? They're taking better care of my kids than I ever could." Gal's twenty years old, has got three kids. They should have just given her a box of Trojans instead of a box of oatmeal.

I would like to see some other form of industry come in besides the mills. That the older workers could do yet. The biggest dream that I would ever have? Is to see the log trucks running again, up and down the highways, full of logs. But knowing that it can't go back, knowing you're not going to see the log trucks running, I would like to see some other form of industry crop up here just miraculously.

I would dream of people getting a sense of pride for living here. Getting the kind of feeling that I have. I'm never going to leave, they're not going to pry me out with a crowbar. And get that kind of pride here, instead of saying, "It's a shitty place to live, and I don't know why anybody would want to live here. If I had the money, I'd go to California. If I had the money, I'd go to Washington. If I had the money, I'd go to Reno." Give the people a sense of pride.

What's important in my life right now is just survival. School. Surviving myself. That, right now, is my complete crusade.

ELLEN TIGART   (age 31) Ellen Tigart has persevered with spirit, working hard at a variety of jobs in the valley and making do in difficult situations.

Sexual abuse, experienced by far too many women, adds decades of confusion to lives already stressed by low levels of education and a scarcity of good options. When women's life chances are undercut by abuse, low pay, mean drugs like "crank," and assistance programs with mixed messages, it guts the community of the kind of optimism and skills needed to move forward.

Ellen, a storyteller and writer, comes from a family of storytellers. Storytelling was a local art in times past.

I was born in Medford in 1958. My mother was raised in Sprague River, Klamath Falls, and Grants Pass. My grandparents were in Portland. My father's dad was killed in a railroad strike in 1912 or '13. And my mother's parents came from Missouri and Nebraska. My mother's family had ten children in Grants Pass.

I'm not sure what my grandfather on my mother's side did. I've got a whole box of letters that indicate he worked in the potatoes over in Sprague River, and in the hop yard over here.

And my grandma, well, she must have been a saint to put up with him and ten kids. The children were always dragging other kids home, so there was between twelve and fifteen kids every day.

I think my parents met over in Klamath Falls when my mom was maybe sixteen or seventeen years old. And Dad was eighteen years her senior. He was a typesetter. But I don't know how long he was a typesetter, because the only thing I ever remember him doing was logging. And he loved it. They got married in Reno. They lived in Sam's Valley together for thirty years in the same house. But it was a rocky road.

Mom and Dad were logging in 1952. I think he had six or seven trucks. He drove a truck, and Mom drove her truck, and then they had some drivers. My mom developed a bad heart and spent a lot of time in the hospital.

I remember a whole summer when I was five years old that I spent on a log truck with my dad. It was a lot of fun. He would wake me up at about four o'clock in the morning. We'd go over to the shop, he'd warm up the truck and put me underneath his coat. I drank dusty coffee with him, right out of the thermos. [*Laughs*] I could curl up on the passenger seat, which was fairly wide in a logging truck, and take a nap going down the road. And that's loud in those trucks, so I can sleep through just about anything now.

Dad's business and Dad's logging people were pretty much separate from people I went to school with. My mom was a drug addict, so I tended to be a loner, even from the start. Which really I don't think was my choice, but you know how every class has the class nerd, and I guess that was me that year—or that six years. I wasn't a very good socializer. And I had a speech problem, too, so that was another strike against me.

We had ten acres. It was a real kind of a little trash house, but Mom kept it up really nice before her drug problem became real apparent.

My pony and I went wherever we could get away and not get caught. There was a pond just across the street and down into the neighbors' field. All of the kids in the neighborhood had ponies, like everybody now has BMX bikes, or ten-speed bikes. And we would take the horses down to the pond and wade them out until they were chest-deep. And then we would skinny-dip and use the horses for diving boards.

I think the last time I went on a log truck with my dad, I must have been about thirteen or fourteen years old. I was fairly mature by the time I was thirteen or fourteen. My older sister escaped when she was sixteen. So that left me the oldest. Well, I thought it was my responsibility to do the housework, to do the cooking, to take care of my mom, and to raise those kids, and to make sure Dad didn't find out. So I didn't have much of a chance to go on the truck.

When I was younger and would go with him, I could get out of the truck and walk about, but Dad had specific places that I could be where I would be safe. I could go up into the woods behind the landing and sit up there on a stump and watch what they were doing.

Once the skidder wasn't doing things the way things should have been done, and Dad was really afraid for the safety of the choker setters. He nailed the skidder in the back of the head with a piece of bark. I was there to see that. He had tried to tell him two or three times, nicely. In a low tone of voice. And I knew my dad. He might tell you two, maybe three times in a decent tone of voice. And then you better listen.

I remember in the back of my mind, he was real upset when someone had been killed. My dad got hurt several times. In what he called these "little accidents." Which would have put a normal man away. Like he was throwing his binders up over his load and he couldn't snap it loose. So he walked around to the other side of the load to unhook it. And some jerk walked by and snapped the binder.

The chain came down and hit my dad in the mouth, and it knocked his teeth out. He was back to work the next day.

He got hurt at the mill one time, when he was putting his trailer back up on the top of his truck, to go back for another load. They were using a tractor with the gaff hook to put the trailer up, and the gaff hooked my dad in the back of the leg and swung him up in the air. Put a big gash in the back of his leg, just above his knee. I think he missed a day that time. But he wasn't off work very long. Truck transmission fell on his head once.

Dad encouraged other young people in the business. In fact, we've got a real close family friend now that I still go see, and I beg him to take me on his truck. I don't think I have the balls for it. In the wintertime the roads are slick and muddy. We've slid down a couple of hills and I didn't like that. Even though Dad assured me we were safe. I mean, I could tell he was scared when we were doing this. You know, he says, "Gonna be OK. Don't worry. Don't cry. We're fine." And we got down the hill just fine, and once we were down there, he'd leave me at the shop. He'd go up for his next load, but he wouldn't take me again. So I knew he was concerned. Even my mom, when she was driving log truck with Dad, if the roads were bad, someone else would bring the truck down off of the landing for her.

During my freshman year I started working after school. I had a boyfriend. We were "in love." [*Laughs*] We decided to get married. We broke up. I married someone else like within three months. I was fifteen years old, and my parents let me get married. My mom let me get married. My dad just sat real silent. But basically I did it to get away from home. I wasn't a very smart teenager, because then I moved next door. [*Laughs*] I still had to put up with my mother. I still took care of her. And then I was trying to take care of my own family at home. Within a year and a half, we started our family.

When I left school in my freshman year, I left in the middle of the year because I already had enough credits to go to high school. But they wouldn't let me go over without putting three years in at junior high. I said, "But I've got my credits." They told me to take art classes. I didn't want to take art classes. So I dropped out. I was planning on going to high school the next fall, but by then I was married, and just shined it.* I had my first child when I was sixteen. My mom died about six hours later.

---

*As in "shined it on"—a West Coast expression meaning "just let it go" or "didn't pay any attention to it." *B. B.*

B. B.   What was your husband doing at that time?

Ellen   Drugs. Lots of drugs. I was working. I did motel work. Yard work.

And then we moved to Gold Beach, and he got a job on a ranch. It was beautiful. We had our second baby there. Basically things were going fairly well as far as the marriage working out. Except that I was just so dissatisfied. I felt like I couldn't respect this man anymore. And I was just so unhappy with my own life. I didn't understand some of the emotions and feelings I was having.

He decided he didn't like the ranch anymore. He decided he didn't like to work anymore. And I decided, Well, we can be on welfare at home, so we came back here and I dumped him. Quickly. I started working doing landscaping with a friend. Five bucks an hour, under the table. And by paying me under the table, I could afford to pay a babysitter. [*Laughs*] I stayed on welfare because it was under the table. So I could afford to pay a couple hundred dollars a month rent, pay the babysitter, and work. I didn't get rich. 'Cause welfare, it's like three hundred twenty-five a month.

After Mom died, I was forced to start to deal with my dad. I don't think that I'd've ever got to know my dad and to rediscover the relationship that we had when I was a child had it not been that my mom died and I got some one-on-one time with him.

I had forgotten about all the times on the truck. And I'd forgotten I was his favorite kid. Which explained a lot, as far as there was a lot of sibling rivalry and I never understood why my sister hated me quite so severely. But after listening to some stories of the things she experienced, it was easier to understand.

I was molested when I was five. That happened at the shop where the trucks were. It was a Saturday, and Dad and I were greasing trucks. It was neat, because they had those creepy-crawlers. And I would get down on those and I would scoot around like this huge skateboard. And get grease in my hair, and grease on my elbows, and grease everywhere.

And Dad gave me seventy-five cents and sent me to the Pit Stop Restaurant, which was just up the road, for a milkshake. It was just up this little dirt path. I'd done it several times all by myself, so he had no worry or quarrel about letting me go this time.

I was walking up the road. There was a man in the ditch. He started to talk to me. Mom had taught me to be polite, and I answered some questions for him. And he asked me if would come down and sit next to him in the ditch. And I, well, that won't hurt anything. He's just lonesome.

So I sat down next to him, and he put his arm around me and told me I was a pretty little girl. And he'd give me a quarter if I'd let him squeeze me.

Easy quarter. . . . And the second quarter was if I could squeeze him back. And it just kept getting a little further and a little further. By the time I left the ditch, I was a buck and a half richer. But I knew that I was in trouble.

I jumped up and back on the road. I looked towards the shop, and my dad was outside watching. Our eyes met. I thought, I'm in big trouble. I just took off and ran up to the restaurant. Dad came up a few minutes later.

I was so ashamed, because I knew what I had done was wrong. And I felt that it was my fault.

Dad came in, and I hadn't even gotten my milkshake yet. And he had sent me with plenty of time to almost be done by now. He asked me how come I wasn't done. I couldn't look at him. He asked me where I got the extra money. I just shrugged my shoulders.

He was real quiet. He talked to the waitress and told me to stay where I was at, and he left for a little bit. When he came back, he said, "Come on. We're going to go home."

And nothing else was said. You know, I was only five years old. I didn't realize until later what had happened. I do remember the police being out at the house later that night. Talking to Dad. It was regarding an accident that had happened at the shop. Evidently that man got roughed up real bad, if not killed. My dad was fiercely protective of me.

See, my sister Karen never heard the story about the abuse. Couple of years ago, when her and I were talking about this, she got real upset. She said that a man had been ran over. Of course, the man was intoxicated and just wandered out in front of the truck, and there was nothing my dad could do.

But a couple of years later, when one of Dad's friends was messing with Karen, Karen went to Mom and she said, "This man will keep his hands off of me." And Mom turned to Karen and she said, "Karen Sue, don't you cause no shit."

You see, I'm thoroughly convinced that man was either dead or was hurt real bad. Because he messed with me. And Mom was afraid that if Dad found out somebody was messing with Karen, he probably would end up going to prison. So Karen took that as, you know, "It's OK to be messed with. Just don't cause any trouble." So that started a whole life of abuse for Karen. "Don't cause no shit." So Karen thought, "Well, then it must be OK."

Working on the landscaping was a fun time because I had finally left my husband. I worked for one whole summer. Then nobody wants landscaping in December, so I went to work at the Southwestern mill. I worked for a very short time — maybe three months or so — and I was developing some health problems. I was pulling planer chain. Which is like one or two steps below greenbelt.

When you pull greenchain, that's where they bring the logs in and they slab them up. It's heavy, and they've still got bark on them. Those boards can weigh hundreds and hundreds of pounds. The only way that you can do this is because they're coming down on a belt that has rollers. So you can roll them down off of the belt and right into the pile that you're stacking. If you're quick and you know what you're doing. If not, you just get smashed.

And the planer chain is after they have been barked, but before they have been sanded. We're talking like two inches thick and twelve inches wide. And real long. It was heavy work. I was the only woman on the chain.

I had to have a hysterectomy. I just knew it hurt to pull planer chain. So I quit my job. Which was real hard. That was ten dollars an hour. That was ten years ago.

Welfare sent me to CETA, and I went to work for an office. Which might have been OK, but there was just enough of my dad in me to know that, man, I was not going to work inside. I was not cut out for office work. My office didn't even have a window. So it was just crazy.

I guess after that I went to work in one of the little cut-stock places out in White City, where they make molding for doors and such. The pay was really lousy — four fifty an hour. Benefits? They let you go to work every day. [*Laughs*] Other than that, they gave you a turkey at Thanksgiving.

It was real hard. It was real tedious. It was hot inside the plant. It was monotonous to where you just thought you were going to die. I would come in in the morning, and punch in on the time clock, and sit down at this dirty old picnic table — it was covered with dust and sawdust and mold. Then the first thing that we would do is go over to the cutting saw — there would be like fifteen- or twenty-foot-long strips of molding that we would have to cut out the bad spots.

There was little blocks of two-by-fours. I still don't know what they did with them. You had to stack them according to their size. It was called a "round table." It was this huge, like a thirty-foot round table. And it just went around and around and around. And you stood in one spot, 'cause the wood always came back to you. And you would just pick blocks up off of the round table and stack them according to size. That's it. For about six hours a day. You could get almost motion-sick trying to keep up with that. The job would just drive you nuts. It was really hard and you got splinters. Splinters were a way of life. That place went through a lot of people. Men and women.

When I was working at the cut-stock company, I think I kicked into survival mode. Because I just did what I was supposed to do and then I came home. And that was basically it. And then I got a job at BluPak, which was the charcoal plant. They made charcoal briquets. Now it's the SureFire plant. It's gone through several different changes. It was SureFire, then a national timber company, then BluPak, and then SureFire bought it back. SureFire is a big company. They've got plants in White City, in Florida, in Wisconsin, and three or four more plants. All these plants made briquets.

I had been in a relationship with an older man. I was twenty and he was forty-seven at the time. He was an alcoholic, and he had become abusive, and he had been unfaithful in our relationship, and I was really looking for a way out. Well, financially, I just couldn't afford it. And I got a job at BluPak, and that basically changed my life for a few years, because that paid eight-fifty an hour. But it was hard work. That was by far the hardest work I've ever done.

They manufactured and bagged the briquets right there at the plant. I worked the bagging line. So the briquets, they'd come out of this huge chute that was on the roof. They put them in ten-pound bags. Then the sewing machine would sew it up, and they'd come down the belt where they would be stacked.

The ten-pound bags would be put in a huge baler bag — it's like a big paper sack that held five ten-pound bags. So the bags were fifty-pound bags, and they would come off the line about, well, let's see . . . I could do a pallet, which would have been twenty bags — I could do a pallet in about a minute and a half. Pallet after pallet. Ten hours a day, four days a week. I was there for three years and I hurt my back. So that's why I'm not doing that work anymore.

I was on Workman's Compensation for over a year while I waited for my back to heal. And it never really healed a hundred percent. [*Sighs*] So the insurance company packed me up and moved me to Eugene. And I was retrained in an optical lab. And I hated it. Hated it with a passion.

I moved back to Medford. I started waiting tables. Good tips.

Twenty dollars a night was pretty normal. If you got put in the banquet room, you could make forty-five dollars. I waited tables through the summer, and then in the fall I got a job at a veterans' facility. I was working in the cafeteria, as a cashier.

It's real funny, because I had forgotten or buried that first abuse issue. And hadn't thought about it in years and years and years. And when I went to work at this place, I was polite and cheerful. But if a man came through that line who had been drinking, my whole attitude changed. My whole everything. That could ruin my day. He didn't even have to say hello — if I smelt whiskey, I was just done for the day. And it wasn't until I went through some real deep soul-searching that I remembered that first abuse issue. I remember that man who had been drinking. So it made it a little more bearable once I realized what it was that I was doing — what was triggering that. I could deal with it.

It was a government job, and that pays six dollars an hour. I had good benefits. Vacation time. Health insurance. I had good health insurance at BluPak's, too. But as far as the job itself, I didn't really care for the job. You know, I'm really accustomed to working with men. But you get women together, and they bicker, they gossip, there's backbiting. And that was just real common. So I worked there two years, I think.

When I started working at BluPak's, it just consumed me physically. And trying to work and date, I just couldn't manage. My oldest boy was having a real hard time dealing with the divorce. So he went to spend the summer with his dad. And then he started kindergarten with his dad. And then it was first grade. And he just wants to stay with his dad.

During the time that I was at the cafeteria, I was really going through some emotional changes. I had just gotten out of a two-year relationship with a man who was very physically abusive. And very heavy into crank — crank is a monster that destroys homes.

We had separated, and it was the first time that I had ever been single. The first time that there never was a man around. Because at fifteen I left my mother's home and was married. And after that, if I wasn't married, I had a boyfriend. And there was a lapse — it caused me to have to look at myself, and that was very uncomfortable for me. I didn't really like what I saw.

That was a real special year for me. I did a lot of soul-searching. I got real close to God. There's a lot of healing that took place. I dealt with a lot of the abuse issues, a lot of the emotional issues.

But I've been single ever since this older guy and I broke up. He was the crankster that I was talking about. The first few months of that was really hard for me. I questioned what was wrong with me, that I was single. But as I got through that year, I became very close to the Lord. I started to have some of these memories again — so many of these memories were just bottled up and put away and I wouldn't allow myself to remember. Because that hurt!

But then I could remember things like Mrs. Ross, who was the lady who took us to Sunday school every Sunday. And how she was so patient when she tried to teach me piano. And she was the one who taught me how to pray. She taught me how to crochet. She taught me how to bake cookies. She was a real special lady.

The church I go to, the pastor is just a real casual kind of guy who shares the Gospel. Jesus Christ crucified. That's it. Not a lot of law. Not a lot of "do's" and "don't's." He teaches if you're in love with the Lord, you won't be doing the "don't's." You'll be too busy doing the "do's" to be worried about the "don't's." [*Laughs*] So it works out.

Then I put an ad in the paper. I started cleaning houses for six bucks an hour, so that was OK, but that's not what I want to do all my life. It killed my back. I'm having a real hard time with it even now, and I'm not working. So.

Since my job was under the table, I would have still been eligible for food stamps. I had a medical card, too. And that's when a new welfare program came open. They talked to me about that and I told them, "Yes, I would be interested." I never, ever thought I would be back in school — especially college, because I quit school in my freshman year. So I spent a couple of weeks getting my GED. And then I thought, Well, maybe college is a reality. Maybe I could do that. And I've been real pleased with my progress.

Being on welfare, it's really kind of degrading. Sometimes humiliating. To have to deal with those people. I'm sure that it's not those people — I'm sure that it's that program. [*Sighs*] You know, it's like, I'm working under the table sometimes, so that I can make ends meet. So that I can feed my family. And I don't see where that should be any kind of offense to someone. I'm not trying to get rich at their expense.

The three hundred sixty-five dollars they give me, even now — let's take a look at my present situation. I had been renting a house for the last year and a half. I paid two hundred seventy-five dollars a month for a one-bedroom trailer. For my son and I. The light bill was thirty-five or forty dollars. There was a phone bill that was forty dollars — and that's no long distance, that's just your phone bill. We had car insurance that was sometimes paid, sometimes not. It was just kind of, "Am I going to get hit this month or what?" So the car insurance is hit and miss. There's gas to get back and forth. Now, already I've ran out of three hundred sixty-five dollars.

This program started out looking really optimistic. Now I can't help but feel like they really fed us full of bullshit. Because they came in with big promises: Nobody's going to bother you, there'll be training programs, there'll be money for car expenses, babysitting expenses. We're going to get you out of this mess, and then you'll never have to be on welfare again.

And the whole program is in the toilet now. I'm clinging by the skin of my teeth to, hopefully, I get to continue college. If not, I'll find another way to do it. If the program goes down and I go to school, I'll be sanctioned. A sanction is when they take my name off of the welfare grant. I am no longer eligible. The only one who would be eligible for assistance in my home would be my son. So instead of three hundred sixty-five dollars a month, they would knock me down to, I think, a hundred and a quarter. Because I go to school. I guess if I just stayed home and was on welfare that would be OK.

I've never been one to stay at home. Not that I wouldn't like to try it. Not that I wouldn't like to be married and have a husband that left every morning for work and be a housewife. But I'm secure enough with myself that I don't have to jump into the first bad relationship that happens down the road. This time I am really being careful about the next man in my life.

B. B.   What changes have you seen in the area?

Ellen   The Mall. [*Laughs*] The mill situation in White City, I guess. I can remember that Dad never had trouble finding a place to leave his load. In fact, he never had trouble finding work. People would call three or four a night and want his trucks the next morning. He'd say, "I can't. I'm on another job. I'll be there as soon as I can." Now that doesn't happen anymore for people.

Some of the big mills that Dad and I used to haul into are shut down. The big mill pond out in White City is empty. The little Tolo lumber mill is gone. It's just like a ghost town. Coronet Lumber in Central Point, sometimes it's there, sometimes it's not.

This is so shallow, you know, but at this point it's not really affect-ing me personally. Economy-wise. But as far as nostalgic reasons, I guess that it bothers me more. It bothers me to go by the pond in White City and see it empty. Even when my kids were young, we used to go out there and park across the street and watch them knock the logs down off the truck and into the pond. And I miss that.

And it's so grown up. I remember driving through Medford and thinking, If my mom was still around, she'd just be lost. The Big Y was the place to shop. It was your everything store — grocery store, variety store, shoe store, hardware store. And it's empty. And there's a mall across the street, which is real big and impersonal. And you've got orange-haired teenagers. [*Laughs*] Hanging around, smoking cigarettes, and looking cool. Wasting days.

We have such a convenient life these days. I mean, we go to the grocery store, we buy our food. We come home and we cry because it takes forty-five seconds to warm it up in the microwave. What happened to the family garden?

I don't really see where church is an answer to the problem. It might develop a lot of hypocrites. Personally, for me, Jesus was a big answer in my life. He pulled a lot of things together for my family, for me personally. I don't want to push my religion down anyone's throat, but I can't stress the difference it's made in my life. I just hope that it's a witness.

When you study our country's history, people came here for freedom of religion. For freedom of speech. Freedom of expression. And it just seems to me that that has been so turned around, now. It's been turned so that we came here for free choice, and that means that we should be able to kill our babies before they're born — that that's what this country was founded on. I beg to differ with that. There's something terribly wrong as far as "I'll do my thing and you do your thing" type attitude that is so prevalent in the community. Everything is OK in your own eyes.

Because when my mom would get sick, we didn't have to call the neighbors for help. They were there. You knew your neighbors by name. And you knew their families. I'm not in a position like that anymore. And I can't think of anybody that is. Whether they live right in the city or out in the country. I'm just as guilty as everyone else.

The changes in the economy don't affect me a lot. I'm already unemployed! What are you going to take away from me? [*Laughs*] I'm not saying it's not hurting me, because I don't know any different. I was born and raised here. People come, transplants come in, and they say, "There's no money here. How did you guys live?" I say, "Well, eat beans. Lots of beans!" And that's OK. I've never known anything else.

They say there's no money here. There's no entertainment here. There's no big culture. And I think that's all OK, really. Keeps a lot of the transplants out! [*Laughs*] I'd just as soon not see you coming.

But they come in looking for, I don't know — cowboys and Indians? For Little House on the Prairie? They don't find it here. Some go back to the city.

The new people say about us everything from, "They're much friendlier than people from the big city," to, we're "sheltered." Naive maybe. For instance, the crankster I went with came from the big city. And he implied that I was naive about life in general. That I'd never left my nest. So how could I know about anything that he'd want to talk about. And he was a crank monster — give me a break! All he wanted to talk about was the drug.

The circle of friends that I chose to run with for a few years, I've learned a lot. I've learned enough to know I don't want to know no more. I've learned it's like a sixth sense. An intuition. When I hear certain slang, or see a certain behavior, the red light goes out, and I'm real careful.

For a few years I moved with a crowd to where I felt that my personal safety was in jeopardy. In fact it was. But I've moved out of that crowd. I've got clearer vision. And I don't know — maybe I am naive. I live in a small town. I leave my car unlocked at night. My front door doesn't lock. I can send my kid to the store and I don't worry about him. If I lived in Medford, I wouldn't do any of those things.

B. B. What about the timber situation?

Ellen I've got a couple of different views on this, I guess. For one thing, I see a couple of bare hillsides, mountainsides. I think those maybe could have been poor judgment calls or something. But all and all, there's a lot of trees. But on the other hand, twenty years ago I can remember that a load of logs were three logs. Three logs if they weren't big. [*Laughs*] And now they come down out of the hills, and a load of logs is twenty. I've sat behind log trucks at stoplights and couldn't count the logs before the light turned green. So the big timber isn't coming anymore. It's not coming down if it's there.

The spotted owl, I think, is kind of a hype. I really don't think that that little bird ought to keep the loggers from feeding their families. I don't think that's OK.

It's not a big issue with me. Because I have a hard time taking the environmentalists real seriously. There's bigger things. Not that what they're doing is not important, and I appreciate the fact that they're taking a stand and staying behind it, as citizens, as that goes. But I don't think they see the picture as a whole. The timber industry feeds this community. I guess we could shut down all the mills and make them all prisons. We could do that, huh?

But the environmentalists — I think that everybody needs a cause, but it would have been nice if they had looked a little further for one. There are big things to be concerned about, you know? Saving an owl isn't one of them. We've got kids starving to death. We've got kids that are getting into some serious trouble. We need work. We need to do what is in front of us.

I was staying in the valley for the longest time because my dad was here. My dad died two years ago. I think I am here now because I haven't had the opportunity to leave. But I'm not sure what I would do when I left the area. I like to write. I like to go up in the hills and just sit. Some people would say that my social life is lacking, and I don't see that at all. Not at all.

If you're real still sitting in the woods, you can see a lot. I used to like to go up on the log landing and sit in one spot and see how much I could see from that one spot. There was the obvious things, like the chipmunks and an occasional deer. But what you didn't see were the spiders, and the earwigs, and the beetles. I remember discovering that in a pond we had out behind the barn. I would look down into the water. There were like these little red spots that were bugs. And little tiny things. And the polywogs were giants — they were like whales.

I picture myself as kind of a bumpkin that just kind of does what she has to, to get by. It seems like life has really been kind of a survival test. And some people can live life and be comfortable about it. And it just seems like I've been in a position most of my life to where it's a struggle. One day at a time. From one paycheck to the next.

People with savings accounts! And retirement funds. And a car that has insurance and runs every day. [*Laughs*] Those things are really foreign to me. And it would be nice to be there, I think. But I don't know that this valley has that to offer to me. Especially not right now. Especially with a bad back. Because I did the mill work for a while, and that's not an opportunity for me anymore. And I don't want to work in an office.

NATHAN CULLENBACH   (age 41) Nathan is a floor supervisor at a Rogue Valley plant. He agreed to this fragment of interview as long as nothing got too personal. Among the big mills and other large companies in the Rogue Valley is Litton Industries, a guidance-control electronic assembly plant that supplies some of the assembly for the Cruise missile. At the time, Litton employed up to six hundred people. Most of these companies are owned by transnational or other integrated corporations. Litton announced the closure of its main plant in March 1993. Nathan's plant was a target for closure in 1994.

I was born in southwest Oregon.

I enjoy working with people. I get myself in trouble sometimes because I am on the side of the workers a lot. So I make waves and want the top levels of management to be honest. Remember that their workers are people, too. Can't shit on them and expect to have good, long-term employees.

We used to have three shifts. It went down to two, and then it got really slow in the area, and we went down to one. It was around 1982, somewhere there. Everybody was wondering what was going to happen next.

Then we got sold. Conrad was a real family-oriented corporation. We had picnics, and would go out for beer and pizza. Really a close-knit place. But then they got sold, and things kind of fell apart.

We sold to Associated Industries. From Texas or wherever. He bought all of Conrad, which included GP Plywood. And he had said, when the timber's gone, he's selling. Four or five years ago. We were real lucky that somebody came along and bought us from him.

He didn't want us. We didn't have any resources like the Conrad lumber part of it. He wanted the Conrad timber. They were well known for their reforestation and everything. Conrad was out there replanting and cutting their own timber. Not going out and buying anybody else's. We were real lucky to get out from under Associated, because he would have closed us down.

At the time it was pretty tough. I had a buddy that was working at GP Plywood. He said he needed to start looking for another job. It was rumored that it would be five years, and that place would be shut down. And it was. It was real close to five years.

I get irritated when people in the area forget the comments that were made way back when. That didn't have anything to do with the Silver Fire, or the owl. It was already predestined as far as I'm concerned. It wouldn't have mattered. Just a snowball effect.

We got bought out by Zephyr, which is a really good company.

Big! Zephyr has more money. They're into growth. And modernizing things. If we can prove to them that our efficiency is going to go up, we can buy anything we want. New machinery, whatever it takes. They don't care, as long as we can make them more money.

Which was never the case with Conrad, 'cause they didn't have the money to give us. It was a nice family unit, a good place to work for, but as far as growing, we were about as big as we were going to get.

Now the Germans own us. So, it's big. I think we're number four or something like that in the United States in our business. So we're trying for number one. That is what their goal is. They make every- thing — microwaves, televisions, chainsaws, refrigerators. They aren't a wood products company. It's a big corporation that is buying everything in the United States.

You can't expect them to be family. We did have corporate heads come here last year. They came in and introduced themselves and talked about what their goals were for us. I thought that was good, to have these guys come to this little small town. The head guy showed a great desire in wanting to make us be successful. And he wasn't a bull- shitter — he was very direct. He knows he can get it done, or else they don't want us.

The changes that are taking place are hard changes, but they're for the better. I think it's one of the better-paying places in this area.

We own another plant up north that gets the raw wood in. It's al- ready in board foot, and they make it into custom dimensions. We or- der it from them. We get stuff that's already been planed. It's oak and alder. We get our oak from the Midwest. And the alder is from the Pa- cific Northwest. The big joke was, we're hoping that the owl didn't go into the oak forest, because we'd be in trouble.

I don't like to talk about the spotted owl issue with people on the floor because I get irritated. We need to be working, so we don't do po- litical stuff. I know pretty much everybody's views. It's understood that you just don't talk about it.

A lot of the people I work with, they're narrow-minded. They can only see one way. It's an absolute fact that it's this way, and they can't see any other alternatives. Somebody says, "The loggers are all starving, we *have* to do it." There's other ways — let's look at the other ways. But I'm not really involved in it.

I probably will be doing this job long-term until they get rid of me. I would like to get into some kind of counseling program. I think we need it at work. They'd pay for it, so I don't know why I'm not doing it. Our company's growing, and we need that kind of opportunity for the people that work there. We've been confronted with so many personal problems, and nobody knows how to deal with them. From child abuse to alcoholism to drug addition to sexual abuse.

They say, "It's paid for, go see a shrink." But you need somebody in the company. You know — somebody might flip out while they're working. Who knows? And they just need to sit down and talk. They're so fearful of losing their job when they're going through personal problems that they start screwing up. They need to know people are there to listen. Instead of, "Hey! You missed three days of work. You're fired!" You can't do that anymore. There's just too much going on.

We've stuck our heads in the sand and ignored the situation that's going on. We've just now started drug testing for new applications. And I think that's OK. But it doesn't say anything for the ones that are already on the inside. We just had an incident where a guy got hurt which I figure was related to drugs. He's in a rehabilitation program, and hopefully he's going to straighten out with that.

The drug part of it was a lot more open way back when. We'd take speed to get a certain amount of production out. It was common knowledge, because it wasn't wrong, really — at that point. You just pass out the beans, and everybody'd go for it and break records and get the work out and have fun doing it.

Now it's a lot more hidden, private. Different drugs. Now it's coke and whatnot. You know where to go. I know where to go if I needed anything. And you don't want to lose those people. You don't really want the boss to say, "OK, you're fired because of all this stuff." You don't want to do that, since it's not affecting you, and then you don't do anything about it at all. There are some people trying to do something about it, but they can't catch them. You know — the word's out.

'Cause they used to go into the bathroom and cut up their coke on the toilet paper cover. I'd go in there and I'd see all of it. 'Course the people that were doing that are gone now. At least I haven't seen any "left over." But I thought, you know, that's bad when you've gotta be doing that while you're working, and all the time.

I think we've got a bigger problem in this area. The people who are making the stuff, and the growers. We've got a problem with our children! If we've got that big of a problem where I work, we're not unique — we're not the only ones in the area that have that problem.

See, I was involved in it some. I never got off on it — coke or crank or any of that. I did it now and then. It cost too much money. And I just didn't like it that much. You'd go to parties. And people'd go into the bathroom and be sneaky, when you knew what they were doing. Geez! The bathroom scene is always the big deal.

Yeah, and we have to deal with illiteracy, too. I guess factory work has a lot of that. Because there isn't anyplace else to go, and it's repetitious work. Those kind of problems can be hidden.

RALPH PENDLESON   (age 35) Ralph Pendleson epitomizes environ-mental contradictions: One of the only interviewees to express blanket ap-proval of clearcutting, and an ardent opponent of spotted owl closures, he is equally supportive of Headwaters, a local environmental group, and the more radical efforts of the international group Greenpeace to protect fish habitat.

Saving wild fish runs is the 1990s flashpoint issue in the Pacific North-west, where activists are fighting irrigation drawdowns, logging practices, and fish impediments like dams by means of the Endangered Species Act.

Ralph is lanky and handsome in a casual, country way. He speaks with passion about the thing he cares about the most: going fishing.

I was born in Oklahoma in 1954. My daddy was in the service for twenty-two years, so we kind of got moved around. We lived mostly on Army bases. I really never was enthused too much about school. Like when I was in high school in Grants Pass, I'd skip school just to go fishing. We had to change busses in the morning. Well, me and my friend, we'd always get off the first bus, ditch it, and head for one of the parks, because we always had our poles stashed in the berries down there. But I never could take any fish home, because they'd definitely know what happened. I let them go. I still do. Probably ninety-five per-cent I catch I let go. I do it just mainly for sport.

I started tenth grade here. Grants Pass High. I was here earlier with my grandfather, for the summer. And I liked the area. He'd take me around fishing here and there. I've just never really cared for the cities, even like going through town here. I'll go around town instead of going through it.

I used to go fish with my grandfather a lot. Salmon, they get so thick at times they're just flopping and rolling. They'll get to jumping at times just playing around, I guess. Several times I've almost had them jump right in the boat. I've gotten wet from them.

My mom and dad were both raised in the country in the North-west, and they just pretty much stuck to it, and we did, too. I think there's less trouble in the country. And with the drug situation, I'm glad.

When we first came to Grants Pass, it was kind of like just another place. Just a matter of how long I was going to stay here. But my folks decided they wanted to set their roots here. Because my grandmother originally was born here. We'd come back and visit family. My folks got to where they liked the area. Because they kind of grew up in the hills themselves. Myself, the mountains are OK, but I'm kinda more used to a little more flatland. Because trying to get around these mountains can be something else at times. Just up–down, up–down. But I enjoy the fishing here. The fisheries are pretty good. Has kind of decreased the past five years due to the population. There's so many people from California moving here.

When I was in high school, I had a motorcycle. So I was able to get around everywhere. I'd take my fishing pole with me. Find a good fishing hole, stop and try it for a while. Then cruise on to the next place and try it. Just gotten to know where the good places are.

When my dad was overseas, in Korea and 'Nam, we'd go to church just because he was gone, but otherwise we really never went that much.

Boy Scouts, all us boys went through. I think out of all organizations, I learned more in Boy Scouts than I have even in school. Just being able to take care of yourself, really — even by yourself, if you had to, for survival. Or first aid. CPR. Lifeguard. I was actually a certified lifeguard when I was about twelve or thirteen.

We used to always go camping, at least once a month. And then we'd have our summer camp in the summer for a week. To this day, if I was to go back in age, I'd go back to when I was eleven years old so I could join Boy Scouts again.

I got into hunting. Duck hunting. And pheasant. Never really went for big game because, for the expenses, like just to go deer hunting is just unreal anymore. For gas and everything else you spend. You'd buy half a beef by the time you're done. And it's a lot better eating. [*Laughs*]

But, myself, I like to go duck hunting. With the drift boat, we just float the river, and they just look at us, till it's too late. You know, like, "Well, are you going to throw popcorn? Or lead?" And I don't feed the ducks.

Planned on finishing high school. Really didn't know what I wanted to do. I took welding. I took woodshop. The automotive department was my favorite, though. It was kind of up in the air. Just trying to figure out what I really wanted to do. I was into fishing.

I went into the service. The military's just full of dope and drugs anymore. One of my co-workers just happened to be into pot and got me started. And there it went.

After I got out, and I was going to community college, someone mentioned to a few of us that there was this mill that had some openings for part-time swingshift. And it was just pulling chain off the planer for about four to six hours in the evening. So we started down there, and it lasted about eight months. And then I went to work in

Medford. And when that slacked off, I go down to the mill and see the superintendent, and he says, "Well, come back and see me in about a week." So I did and got a job. Working swingshift. On the fingerjoint machines. Just gluing blocks of pine or Doug fir or whatever back together to any length desired, to use for molding or door frames or whatever. There's no heat drying into it, it's just a matter of pressing it. The glue joint itself was actually stronger than the wood. 'Cause we'd try to break the boards by hitting them on the floor, and the wood would break first.

It takes a lot of coordination. Especially feeding the machine. 'Cause, well, you can be feeding anything from seventy to a hundred and fifty blocks a minute. Into what they call a lug chain, so it cuts the ends. The lug chain puts the fingers in the end of the block. And then it would go through what they call assembly press. It's just a person standing there just putting them together on these rollers. As they would go through the press. And it would hit a microswitch that would cut the board to any length that we set the machine for, and it would press it.

It was interesting at first. It kind of grew on me. And I got to where I was doing all three jobs on the machine — feeding lugs, feeding the press, and the offbearer, which would just stack the lumber as it come out of the press.

And then one day I was up feeding lugs and smashed my hand in the lug chain. So I went and had that taken care of and came back to work the next day, and my boss says, "Well, what do you want to do? Clean up, tail off, or try forklift?" I says, "I could drive." So he started teaching me, and I drove from there for eleven years.

I was constantly busy. I'm not one to just stand around. 'Cause it's just not me. For a while I'd work through the whole mill and all the different departments. That's where I got to know the whole system of it.

But then the business finally slacked off, mainly due to the price of lumber. For the most part it was the price. Other companies back East, and Canada, can supply the wood so much cheaper anymore. And then for a while the price of lumber — they would sell their product for almost what they paid for the lumber. They could just not get the price they needed for it. I talked to a few of my friends down there the other day, and they kinda give the mill about six months. Mainly just due to the supply of lumber. And the price. They just can't afford it. Making too many changes down there, just not making a profit.

I've seen change in the mill go from molding to door manufacturing. What they call a secondary wood product. And that's where the fingerjoint machines come in, 'cause they would take blocks of wood with solid knots in them. And would use that for door stock. They would run it through the molders to surface it. And they would glue clear Doug fir edge strips on the sides. Then glue clear strips of veneer on the faces. To where it looked like a clear, solid piece of wood. But inside it's nothing but knots. They're using junk for prime material. And then you wonder why these houses cost so much anymore, the stuff that goes into them.

I've been in veneer plants — a few of my friends worked there — and they'd leave a lot of gaps in the veneer. In the pressing system. And just putty the ends to cover it up. And then you wonder why half this veneer comes apart with a little moisture. The chipboard anymore is better than the plywood we're supplying. 'Cause they use just such a high-density glue.

B. B. Do they make chipboard around here?

Ralph No. 'Cause most of the chips go to the coast. Mostly for paper anymore. Then I know one paper mill did shut down over there. But the price of chips going overseas — they're paying twice as much for it overseas than what we're getting for it. And Japan, they'll buy all the chips they can get. Oak, pine, fir — it doesn't matter.

B. B. What do you think about the changes in the area?

Ralph Just gotten to be too many people move here from California. Buying all the river property. Anymore, to go fishing, the only place to get to the river is mainly at the parks. County and state parks, and then there's really not enough of those. And then there's just big dead calm holes there. Most of your fish are in the riffle areas. And that's all in between. And with all the private property, most people just don't want you going through their yard. Which I don't blame them.

There's a mobile-home park on the river that ever since we moved here, I'd been going through there for like fifteen years. Ride my motorcycle or drive my truck through there. I'd even take my dog at times. The manager I had talked to quite a few times. He'd even ask me how I did fishing down there. He said it was OK to go down there. There was never any problems. Everyone kept it clean.

And one day I went to go fishing down there, and some man stopped me and asked me where I was going. And I says, "I'm going down there to go fishing."

And he says, "No you're not."

And I just says, "Well, why not?"

And he says, "Well, I'm the new park manager. You live here?"
"No."

"Then you're definitely not going down here. Not unless you live here or you have relatives here. No one's allowed down here anymore that doesn't live in the park. I'm shutting her down."

So him and I got into a little squabble over it. He's from California. He'd taken care of some mobile-home park down there, and thought he'd move up here.

I know many, many people who go down there fishing, and some of the retired folks that live there knew me by face real well. They'd come down there and see how I was doing, even.

I'm not much for salmon fishing. But I can catch them, no problem. Steelhead's my favorite. So I'd go down there fishing for summer steelhead, when the fall Chinook are in real thick, and I'd accidently hook into a fall Chinook, and you know, some of the people'd be watching. And I say, "Well, anybody want to fight this fish?" And they'd all jump up at once. Myself, I enjoy seeing other people catch fish more than I do catching it.

Guy closed it off for us, and no one's allowed down there. So the only way to it is by boat. Anymore if you don't have a sled boat or a drift boat, you're really limited where you can go. Unless you go way downriver. But then you've got a lot of walking and climbing to do, because of the canyons.

But like my one daughter, last year she hooked her first summer steelhead. And lost her first steelhead. And she still to this day has what we call steelhead fever. Once you hook one, you're hooked. She was just bouncing her bait along, daydreaming, and it hit her so hard and fast she didn't realize what was going on until I told her, "You've got one of my babies on there!" She seen it come up, and she just about went hysterical. And she was just using a little trout pole, and the little reels — they're either all drag or no drag. And when that fish tried to take off, it just happened to be all drag, so it just — that fast — was over. And her face just fell in the river. And to this day, she still wants to use that fish club and my stick on the next one. She says, "I'm going to hit him hard!"

You can't use trouble hooks on them anymore. They all have to be single hooks, because of it snagging salmon. It's just been too much trouble, and the people just taking too much fish out. Just more people taking more fish. It's gotten to be, in Josephine and Jackson County, there's sixty to seventy guides. Which is a lot of guides when you figure two people per guide per day. Anywhere from four to eight fish, if they're doing good. Times sixty, seventy people a day? That's a lot of fish.

But all these years, I had only caught one hatchery steelhead. That was a summer steelhead last year. They clip the dorsal fin, so it's kind of deformed. But this winter — I do a lot of winter steelhead fishing — and this winter, I finally caught two hatchery winter steelhead. The first ones ever. And I caught 'em both in the same day. They looked like twins — same size, same weight. You know, I thought, Finally paid off, even for myself. Throwing all them hatcheries back. Because come next year, that's all you're going to keep, is the hatchery steelhead. And they've lowered the steelhead limit size from twenty inches down to sixteen. Over that you have to tag them, or throw it back.

Like I tell a lot of people anymore, you can always enjoy the natural high of life. You don't have to be high on drugs to enjoy the natural high. Just a matter of being clean and sober and having fun.

B. B.   What about the changes around Grants Pass?

Ralph   A lot of it's kind of depressing, really. I've even thought about relocating out of this valley. 'Cause of just so many people moving here. I'd probably move towards Puget Sound in Washington. There's a lot more work up in the Puget Sound area. In fact, one of my old bosses from Jebson sawmill is working for Pope and Talbot up in Puget Sound. He told me, if I ever need a good job — good-paying, benefits, and all — to let him know if I wanted to relocate. I would, if the economy gets any worse around here.

B. B.   You got laid off?

Ralph   Yeah. We had a mill shutdown, been about two to three years ago. Because the market just collapsed. I was off work for one week and went to work for the Jebson sawmill. It was all Japanese export. That lasted for about eight months. Then they shut down because the Japanese pulled out. They're hard people to work for. It's either perfect or not at all. It's just the way they were.

We kept improving our shipping methods and procedures, but it just could never seem to please the Japanese. They'd gripe about anything. It just gets to be so much. They had a Japanese representative there every day. And then about once a week there'd be three or four come over. And about once a month it seemed like the whole family would come over. You'd turn around and there was Japanese everywhere. And you just have to be on your toes then.

We was putting out a good product, but they were just having a hard time getting raw logs. I think a lot of it was due to price. And availability. That's when the spotted owl started to really get going with the environmentalists. And just trying to find a job site to buy logs from was getting pretty hard and slim. Most of it was private. And then, people only own several hundred acres, there's only so much timber there.

We didn't like it at all. We was making up tee shirts for open season on spotted owls, and game seasons and everything. Hats and the works, we had out there. The Japanese liked it, too. I even had a pigeon one day, we had shot, and I'd put a tag around its neck, said, "Spotted Owl." Had a rope around its neck in the forklift. The Japanese loved it.

It's really hurting the timber industry bad, 'cause if it's not spotted owls it's gonna be something else next. And it's just pretty well shut the woods down. It's gonna hurt the whole state. And everybody else around it. Because if there's no wood, there's no new home construction. Or business construction. The price is going way up. It can only go so high. And it's got to stop.

Like the old-growth timber—it's got to be harvested, or it's going to die and rot. Then you have a big fire danger. You know, it's part of a recyclable resource.

As far as the spotted owl, having to have old growth is a joke, I know for a fact. They migrate. Move around. So you take several hundred million feet of lumber out—it's a slow process, to where the wildlife knows something's going on, they got to move. Just like a fire. They move on to the next grove. They've found spotted owls in lots of second growth. And even smaller.

And as far as being protected, they're protected anyway by law. Any non-game animal or bird is protected. Except for in season. And the spotted owl is not a game bird. The way the situation's going, I think it should be.

Especially when they interfere with people's jobs. Climbing trees and get in front of log trucks and everything. I think if I was a log truck driver I'd just say, "Well, I just ran over a bump! I didn't know it was EarthFirst!" And like climbing these trees, sitting in their platform, you know, if they want to stay up there, let them stay. Drop the tree. Tell them, "Here comes EarthFirst!"

I know a lot of them are getting paid for it. It's just something to get in someone's way, I guess. Cause a ruckus and try to get their way. They're only looking at one side of the situation. And it's theirs. But toilet paper's made out of wood. Wait till they run out of that. They're going to have to use EarthFirst! Mother Nature as leaves. And I hope it's poison oak when they do. [*Laughs*]

Headwaters has done a lot of good, I think. They haven't raised all the ruckus like EarthFirst! does. All their protesting and everything. You know, their protesting doesn't get them nothing but jail time. And some of them are getting it. There's other ways to go around — getting things in the legislature or Congress to see the side they're trying to point out.

But like — oh, what's that one ship? For saving the whales and all? Greenpeace. Now, they've done a lot of good. 'Cause, like the fisheries, a lot of the problem there, too, is overseas harvest. All these giant nets they have — fifty miles long. It takes everything. That's a lot of fish. They've got proof where they're throwing dead steelhead over the ship! You know, I've caught a lot of steelhead this winter that had net marks on them. I was amazed how many. I think I only caught a couple that didn't.

B. B.   The mill laid you off again recently?

Ralph   Um-hmm. Quite a few. A good half of them are gone now.

B. B.   What are people doing?

Ralph   I know one guy, he is going to school. In pipe-laying. I know a few of them have moved out of the valley. Few have tried to find work in Medford, and Medford's getting just as bad as far as timber industry. 'Cause one of the main sources of lumber, we was getting from Double Dee Lumber in Central Point. They shut down. They can't get the logs anymore.

They're all going to have to find something else. Like on the news last night, about the timber industry and new job relocations and all — I don't see the state helping any, to help retrain all these millworkers.

You know, you're making anything from seven to twelve dollars an hour. That's fairly good wages. So you get your budget accustomed to it. House payments. Truck payments. Cars. Then kids anymore! That's another big expense. Medical bills are just outrageous. A lot of them, they have to drop down to a five-, six-dollar-an-hour job. And they wonder why people are losing their homes. And going on welfare and food stamps. They just didn't have any choice, you know. Their unemployment only lasts so long, so they have to draw welfare and food stamps just to survive. If not, what else would you do?

Yeah, I think it's going to be left to just the major big mill industries that will be left. And all the middle and little guys are going to dwindle away. They just won't be able to compete. Yeah, I think the timber industry — I'd say another five years and it's going to be just about over. Except for the big outfits. If you plan on building a home, it better be out of brick.

Clearcutting, it can be ugly for a few years, because there's nothing there. But as long as they replant it, it's been going on for years and been working out just fine. And then they can go in there and log the whole thing in another fifty years, and it's all the same size logs, pretty much. And certain mills are set up for the smaller timbers. That's what they want.

B. B.   What would you like to see for the area?

Ralph   I'd like to see them get this timber industry situated. Better management of the forest. It's a recyclable resource. They've got to take them old growth. Or they'll just get so old they'll die off, rot, bug disease. Then it's wasted. It's mulch. It's just Mother Nature's fertilizer. But with the fire danger — all that downed wood is what the Forestry goes out and tests for fire danger. And you could really care less what's standing and green — it's what's laying down, all that dead fuel wood.

BLM, all the Forestry departments, it's just a matter of getting together and managing it and seeing what does need to be taken out, or should be. And how old it is. And just keep EarthFirst! out of everyone's way so they can do their job.

Grants Pass has always been pretty much of a retirement town. But I know property around here is just actually selling good. But not to Oregonians. It's Californians that are retiring, selling their business and homes. 'Cause they can buy their homes up here for half of what they sold their home for down there.

And then they gripe 'cause California has so many taxes, and then they move up here and gripe about property tax. I told one man, I says, "They're going to get you one way or another. Don't pay taxes, there ain't going to be nothing happening." That's what keeps things running.

Years ago, camping was free. Go out in the woods and go camping and have fun. Fishing, or just goof around. Didn't cost anything. Now it's — what? Seven, nine dollars for a night? It's almost as cheap to get a motel if you want to just go out. I know my camping's stopped a lot. Not really because of money. It's just — like Jackson County, all the county parks cost you a dollar just to drive in. You know? And they have their taxes. Josephine County parks are doing just fine, really. Maintenance-wise, and beauty. But then, Jackson, they got to charge you a dollar just to drive in. To dump your boat or to go to the bathroom. It's ridiculous.

They have a seasonal amount you can pay. I know one river guide got in a big fight with the sheriff over there one time. 'Cause he didn't want to pay a dollar just to drive in to dump his boat. And that sheriff was going to arrest him. That's crazy. Here everyone pays their taxes for them parks, and then they got to charge you just to drive in or walk in. I know one of them's a quarter just to walk in.

And there'll be more of it. I can see where some of these rate fees for camping, just the cost of maintenance and everything going up. Ends got to meet somewhere. The demand's a lot. But like my wife and I, we usually just pack the drift boat and our camping gear and tent, and we just float down the river and camp out. Where it's secluded, quiet, and free.

I have taken a lot of people fishing privately. They've always enjoyed it, and we've always gotten fish. A lot of people have told me, "You ought to get your guide license." And I says, "No, it just ain't worth it anymore." With all the new fishing regulations and restrictions, and fees and insurance. The guides used to make good money. But now they make just as much as a low-paying millworker would. But even the fees for clients is gone like from fifty dollars years ago to eighty-five dollars a person per day! And you figure your limit's two fish? That's expensive fish.

I just hope something busts loose with this timber industry. There's going to be a lot of people without, and move out. I'm just kind of waiting to see where it's all going to bottom out. And what's going to start up first.

I've always gotten along good with animals, and birds and all. And when I was a kid, I kind of thought about being a veterinarian. I had thought about going to work for Fish and Game. But it's just a matter of going back to school and getting the training. I'd rather get training and knowledge, 'cause why do something you don't enjoy? You're not going to be happy with it, you know?

CAROLINE COLDBROOK   (age 41) Caroline Coldbrook summarizes the current economic situation, including the beginnings of a "runaway industry" movement, as some timber companies transfer their economic focus to the U.S. South and the Southern Hemisphere. In addition, she turns a critical eye on the old idea that "women's issues" are separate from "real" economic development issues.

In 1992 Oregon became infamous across the country for a statewide initiative mandating discrimination against homosexuals. Complicated resentments arising from battles over the environment and gentrification crossed over into the fight against this anti–civil rights measure, and the issue became even more polarized and murky. Stereotypes of "pinko faggot environmentalists" were pitted against stereotypes of "bigoted redneck logger types." Measure 9 lost statewide but was approved by wide margins throughout rural regions.

We sat in Caroline's back yard, which was full of flowers, ornamental trees, and vegetable plots. She spoke with a droll mix of experience, hope, and exasperation.

I was born in Klamath Falls in 1949. My parents lived in Cartwright, Oregon. My grandparents had moved to the Tule Lake region to homestead during the height of the Depression.

My great-great-grandparents came to Oregon. I'm fifth-generation. My great-great-grandfather came around the Horn in a German ship, and then jumped ship when he got to Coos Bay.

That was my grandmother's grandfather. My grandfather's grandmother and grandfather came across the country in a Mormon wagon train. My great-great-grandmother was betrothed to the Smith that had something like ninety wives? She didn't want to marry him, so she and my grandfather left the wagon train in the middle of the night and came the rest of the way across the country alone. I guess they had a lot of adventures. They all settled on the coast. My grandfather came over to Tule Lake.

My father is from the South. He's the youngest of thirteen children. His mother died when he was nine or ten. He went to live with one of his older brothers in Florida, and helped his brother run a night club. He and my grandfather and my mother's brother all started farming together. They raised potatoes and alfalfa on leased land down by Tule Lake.

I got real sick in elementary school. I was home for a year. They couldn't get any school help for me in Cartwright, so that's when we moved to Klamath Falls. I guess my parents' marriage probably wasn't very good by that time, but it wasn't something that I was as aware of.

But when we moved to Klamath Falls, my dad stopped coming home nights. My mother really had a hell of a lot of responsibility. She had me, I was home sick. We didn't have enough money. My dad was seeing another woman, the woman that he eventually married. Shortly after that my dad left.

My mom just wasn't making it. She had no skills, no money. She was just totally depressed. She spent about a year trying to keep us and keep a job in a supermarket. We came home alone after school, and we were pretty young. She was feeling real guilty. She sent me and my sister back to live with my grandparents. My grandfather was very absent most of the time. Although to this day I feel like he was a real strong influence in my life, in that he really valued my mind. He would talk to me like I was another adult.

And then the summer after we were in the sixth grade, somebody broke into my mom's house. She was just terrified. She moved back down to Cartwright where we lived, and we lived in this teeny, tiny, itty-bitty apartment. It had one bedroom, and a Murphy bed in the wall in the living room. My sister and I shared the bedroom, and my mom slept in the living room. She was very depressed and out of control that year. It was really an awful year for me.

When I lived with my grandmother, there was a group of four of us who lived on the same block who were my age and a year older. Rita was a dyke when she was five. [*Laughs*] She was one of those girls who was born a dyke. Rita was born with grease under her fingernails. She didn't have a horse, but she wanted to be a cowgirl. I had two other friends—Cheryl was a Mormon, and Peg was a Catholic. They would kind of eye each other, but I loved both of them. We were left to run wild, and we just sort of lived in a pack.

When we moved back to Cartwright, it was like "back home." It was little. There were only seven or eight hundred people there, and we knew every one of them. My grandparents had lived there, my cousins, my aunt. Potatoes. Alfalfa. Sheep. Cattle. My dad would come and get us on Friday.

The other thing I remember about Cartwright is real hard drinking. By the time I was twelve, I had lost several of my older friends to drunk driving on the backroads at night. I was drinking by the time I was twelve. Hard. And that's what everybody did. We'd go out to the gravel pit in cars and get drunk. The boys would race and the girls would get laid and everybody got pregnant by the time they were fifteen. That's just what life was.

My mom was doing better. My dad was doing better financially.

She bought a nice little suburban house — you know, fifties ranch-style house. So by the time I was in high school, it was pretty nice. My mom and dad lived within a few miles of each other. We spent a lot of time with both of them. In the fall of my freshman year I got gang-raped by several of a girlfriend's friends. And then I just, you know — I'm not going to have much to do with this kind of people anymore! I took a lot of measures to really protect myself. Getting along with my mother, seeing my father, and made these new friends.

I met my first woman love in high school. Her name was Dorene. Dorene and I would talk for hours about what we were going to do. Her family was from the South. Her mother did cleaning. They lived in this little tiny house. Then Dorene went away to college. She went to summer school over here at SOC, and she came back married and pregnant. A year later she was crazy. She was having periods where she would black out, flip over into another personality. It was just so scary. It was like, Where did my Dorene go? And that son-of-a-bitch that she was married to I'm sure was abusive to her. He had her committed. She disappeared. I've never seen her since then.

It's like, Well! If you're homosexual, what happens is that you go crazy. Just like they say. I think her husband called her a crazy homosexual. Somebody did. I heard that. Maybe what they called her was queer — "crazy queer."

What I wanted at that point more than anything was to be normal. My cousin had gotten pregnant and had gotten married when she was sixteen. A lot of my friends got married before they got out of high school. I had a teacher in high school, she was just like the light of my life. I could talk to her about anything. And she just kept saying to me, "Don't give up. Wait till you get out of here. You'll find that there are other people like you. You'll find that there are other people who appreciate ideas and people's differences." She really kept me going.

Somewhere in there I just really determined that I was going to be an independent woman. Then I came over here to SOC. I really wanted to go to the University of Oregon, but Dorene was over here. And I was really worried about her by that time. I got a tuition scholarship to SOC. I was into "excitement." Hah! I dated a number of men who had been to Vietnam. They were all crazy. And I dated a number of drug addicts.

Anyway, I met a group of women with whom I am still friends. We proceeded to have the most outrageous four or five years. We were going to school in the mid-sixties. I was like drunk on ideas of the mind. It was just so exciting. People started doing marijuana. And then acid. And then speed. And then speed and acid together. It's just amazing to me that they all lived, and all came out with their brains intact.

Some of the guys didn't. One of them was a real down-and-out alcoholic for twenty years. Our friend Pete was killed in a log truck accident right after we graduated. Stoned, driving a log truck. Arlo went out into eastern Oregon and went crazy — from post-traumatic stress syndrome, I guess. Only one of the guys came out *fairly* normal — he's a psychiatrist.

I still think I was really affected by Dorene's being hauled off to the state mental hospital and being given shock treatments. My perception was, she was never going to come out again. That's what they did to lesbians. And I didn't want that to happen to me. So if I could sort of be safe with my best friend, that was OK. But to have to actually go out and find somebody? Excuse me, I don't think so. [*Laughs*] I stopped being involved with men, and just wasn't sexual for several years.

When I graduated from college it was in 1972, and it was like, what, the first recession? Not a lot of jobs. I was an English major. I had worked at a bunch of shit jobs to get through school, one of which was working in a nursing home. So when I graduated, I just went to work for them full-time. And then I went to work, eventually, for a poverty program in the area. Which was really fun.

I got involved with this little unincorporated area north of Medford. And mostly what I learned was, there is whole group of southern women out there. It was like, "Oh, hallelujah! I'm home!" I really had not realized, first, the poverty of the area; or, second, the number of southern transplants.

It was also interesting in that the women's groups were still sort of focused on their families, and they weren't seen as the "real" activists. The two guys that I worked with saw themselves as the real organizers, and the men they worked with as the real activists, and their groups were the important ones. I had trouble with that, but I didn't know why I was having trouble with it. I thought they were full of shit, but they were intellectuals, and they could just talk their way around me in circles. I was kind of, you know, we get these people together, and we do something useful for each other and in the meantime we talk about what we need and then we'll figure out the next step. And it's like I'm sort of plodding along. So I would sit there at these meetings where they were doing their dit-dit-dit-dit-dit-dit-dit. And I'm going, "Gee, there must be something wrong with me, 'cause I don't do that."

It took me twenty years to figure out that's not true! What I was doing was the real stuff, and what they were doing was bullshit! We deal with what's real. We teach people to can. We teach people to sew. We start something for their kids. Then if they go on from there, that's great.

Somewhere in here I decided I needed more credentials. I went to live with my mom so I could go back to school.

I got married here in Ashland. When he and I were first together, it was nice, and it was exciting. Then, probably from the time Jesse was born, I knew I didn't want to be married. And I had this inkling of why. I wanted to be with women. I just didn't know what to do about it. It just scared the shit out of me.

And the economy was getting harder and harder, and it was getting tighter and tighter. My husband decided that he wanted to go back to Peru, where he was from. And then I got another job and met Lois, and the rest is history. I just, I mean, I fell in love with her the minute I met her. There was just no other woman for me. [*Laughs*] "You're it! How would you like to be the candidate?"

B. B. What about being a lesbian in all the work you've done?

CAROLINE Oh, God! It's been real scary, sometimes real dangerous. I feel like it's not something that I ever say out loud. But, on the other hand, I don't hide it.

There are points at which you simply lose credibility. Like when a program becomes too mainstream. I can take things up to a certain point, and then I have to let go of them, and other people go from there. And make it more mainstream.

At times that's been hard. But really, now that it's happened several times, it's easier. I mean, morally, emotionally, I don't want to pass. I am who I am. I'm not going to leave. This is where I live, this is what I believe in.

It's interesting. When I was deciding to come out, the lesbian community was real important to me, but where I really live is in the straight community. I have some other lesbian friends who've grown up working-class, mostly. I mean, we love this neighborhood. We bought a house here. It's a great neighborhood. It's a real mix, but it's basically a working-class or a working-class-roots neighborhood.

One of the things that really strikes me is that I expected when I got a degree that I would make good money. I would really be able to support myself. But for several years after I was divorced I could barely make enough to live on. That was seventy-nine. Not a good time to enter a new profession.

I got this little apartment and I was working. And making, I don't

know—eight hundred dollars a month? But because I had these humongous medical bills from a severely broken leg, I was left with five
or six thousand dollars worth of bills, and I was just barely eking it out
every month. And I'd been on welfare for about six months and had
accumulated other bills, and it was just really tough—had been out of
work for nine months. And just couldn't get these bills paid off. And
eat. And pay rent. And pay childcare. And drive to work.

So at the end of every month, we would be almost without food. I
would buy lots of rice and beans and canned tomatoes. At the end of
every month, we would live on rice and beans and canned tomatoes.
Jesse to this day will not eat canned tomatoes. She still loves beans,
though. [*Laughs*] It's a good thing.

And that was real tough, but, you know, when I see what's happening to my mom, it's even tougher? She's worked thirty years. She's
going to retire this year. Now she's going to retire on six hundred dollars a month because of changes in the retirement plan where she
worked. That's all she's got. And she's got a good loan on her house,
because it's a low-income loan? She only pays like three hundred dollars a month. But she's not going to be able to stay there. So here she
is, she's worked all her life just to have a house to return to, so she'd at
least have a place to live and feel safe. And she's not going to have it.

And then my dad, he had made enough money that he was living
on a ranch again, and was ranching. As well as doing his other job.
And was making fairly good money. And the bottom dropped out of
the economy. The bottom dropped out of the cattle market. He's had
to sell off most of his farm just to keep a half an inch in front of the
bank. He won't even live there now. He won't talk about it. It's like it's
dead. He and my stepmother are working their butts off, seven days a
week, twelve hours a day, so they have some money to live on when
they're older.

Some really good friends of theirs had lost their farm, and these
guys had been on this farm for fifty years. The wife died shortly after
that, and it just blew my dad away. And it was clear to me that he was
in the process of making a decision to either lie down and die or figure
out a way to fight back. He decided to fight back, but it was real scary.

You know, I always thought of farming as being a gamble. But it
had never been that much of a gamble. It'd never been the kind of
gamble where people died. And that is what it seemed like to me. I
mean, particularly because the people I knew were in their sixties and
seventies who were losing their farms. And because they simply lost the
will to live after that happened to them. In some ways it seemed to me

like the banks were committing murder. These were all family farms. And do you want to make a guess about who owns all the farms now? Corporations! Corporations own all that land. My stepmother knows all of them, by heart. And recites them.

I started volunteering with women's organizations. It's 1979, 1980. There are no jobs. Women were going into service jobs. Minimum wage. For the first time there was some connection for me about the economics that women faced. I didn't really understand it, but I knew that everybody was getting screwed. This one woman just stands out real clearly in my mind. She'd been married to this guy who worked in the mills for twenty-five, thirty years. And one day he came home with a friend of her daughter's. And said, "Well, I'm leaving you now."

He had lost his job at the mill. I mean, his self-esteem had gone plummeting. And he had gotten involved with this young woman. I heard this story time after time after time. Men would lose their jobs, they would leave their wives. Everybody was falling apart. There was no place for people to go to work.

I mean, I had been out of work for nine months myself, and I had a college degree! And I couldn't find work. It was terrifying. And I had been able to fall back on welfare. And while welfare was *tough* — I think Jesse and I got two hundred eighty dollars a month, and food stamps — at least we got something. And to see these older women who couldn't even qualify for welfare. What the hell were they to do? There was nowhere for them go.

We were moving from a resource-based economy to a service economy. We were losing literally millions of dollars a year in payroll in this area, and the effect that that had on people, over and over again, is that men would leave — leave their wives and leave the area. It meant that those women were out of any source of income. If their husbands were out of the state, there was no way anybody was going to collect child support. They were just flat on their own.

At the same time, welfare had changed so that anybody who had a child over the age of three was required to look for work. So there was no way that these women were able to do anything to improve their lives. I saw battered women who would go back again and again and again because there was no way for them to live without being dependent on a male partner.

I had a friend who had been volunteering at the battered women's shelter for a couple of years. A woman had called — and it was way before restraining orders or any of the legislation that ever made any difference — this woman had called her in a small town near here, and she was going to meet the woman in front of the police station. She's in the process of putting the woman in her car, and this bullet whizzes past her ear. She just sort of shoves the woman in the car, jumps in after her, and drove off. You know, sort of mindless. And that's what it was like.

It's hard to tell whether the recession made things worse. What does what. Because there are so many Survivalists around here, there are so many counter-culture people living out in such isolated situations. And the culture around here is fairly violent anyway. I think that when people are frustrated and beaten down and oppressed, that they turn around and oppress other people. Whoever's the biggest and the meanest wins. And that continues to be the case.

In the town that I grew up in, women just didn't see that they had any choices. Birth control wasn't available, abortions weren't available. Education wasn't available. There was no college where I lived. There were no jobs for women. Why go to college? — there were no jobs. You could be a nurse or a teacher — and the people that did those were outsiders and weird.

And I don't think anybody else wants to be where women are in the service economy. I think of mail-order fruit companies, where it gets into production of food products and mail order, as service economy. And then the tourism industry. I mean, what kinds of jobs does tourism create? Maids. Working in a restaurant. There was a study done about the income that is produced in the state of Oregon from tourism. And they were talking about, Well, it's seven dollars an hour. But you read further down the study, and it says that kind of income comes from entrepreneurial development. And who does that? It's men. And the women that work for them making three dollars and thirty-five cents an hour. Part-time. Seasonally. Nobody, still, is talking about that.

We continue to look at economics as if women didn't exist. And we'll deal with the "real" economic development, which is white middle-class men — this group of white middle-class men who are coming in and telling all the rest of us what is the economy, and what should be. I mean, nobody's asked us what we think economic development should be.

One thing that's clear is that the whole of economic development is much more based on entrepreneurship, rather than bringing in large corporations. Yet they're still saying we need to bring in the forty-million-dollar huge destination resort development like they're looking at in both Ashland and Rogue River now.

And in the meantime, what does that mean for the rest of us? We're right on an I-5 corridor. We're certainly all able to link up through computers. And fax machines. Why aren't we looking at broadening the economy? Does it all have to be out of serving rich, snotty people and old people? I'm not interested in doing that for the rest of my life.

A lot of my neighbors work in the mills. We were talking the other day about what they see as alternatives. Like the neighbors up the street. He works in a mill, she works at a low-paying discount store. He sees his alternative to his very good-paying job in the mill as working in a discount store. He knows that he doesn't really have much else to look for anymore than his wife does. His sister works with him in the mill. And she's been there for a long time. She's a single parent.

I have real mixed feelings, because I think that we need to be sensible about cutting old-growth timber. And I think that the people in the mills are being fed a line of bullshit. I think they're being told that we have to cut old-growth timber. But I'll tell you, Lois and I went to Coos Bay three months ago, and the road between Roseburg and Coos Bay — it's clearcut. There's this little teeny, tiny corridor of trees along the highway, and then it's just raped. It's just stripped.* And then you get to Coos Bay, and the logging mills are shut down, right? And there's mile after mile after mile of timber decks sitting there waiting to be shipped to Japan. Mile after mile! It's got Japanese names on it. I mean, it's not like maybe it's going to go to a sawmill somewhere else. But we're being told that we have to cut down old-growth timber. Well, bullshit.

In the timber management plan, they're counting on private reforested land that's been reforested for twenty or thirty years. They're looking at it being available at about year forty. But when they went back and reexamined that plan, what they found was that twenty- and thirty-year-old timber has all been cut and sold to Japan. So we don't even have that to count on in a couple years.

There's so much lying going on. And again, I think it's white middle-class men or upper-middle-class men doing it. Just putting out all this crap that we're supposed to believe. I don't want them to be in charge of deciding this economy. As far as I'm concerned, they've done plenty much to screw it up. Some of the rest of us need to start making decisions about what the economy needs to be based on and how we're going to manage it.

*This area is private industrial land adjacent to BLM land. *B. B.*

One of the biggest changes around here is the fact that women have to work. Both because half of marriages end in divorce, so most women are on their own; and even in those families that stay together, there's not enough money from one earner to support the family.

The other is the change in the economic base from agriculture and timber. You know, people make fun of the people in Klamath Falls for wanting the Salt Caves dam. And it just makes me furious.

We have some friends who moved here from the Bay Area. Their parents have lots of money, and they have an education, and they're professionals. They have access to the retirees from California who come up here and need their services. They have no idea what it's like to be a farmer or a salesman over in Klamath County, where you've lived your whole life developing some personal economic base only to see it all absolutely washed down the drain. You've lost the Air Force base in seventy-six, seventy-seven. Then you lose the timber base economy. Then, right on its heels, you lose the agriculture. And all of your friends have lost their means of making a living.

So you begin looking for any way to bring some money into the area. The I-5 corridor has some chance of developing tourism. But what have you got in Klamath Falls? You look at the one resource you've got left, and that's hydroelectric power. And you come from a place where resource development and resource extraction has been a way of making our livings for generations! So it makes sense to look towards more resource extraction to support the economy of the area. Jesus! They need to be able to feed their families.

So when this friend of ours started making fun of the people from Klamath Falls and the Salt Caves dam, I almost broke his foot. We don't discuss it anymore.

I see a lot of people who are environmentalist—I mean, I think that I'm, at least to some extent, a modified environmentalist. But on the other hand, I remember in the sixties when they talked about radicals as effete snobs. And I got real whacked out when I heard that. Now, sometimes when I hear a lot of the environmentalists who come up here and criticize, I think the same of them. They come here from California, which has been raped and ruined, and then talk about how we—who are these "dumb Oregonians . . ." It's real irritating. It's just real irritating to see people from the outside not really want to have any understanding of where people are coming from. And the fact that they don't see themselves as having many choices. The women and the men. People who've grown up here and have not had the opportunity to go on to college—and people who've grown up here and *have* had the opportunity to go on to college! — see themselves as not having a lot of economic choices.

I mean, a number of the people that I graduated with, from college with! — went to work in the mills. 'Cause that's where they could make the money. And are still there.

No one's calling the timber companies to task. People don't see what they can do about it. I think lots of us feel that way. It's like, So what can we do about it? And that's hard to deal with when what you're looking at is an economy that's going downhill fast.

And there's not much discussion about the fact that private timber is being sent to Japan. And there's not much discussion about the fact that lumber mills are not real willing to retool. It's cheaper for them to shut down and move elsewhere than it is to retool.

Weyerhaeuser has been moving into the Southeast for years. Since I was a kid! Weyerhaeuser is like the center of the economy in Klamath County. And it just so happens that my dad's family is from the South. So it's been real clear to us the kind of movement that's going on from Weyerhaeuser in Klamath Falls to Weyerhaeuser right outside of where my relatives live in the South! Just as the operation shut down more and more in Klamath County, when we go down there to visit, more and more land is owned by Weyerhaeuser. More and more people becoming employed by Weyerhaeuser.

And the people down there have always worked for lower wages because they've worked in the textile mills. The textile mills are all closing down and moving to other Third World countries. And so those people that were working in the textile mills are now available to work in the sawmills. The last strike that they had in Klamath Falls, they lost. Because they're just saying, "So? You want to shut down? Fine. We'll shut down. We don't care." And they go work somewhere else. I mean, it's no big deal.

And they're not reforesting the land that they're cutting. Like between here and Klamath Falls? Look at the Weyerhaeuser land. It's not being reforested! They could give a shit. You can go by and watch clearcuts for two and three years just sit there. They don't even clean the slash.

They're sort of finishing out the land that they own up on the Green Springs. It'll be real interesting to see what they end up doing with it. If they reforest it, if they actually tree farm it, or if they just throw a few seeds out and leave?

The whole family system — I mean, what family system? It's like: What is left? It's Mom and the kids. And Dad's out somewhere trying to find work. And Mom's working part-time, temporary, seasonally. Relying on welfare in the off season.

I mean, that's the other thing about these shit jobs, is that we're subsidizing them by paying for those women to be on welfare the rest of the year. As far as I'm concerned, we subsidize the big mail-order fruit businesses. We subsidize the tourism industry. Because people work for them for nothing in the summer, and get childcare and food stamps and rent subsidy. And then in the winter they get welfare when they can't work. Until this welfare reform, forcing them to go do so. They didn't have a choice. They did that or they were taken off welfare.

Women in this area, I think, are seeing that they need to do it together. More than men are. Still. I think that men see they need to do it together in the context of the union, but once the union fails — and it has, around here — they don't turn around and organize again as a group to look at the economy.

But I think it's coming. I think it'll be maybe ten years from now, but I think this is an area where we're going to see leadership by some women, and men will follow. And that's OK.

Language, complexity, and power: life stories and a community in transition

Throughout the interviews in this book runs the question of who will control the Northwest's lands and forests. Will it be transnational corporations, in-migrants/environmentalists, or the federal government, serving either the corporate or environmental interests? This is, then, a book about land and power.

Land-use changes, a plunging economy, and the cultural ascendancy of "outsiders" define the action. The details are played out at the micro-level of everyday lives. Consequently, these interviews are as much concerned with family violence as the loss of timber jobs. They are as much concerned with women's decreasing sense of safety as they are with gentrification. Men and women's lack of access to good education, birth control, and jobs that pay well is intertwined with diminishing public access to land and rivers. These narratives are very much about the desire of poor and working people to have a say in the direction of their community as well as their personal lives, and the reasons why they think that will not happen.

Public debates in the Rogue Valley are often framed by people with a national political agenda. From the top down, people pursuing ideological battles try to impose their theoretical concerns on local problems. From the bottom up, local people try to fit neighborhood or topical concerns into someone else's theoretical or scientific fight. The concerns of poor and working people often do not fit. Instead they are swallowed up in predefined environmental, or religious-right, or tax-revolt debates.

This book suggests that people's own life stories are the source material for understanding and acting upon the complexities of change. If the individuals in this book, and their friends and neighbors, create an effective voice within their own communities, it will probably arise through independent groups of poor and working people, gathered to analyze, develop, and define their own experience on their own terms. The ability to challenge the agenda of the more formally educated, or the more powerful, or the more vindictive elements of a community lies ultimately in the ability to organize in a way that fits working citizens' own cultures and daily rhythms. One hopes, in the tradition of the best social movements, that these efforts will take place not in intolerant self-interest, but with a vision of a diverse and reciprocally respectful community life.

PUBLIC AND PRIVATE LIVES

The amalgam of private and public lives in these pages may seem at first to be confusing the issues. But the overall shape of a tree reflects the same pattern as its smaller branches, and the smaller branches reflect the pattern of the whole. So social scientists see economic trauma as the source of individual and family crisis; and feminists and scholars of color see authoritarianism, prejudice, and violence reflected in our macro-economic and cultural realities.

Therefore this mix of public and personal lives addresses the ways in which perspectives on public affairs are filtered through private responsibilities and tensions. In this book, political and social opinions are built upon real experiences, from drug use[1] to exclusion from community affairs because of race, gender, or sexual orientation.

Context is everything. Against the complex background of people's lives and the local economy and culture (including a tradition of tall tales), bumper stickers such as "Save a logger, eat an owl" make sense as a form of resistance to something bigger than federal logging plans. Journalists who visit our region to interview men who are laid-off millworkers[2] ask questions only about the timber situation, and receive answers only on the timber situation. These answers might lead one to believe that plywood linemen find their personal identity in mill work, and that their anger about being laid off means they are in sympathy with the mill owners, and that the focus of their ire is environmental activism.

But these interviews, as well as other work,[3] indicate that mill-

1. There was substantially more discussion of drug and alcohol abuse, and family violence, in the original interviews than my agreements and personal commitment to protect anonymity permitted me to include.

2. Women represented up to 23 percent of laid-off millworkers in one cluster of layoffs involving several mills according to the staff of the RCC Employment and Career Center (personal communication, 1992).

3. David Halle (1984) also discusses the lack of identification with occupation. Some fallers and other woods-workers do identify with their occupation, however, as I learned from personal conversations, especially with Phil Wickham, a forester (Grants Pass, 1991; also see Carroll, 1989; Carroll and Lee, 1990).

workers, given more space to talk, do not necessarily identify with mill work. Their distress over layoffs arises from a much more fundamental set of experiences that touch on region, culture, and class. For the most part, these men and women do not like or trust the companies (indeed, as is evidenced in these narratives, many forest workers are bailing out early and seeking other opportunities), but neither do they automatically trust the motives of people professing to be protectors of the environment.

For women, safety is a primary concern. Disappearing access to neighborhood and backwoods areas raises concerns about safety outside the home. Women in southwest Oregon had been accustomed to walking with very little fear. Places to walk freely around the neighborhood disappear. As the population grows and, increasingly, is polarized by culture and income, with the attendant increases in violence, many women have told me that they no longer feel safe walking alone in areas that are still accessible. Some no longer feel safe from intruders in their homes. This is a change that has taken place over about fifteen years, since the late 1970s. It hits hard, because freedom to wander in safety has always been taken for granted by women in our area — a privilege that offsets disadvantages of low income and isolation.

Violence *inside* the home affects boy and girl children as well as women. The educational future of children is steered by the outcomes of family discord, as we see in the interviews with Kevin Sjorn and Rhonda Marshall and Ellen Tigart. Without an opportunity to acquire high-paying employment outside the wood products industry, young people have to depend upon the kind of low-education jobs the now-scarce mills have provided for decades. Women like Kathy Dodge are sometimes paralyzed by the threat of physical harm and kept from pursuing any options. Is this connected to the ambivalence and fear with which she anticipates a more racially mixed Oregon? In turn, lack of education creates a community unable to attract the best entrepreneurs or companies. Instead, the Rogue Valley is likely to recruit the worst of industries in terms of wages, expectations, and racial/gender prejudice.

The language of public debate — usually defined by the most powerful participants — makes it difficult to see or value the complexity of overlapping themes of local community concern. Women's safety is, I believe, a barometer of the health of a community, and development that closes off access to trails and blackberry brambles threatens women's safety by funneling more people into smaller and more exposed places for recreation. It is unlikely, however, that access will be discussed in terms of women's safety; rather, the issue will be evaluated in terms of letter-of-the-law private property rights. And if blue-collar families with deep roots in the area lose their homes and leave in large numbers, their exodus is unlikely to be discussed publicly in terms of gentrification, but rather as an outcome of the spotted owl controversies and the *personal* misfortune of "dislocated workers." Family violence is more likely to be discussed as psychological "dysfunction" rather than as a crisis with roots in cultural, gender, and economic inequalities.

In other words, if public debate does not include diverse voices, including the organized voice of poor and working women and men, complex problems get collapsed into single issues. Matters of importance to working people — the closing of formerly public space, economic pressures to relocate, gentrification, the health and safety of the workplace and neighborhood — are displaced and translated by political opportunists into the sound-bite slogans of "tax revolt," "saving our forest jobs," and "traditional values."

In this war of rhetoric, it is the industry and the far right, which purport to care about working people, who *appear* to win the (rhetorical) sympathy of working-class citizens. Environmental activists often perceive popular rhetoric as an expression of the real issues at hand, and therefore commit the blunder of treating anti-environmentalist, anti-tax, and anti-urban concerns as "stupid" or — interchangeably — simply "redneck."

WORK, LAND, AND COMMUNITY

For the people who grew up in the Rogue Valley between the thirties and the early seventies, southwest Oregon counties were small, intimate communities. Friendship and extended family networks were central, as they remain today.

Locals who had managed in the past to get by when the mills slumped found themselves less able to ride out the more recent economic shifts and national recessions. Through the previous decades, individuals and families often bounced from poor to lower or middle class, then back again, following the market for labor-based jobs. Middle- and upper-income people who arrived in the late 1970s and 1980s have marketable skills and incomes much higher than those of most people who have grown up in the area. Low-income and working women and men — the majority of in-migrants in previous times — now represent a small portion of transplants: Few can afford to relocate to what now is a notoriously high-price, high-unemployment area.

Local people once dealt with the local poverty and uneven employment by trading the possibility of better wages elsewhere for access to the beauty and bounty of the region's vast acreage of forests and waters. But easy access to land is disappearing with the proliferation of fences and "No Trespassing" signs. Rural zoning regulations unintentionally reinforce these changes. Newcomers, with a shallow connection to the land, dismiss local irritation about the new prohibitions: "That way of life is gone forever."

Meanwhile, the higher-paid blue-collar jobs are disappearing. The recession and the emerging service economy, designed for the newcomers and tourists, holds down non-professional wages. Benefits such as health insurance are severely cut back, or vanish. Women, with low-wage, seasonal jobs in tourism and other poorly paid service industries, are hit the hardest by cutbacks. Local people find themselves under a quadruple burden: loss of income and benefits, the threat of being priced or taxed out of their own homes, diminished access to forests and rivers, and an increasing dissolution of neighborhood and community coherence.

Most official reports on the changing workforce and the new service economy focus on jobs and wages as an answer to the troubles of the rural Northwest. These interviews demonstrate that the loss of assets — public and private — is as important as the loss of wages, and possibly more important in the long term. The private value of home, property, tools, and so on is self-evident, but the rights of access to forests and waterways, free movement across the countryside, and the ability to fish, hunt, and gather are public assets with critical importance in individual and family economies. Too often the role of these public assests in community well-being is overlooked.

The middle-class 1980s newcomers, and the counter-culture in-migrants of the previous decade, were urban people with the desire and the skills to organize politically. In southwest Oregon, three constituencies benefited from the urban-to-rural population shift: the formal environmental movement, orchestrated antitax campaigns, and Christian political activism. Old networks of long-established business owners were accustomed to setting the agenda for the region; the newcomers challenged their public power-brokering. (Industry, including the timber industry, usually operates behind the scenes.) Leadership in these citizens' groups in the Rogue Valley is drawn primarily from people with middle- and upper-income backgrounds. "Progressive" groups include many who are well-educated and downwardly mobile by choice.

In contrast, there is a lack of effective political organization among working people — men or women — throughout the Rogue Valley region.

Strong unions, local low-income pressure groups, and the like are absent from this book. Consequently, the political power struggles in the region were skewed sharply towards middle-class issues in the 1980s, leaving a vacuum in political advocacy by and for working people, even though this was a time of economic crisis for many.

"Yellow ribbon" campaigns against the cutbacks in timber harvest, which gained national attention, attempted to create a blue-collar counterbalance to environmental victories. These groups faded from prominence, however, most likely because they were industry-sponsored and promoted. Many millworker families, as the interviews show, view the companies with an equivocal eye. The companies provide jobs, which are appreciated, but the mills also push workers' bodies to the limit. National corporations are in the area only for the bucks, pulling up stakes whenever it becomes convenient, ready to cut workers off at the knees whenever there is a conflict between people and profits. Except for a few locally owned mills, corporate forestry practices are far more unpopular than the industry would have the national public believe. But there is no great love for the other side: These interviewees perceive the "well-off newcomers," the "counter-culture," and "environmentalists" as sharing sympathies and social attitudes. These groups, like the timber industry, represent people with more education, money, and powerful connections who would impose their will on the local working-class community, even when their lives might be torn apart by the consequences.

EVERYDAY LANGUAGE AND POLITICAL SYMBOLISM

Public debate is framed in the language of the social groups who are organizationally sophisticated. Arguments become confused as symbolic speech of dominant groups is appropriated by all other parties — but with altered, multi-layered meanings.[4] For example, "environmentalist" means something substantially different to Peter Alten than to Art Downing, whose interview winds up this book. Access to public spaces along rivers and in the woods, and the free use of forest resources such as mushrooms, cover one aspect of "environmental" language. The fear of losing crucial assets such as homes and land to gentrification and income-discriminatory zoning is another aspect. These meanings exist

4. Ann Hawkins and Frederick Buttel (1989) discuss the many-layered "environmentalist" language that is institutionalized and co-opted within international development agency policy, or appropriated pragmatically by various nations' non-governmental organizations in order to debate broad issues in a language less threatening to governments than a direct challenge to authoritarian power structures.

alongside those implying ecological protection, which is championed in one way or another by virtually all long-term residents.

But the word "environment" strains to cover all these concerns: The language is no longer adequate for the situation (White, 1984). Instead, we are conducting arguments in a terminology "in which the interpretations follow wildly divergent paths in accordance with vital interests" (Scott, 1990, p. 100). For example, the various meanings of "environmentalist" in this book—ranging from a synonym for EarthFirst! to an almost generic description of urban newcomers or retirees—raise questions about the interpretation of anti-environmentalist statements. As Margaret Norman explained to me (off-tape, unfortunately), "environmentalist" is often a catchword; environmentalists are people "coming up here from southern California" who "didn't know shit about the area and didn't give a rat's patoot about the people here." If you said you were an environmentalist, she explained, that meant you were in alliance with the "southern California" bunch who are pushing local people aside. I asked if she meant that there was no way for local working people to express concern about the environment without betraying a sense of self and community? "You got it," she said.

There is almost no independent, citizen-based opposition to the environmentalists *or* the large timber companies, despite the wariness towards each expressed in these pages. Local people are neither indifferent or passive, but in the face of the new power structures in the area, they choose—or feel compelled—to center their lives in friends and family, in a more isolated and personal community. Community sports and some church-based activities continue, and perhaps take on more importance, but the sense of the town or county as a community of which one is an integral part diminished. As Barbara Roland notes: "The town got bought out from under us." Indeed, many poor and displaced blue-collar workers have pulled up roots and moved on.

NETWORKS AND DIVISIONS

Inequity suppresses interaction among groupings of people whose lives and well-being are in fact tied together ecologically; and, without interaction, community—particularly a dynamic, interactional form of community—cannot exist.

—Kenneth P. Wilkinson

During the last decade, local working people lost not only their economic footing in timber but also more than six hundred electronic assembly jobs, following the nationwide decline in manufacturing and military-based industries. The region was not ready for this switch; there was no substitute infrastructure that would provide decent wages. As is true across the United States (Bennett and Bluestone, 1988; Lovemann and Tilly, 1988), most of the newer service jobs pay little and hold a lower social status. Women's jobs generally pay the lowest scale, which, in addition to complicating the finances of healthy families, compromises the ability of those women in violent or abusive home situations to leave.

Meanwhile, counties lost their percentages of federal timber receipts. Schools lost ground against inflation with the repeated defeat of school levies. As the county with the most severe impacts in the region, Josephine County suffered additionally when several prominent doctors and educators sought jobs elsewhere, citing the poor schools and community infrastructure; doctors who remained in the county found it hard to recruit medical personnel to Grants Pass. These losses, along with the population transformations of the area, happened so fast that both Jackson and Josephine counties have yet to gain a new footing. Urban habits of social isolation combined with effective political organization counterweigh against the disorganization and economic distress of the long-time poor, lower-middle-, and fragilely middle-income local communities.

The area lost its equilibrium and, as in so much of the urban United States, began to segregate more rigidly in several dimensions: *culturally*, as the urban newcomers brought a distinctly city-based set of values to an area with a small-town and rural orientation; *socially*, as the social barriers notably increased between people employed in blue- or pink-collar jobs (regardless of income) and people supported by professional and white-collar jobs or investment income (regardless of income);[5] *economically*, as a two-tiered economy separated people into the economically comfortable and those who are not, with a diminishing middle ground; and *physically*, as once-open land is posted "No Trespassing" or becomes accessible only by lottery or payment of users' fees. Income-exclusionary zoning contributes another layer of restrictions.

Racial segregation and racist intimidation, long an unofficial southwest Oregon tradition as these interviews testify, are reinforced by the influx of "white-flight" newcomers hoping to leave behind the troubles of racially conflicted cities.

Until recently local networks were dense and interconnected. This

---

5. For instance, a landscaper might make a middle-class income, but is less likely to travel in overlapping social circles with her or his clients.

was by no means a model community, but the sense of inclusion was definitely broader among residents. Now people from separate income and social groups share common geographic neighborhoods, the same streets and landscapes, but almost never share intersecting lives. The antagonisms that arise among strangers begin to define the community.

Meanwhile, environmental organizations pull their constituencies from a relatively small network that shares cultural and social (often liberal-to-left) attitudes with a middle-class, urban bent. Rural working people concerned about the forest environment are unlikely to ally with these social networks. Federal and state programs of "displaced worker" retraining, "welfare reform," and economic planning are designed and run by agency directors, usually educated in-migrants who share few social or cultural perceptions or experiences with the people they are mandated to serve.[6] Economic planning groups focus on tourism strategies targeted at people with above-average incomes.

In these settings, cultural prejudice against local working-class people often prevails at the policy as well as the personal level. Several of these interviews reflect the indignation local people feel when they and their friends are belittled as backward and stupid. Public policy strategy that offers a new economy promising low pay and low status does nothing to mollify these insults.[7] Appalachian counterparts are called "hillbillies"; here, working-class locals are simply called "rednecks." Indeed, the desire to maintain dignity may be a powerful motivator when local working people choose sides in any regional issue.

COMMUNITIES OF AFFILIATION

Neighborhood and workplace networks dissolve in a highly segregated community. "Communities of affiliation" take their place people who share a similar social class or culture and specific social values or church

6. Because living on a piece of land helps blunt the effects of poverty, many women involved in welfare reform programs resist moving into towns where there are somewhat better job prospects—much to the consternation of their instructors and caseworkers, as a Family Service Act employee observed (personal communication, 1992).

7. A large manufacturing company negotiating with local planners to relocate to the Rogue Valley was known to be interested in busting the union that represented its workforce (predominantly African American and Latino) in southern California (personal communication, 1992). T. A. Lyson (1988, p. 271) notes: "As the US Commission on Civil Rights recently reported, to the extent that tax abatements, guaranteed loans, subsidized vocational training and other forms of public assistance affect the decision of a company to locate in a particular county, their net effect is often merely to shift jobs from one place to another rather than to create any new employment opportunities." These shifts often, as cited above, place racial and cultural minorities at an even greater disadvantage in the factory recruitment roulette.

or occupational concerns within more or less closed networks. These new networks do not necessarily encompass a neighborhood or a region or even a single state (Lee, 1991; Machlis and Force, 1988). Although political pressure groups representing only one segment of the population are nothing new, differences of degree can transform their impact. In our region, the proliferation of single-visioned efforts, and the lack of public coalitions, has produced a distressing myopia: Most political efforts have come to disregard the well-being of the town or region as an important public entity in itself. In describing efforts to analyze constituencies concerned about specific environmental questions, R. G. Lee (1991, p. 36) notes, "There is limited communication between individuals in separate social circles, and such communication is usually limited to a rather narrow segment of concerns." As is documented in these interviews, the social coherence of towns within the Rogue Valley is already unraveling as class and cultural differences deepen: At risk is the value of community, measured not as an economic or demographic category, but as a public activity.

Because communities of affiliation — such as organized environmentalist groups — represent vocal constituencies, it is a short step to promoting communities of affiliation as the groups with which to negotiate most effectively to formulate public policy (Lee, 1991). In the Rogue Valley, social divisions devolve into a kind of identity politics ("Environmentalists," "Progressives," "Evangelical Christians," "Business Leaders") that threatens all with perpetual gridlock, where all in-group communities of affiliation hold significant power, and none are ready to back down.

As an organizing strategy targeting short-term goals and successes, community-of-affiliation tactics can succeed; but single-focus middle-income-controlled groups are usually willing to sacrifice the well-being of poorer groups for the sake of the "issue." Low-income women's interests are rarely even considered. Thus owners who fence long-used trials running across their high-priced property bordering public land may be exclusively concerned with protecting their own privacy, even when doing so would cut off public access to the vast federal lands and public waters behind them. In creating a privatized buffer zone around public lands, owners retain privileged access from the backside of their property. Private timber companies, cheered on by some unions, lobby for more access to public timber to maintain their profits, even though their current level of harvest will inevitably bankrupt labor, community, and environment. Environmentalists litigate to close forests, with scant attention to the effect on working people. Tourism — a development goal guaranteed to aggravate a dual economy — is promoted as a key to economic recovery. Rural zoning regulations, as they now exist, guarantee an eventual concentration of wealth in the countryside and poverty in the towns.

In each of these cases, the private struggle for gain devalues lower-income, lower-status citizens and their interests. Even if social or business circles rarely overlap, people share *space* — a physical and political "commons." Once again, few effective low-income or working women's or men's organizations exist in our area to challenge the decision-making that is taking place among the more powerful and effectively organized communities of affiliation. The few ideologically driven conservative groups that attract some working people have not worked towards constructive solutions, structural or reformist; they instead have become a nay-saying phalanx, a resistance with no place to go. As Henry Dubnik notes, referring to the defeat of levies to fund schools: "You're starting to feel controlled in just about everything you do. . . . They still can vote 'no.' Or they still can vote 'yes.' And so you get a bunch of different factions who are all thinking different things, but the end result is that the schools are having trouble getting funded."

When poor, working, and fragilely middle-class people are socially and culturally excluded from decision-making arising out of their own concerns, the accumulated tension and resentment rebounds on all residents. Hostility increases; petty and bitter attacks on all levels of state and local government persist, with no willingness to participate in a solution; crimes against property increase; and civic pride in the area deteriorates. It is in this context that battles over the spotted owl must be analyzed.

SCIENCE AND THE LANGUAGE OF GENTRIFICATION

If ever an issue impacted working communities in Oregon, it is the environmental war over the future of the forests, symbolized nationally by the spotted owl. Yet despite the real concern expressed in many of these interviews over the mismanagement of the forests, the owl comes in for scant sympathy.

Battles over the Endangered Species Act and the old-growth forest have been pursued by a fairly narrow segment of the local population — usually counter-culture or middle-class in-migrants of various political points of view — with broad urban support across the nation. Virtually all the organizing around these environmental questions has moved through agency review processes, legislatures, and the courts — arenas for the highly educated. While the timber industry pursues forest policies in its own narrow economic interests to the detriment of the environment and workers, environmentalist concerns are also framed narrowly. Characteristically these are argued as scientific matters of ecology, forest management, biodiversity, and so on.

Middle-class environmental reformers who become adept at sparring with agencies like the Forest Service, BLM, and Fish and Wildlife discover that "science" is the language of the battle: "Value-neutral" scientific reports take precedence over social concerns like widespread unemployment. In this process, environmentalists and agencies engage in ever more detailed and specialized internal negotiation or technical litigation. Policy becomes an inside job, carried on through agency networks. Social issues are bypassed or referred to government social service agencies. While most people are aware that science is far from "value-free," if they are not able to present their case in the language of science, they are cut out of the argument.[8] (This tendency has been aggravated by the legal issues in spotted-owl-related court cases, which are being adjudicated on the basis of scientific evidence.) Not surprisingly, the people I interviewed viewed "scientific" studies with some cynicism. Without independent pressure groups to develop arguments on their own terms, poor and working people receive little more than rhetorical nods toward "job creation" and inadequate or relocation-oriented retraining programs.[9] Attitudes, however, show up in everyday conversation, in which "rednecks" (working-class white people) are considered dupes of industry and therefore obstacles, as well as a social inconvenience, to "progressive," development. This is understood locally as gentrification with a vengeance.

Although most environmental activists and working people in these communities appear to have few class interests in common, they share many concerns about the environment. These interviews usually include disapproval of clearcutting and poor reforestation and watershed management. Some of these same individuals do not hesitate to vent hostility towards organizational environmentalists and the spotted owl debate. At a time when environmental concerns about the forest are converging across class lines, the social concerns of working people and middle-class reformers are diverging more than ever.

In at least a portion of these interviews, the phrase "spotted owl" is used as a shorthand for gentrification. Does local resistance become more intelligible if the owl symbolizes the ability of middle-class newcomers from the city to unilaterally enforce their agendas through agen-

8. I acknowledge Theodore Lowi's intricate unwinding (1986) of these issues.

9. For a case study of the limited effectiveness of retraining programs, see Zippay (1991). See also recent U.S. Department of Labor studies questioning the usefulness of "retraining" (cited in "Retrain for What?" 1993). In an economy that is producing few jobs, "retraining" can be a false promise.

cies and the courts, and in the process cut local people off from homes, land, good employment, and social respect? The antagonistic interests of people from different economic and cultural backgrounds have worked against this comprehension. Consequently, the timber industry is able to play the interests of poor and working people against environmentalists, and this may signal a tragedy in the making for both the community and the forests.

CONSCIOUSNESS AND POWER

Some theorists question whether poor and working people are capable of thinking independently on these issues. They argue for a "false consciousness" among the least powerful and a "hegemony" of public opinion-making influence by the most powerful members of society (for instance, in rural Oregon, the timber corporations and their political allies). In this view, stated in a simplified form, the interviewees are angry at environmentalists because industry and political leaders have convinced low-income and blue-collar workers that industry's and working people's interests are one and the same. A variant on this argument is that in the face of the enormous political and economic power of the timber industry — power over media, community affairs, and employees — working people choose to side with those in power, taking on the "dominant ideology" the industry promotes, even though it actually harms their long-term interests.

More appealing is James Scott's argument (1990) that the preexisting public language of political debate is used by people to promote their own interests. The terminology might be the same, but the meaning is different: Peter Alten and Larry Lyon, for instance, defend the timber industry at one point and damn it at another. Either set of comments could be pulled out of context to support the industry or environmentalists, and therefore the dominance of either of those two powerful interests. But together the comments suggest either that Peter and Larry have no idea of what they are talking about and are fatally self-contradictory *or* that something else is going on. The same is true in a number of the interviews where the narrator is torn between the interests of the industry and or the environmentalists. In the course of going back and forth in analyzing sides, they are actually staking out a separate ground for which there is not yet a straightforward language (or none they were willing to use with me at that time).

Again, at this time there are few *independent* low-income or blue-collar or women's political advocacy groups to articulate and promote those interests, or even to investigate them in depth. If such groups existed, these interviews suggest that the timber corporations would face questions about their working conditions, cutting policies, and raw-log exports. The rights of national timber companies to the logs themselves might be challenged by locally based firms with substantial worker input. The environmentalists would be challenged to include the well-being of working people and local culture in a much broader context than simply "jobs." (And this might bring up the crux of class conflict: Does a middle-class community — environmentalist or otherwise — that depends on low-paid service and tourist workers really want working people to organize and protest?) New language might also include ideas about access to land and resources that would restructure the understanding of timber industry and government-land administrators' notions of "public" and "private" property rights. Rural zoning might be expanded to include provisions — similar to those that exist for urban areas — for new low- and moderate-income housing inside hamlets, or in land-trust clustered housing with strong covenants for maintaining rural character. In a discussion where women's voices were prominent, the creation of realistic economic, environmental, and personal options for women would be at the top of the agenda.

NARRATIVES AND DIVERSITY

Narrative is used in this book not only as a means of identifying themes of concern in the community but also as a means of moving forward to meet those concerns across the silence of the social divisions that isolate poor and working-class issues. Personal narratives bring unexpected themes to the fore — themes that arise from a diversity of life situations instead of rigid ideology or economic determinism. Getting real people to talk to each other about their lives is effective because, unlike theory, life narratives are supple and surprising, and convey a respect for the inevitability of change.

The Highlander Center in Tennessee, Christian base communities in Central and South America, Paulo Friere's work in Brazil and Guinea, and "consciousness raising" groups of the women's movement use peer education, the foundation of which is personal narrative, to build the themes on which social movements have been based. To be politically effective in developing a "voice" for low-income and blue- or pink-collar workers, this kind of narrative needs to be shared among diverse equals. The "voice" we are trying to hear is not an individual anecdote, testimonial, or survey statistic, but a collective expression accumulated from real conversations among people at the root of community (Hawkins, 1991). Social equality is necessary so that speakers are not intimidated or belittled, so that they can create a collective voice with which to challenge the more powerful. Diversity is necessary to broaden the overall vision. Looking at the broader situation is crucial: When Peter Alten, Caroline Coldbrook, Wayne Douglas, Gary Carter, and Dorothy Harris joined the military or attended a racially mixed college where they were on the same footing with people of different races and cultures, their sense of inclusive democracy widened, and their ideas about the world were fundamentally altered.

However, the efforts to bring together people from different sides of an issue in our area have been confined to activities like the "round-tables" set up by the Forest Service, which assemble groups of people who are essentially unequal: mill owners, politicians, veneer pullers, secretaries. The meetings are informative, but such attempts to find common ground must fail unless the less powerful participants are independently organized. In southwest Oregon, as elsewhere, Frederick Douglass's message in 1855 remains the foundation of all policy debate: "Power concedes nothing without a demand. It never did, and it never will."

The purpose of this project is not only to document that poor and working people have complex political ideas about the communities in which they grew up and live, but to suggest that their ideas be listened to as carefully as those of professional planners, politicians, environmentalists, industry representatives, or economists. Political agendas and the economic structure shape events in a region, but it is shared stories and memories that give events meaning. Histories (like this one) of childhoods, on-going family situations, jobs, and recreations — of people who are not thought of as "prominent" — are the matrix in which the meaning of "community" exists.

Narratives inform us not only about individual lives, but also about personal fears of bucking the system. Stories of how "just folks" and "small people" have initiated transformative social change in spite of roadblocks can inspire more success. We need social justice groups that identify with working people's problems — rather than viewing working people only as a constituency — to catalyze and support this kind of peer education.

The organized voices of poor and working people will change the agenda of the debate. In order to enter into common-ground coalitions with the lower-income majority, environmental and other "progressive" groups must challenge themselves: Are the rural communities in the forested Northwest important as areas where poor and working communities struggle to survive massive transitions, or only as places with nice trees, great views, "ecological significance," and a cheap labor force? Are environmental and "progressive" groups satisfied to administer the lives of lower-income people through public agencies and unilateral environmentalist agendas, keeping the people themselves at arm's length? Policies that blithely roll over working people's regional cultures will always produce a backlash, which right-wing ideologues have shown no hesitation to cultivate.

As for building coalitions, most people, but especially poor, lower-income, and fragilely middle-income women and men, avoid political pressure organizations because they pull people away from the rhythms, complexity, and respect of everyday life into a structured, high-pressure environment offering few rewards. "Experts" dominate the agendas of interminable meetings; demands on time, energy, and money seem endless. Narratives can be a bridge to a different kind of activism, based in the expert knowledge people have of their own lives, combined with the everyday experiences of people with similar problems.

If we consider the narratives in this book as a peer-education workshop captured between two covers, several ideas (among many others) suggest themselves. Strong unions and other low-income and blue- or pink-collar community-based organizations are essential to express the interests of working people — in the controversies between environmentalists and the timber industry, and elsewhere. If they do not exist, industry, demagogues, and promoters of authoritarian religious agendas will step in.

Gentrification — what locals call "people with money moving in and taking over" — is a pivotal concern to many working people in southwest Oregon, and is the issue through which many working individuals evaluate other public debates. Nowhere in these conversations is there the belief that people of greater social status have a unilateral right to impose their own interests at the expense of poor and working people, whether through overtly income-exclusionary policies or a mainstream environmental agenda that ignores complex social impacts. Similarly, large corporations have no moral or economic right to determine the future of the forest on the basis of profit margins.

There is, within these interviews, a burdegeoning concept of "environment" that situates local concerns in the framework of the environmental justice movement: "The environment is where we work, where we live, and where we play." Environmental justice includes "making sure people have the right to speak *and* have their issues addressed" (Alston, 1994). In southwest Oregon, environmental justice could be served, in part, by the institution of public schools that hold the interest of adolescent young women like Kathy Dodge and Ellen Tigart. Voluntary organizations, school personnel, and trusted neighbors could offer refuge for young people whose families offer none. There is an urgent need for activities that orient and prepare the majority-white communities to become mixed-race communities, as they will inevitably become. Informal economies based on natural resources occupy a central place in many poor and working people's lives: The maintenance of the public commons — free and open public land and waterways — is fundamental to economic and political democracy.[10]

Our lives are bigger than our livelihoods. People want, not only decent jobs that anchor them to a wage economy, but secure assets, both the public assets of common-property access to land and water, and the private assets of homes, gardens, and livestock. They want liveable neighborhoods and trustworthy families to provide buffers against a narrow money-based economy: The job-creation strategies that link national political interests and many environmental organizations focus far too narrowly on solutions based only on a cash income.

The diversity of issues in a community need not paralyze an organization — or a community — but can inform it. In the end, the willingness of most poor and working individuals to change, to challenge the powerful within their own community, is embedded in the possibility of maintaining a decent everyday life (Chambers, 1987; Flacks, 1989) in the culturally diverse and shared public space of neighborhood, town, and nation. The key is to challenge the power of industry and the narrowly focused interests of the privileged. To do that, lower-income people

10. It is important to note that some countries have approached rights of access to private and public forests in very different ways than the United States. In Finland, "everyman's right" guarantees Finns the right of access to public *and* private forest lands. "The tradition of everyman's right creates the basis to man-nature relationship in Finnish culture. Many Finnish people have strong feelings toward nature, and the everyman's right offers an opportunity to keep it alive. The tradition helps citizens to be aware of the limits of recreation behavior. Both rights and duties are in common consciousness of Finnish people" (Sievänen, 1992, p. 112). "In Finland, the picking of wild berries and mushrooms is a public right of access; every person can freely pick berries and mushrooms in forests and peatlands" (Salo, 1992, p. 135).

Louise Fortmann and John W. Bruce (1988) discuss various layers of ownership of trees worldwide: For instance, one person may own the land, another the tree, a third the fruit of that tree. On national lands, a village may own the rights to gather livestock feed from a section of public forest.

In the United States, estimates of the worth of the informal economy based on natural resource use can be found in Shanna Ratner's work (1984). In her survey of one northeast community, up to one-seventh of the equivalent of total cash income was provided by use of natural resources in the informal economy.

must generate the space to define their own agenda and then make strategic alliances on their own terms—perhaps with the part of the labor and environmental community that has not abandoned concern for social and economic democracy.

A successful democratic society depends on the constant interplay of interests among equals. People of traditionally lower status will break through the racial, gender, and social segregations of our society, to listen to one another, to pay attention, as Art Downing says, to "the similarities instead of the differences," when there is a realistic opportunity to make a change. In order to achieve leverage in the Rogue Valley, low-income and blue- and pink-collar men and women who are grounded in the rural culture of this area must create independent pressure organizations and enter the public debate with power of numbers behind their words. This book is offered in the spirit of the best efforts of this kind— those which are devoted to economic and social justice embedded in local community.

An environmentalist reflection

ART and PAULA DOWNING   (ages 44 and 50) Art and Paula Downing were two of the founders, in the early 1970s, of Headwaters, the most important Rogue Valley public lands environmental organization. They are among the rare local activists of blue- or pink-collar origins.

Art   I had some thoughts come together recently, kind of looking back over the history of Headwaters and the history of what's happened in this region in terms of environmental activism.

Kind of a catalyzing event for me was, I picked up a young hitch-hiker last time I drove to California. And I tell you, it was like picking up me, having a conversation with a younger self. It was eerie in a way.

This young man, eighteen years old, out of high school, disenfranchised from his Republican parents. Obviously overprivileged. But hyperconscious and aware of environmental issues. His words were, he really "wanted to do something to save the woods." He was on his way to rendezvous with the EarthFirst! people in Laytonville [California] for the Redwood Summer.

I found stuff coming out of my mouth that I hadn't really articulated before because I was talking to this young man who was just so gung-ho and so EarthFirst! So radical. And so opinionated.

I found myself trying not to lecture him too severely. What I said was, There's no question that when you think through the environmental issues, when you really come to understand forestry, you really get into the issues on the intellectual level. You can become so acutely aware of how stupid the system is. How utterly wrong it is. Intellectually, logically, philosophically, you can be so hyper-aware of how wrong it is, that you can get into having the power of being right. And you end up taking extreme postures.

So I was telling him that I was really concerned and disapproved in a basic way of the positions I saw EarthFirst! taking. Not so much the positions, but the kind of polarization that they catalyze.

And that led me to talk about fear and ignorance. Economic terrorism. We're all victims of the same terrorism. We've got people who are just scared to death of being out of work. And you don't do yourself or your cause or the woods any good by alienating those people—just because you're right. Just because you're right doesn't make it work, you know?

So we talked. It was a chance for me to reminisce about the history of Headwaters in the context of current events. And think about some of the mistakes that we made. Some of the mistakes that I think are still being made.

Until we can put together a real cogent strategy that addresses the bottom-line issues of fear and ignorance that underlie all the issues, we're not going to make any real changes. People are going to become more entrenched, and we're going to not communicate on some vital issues.

The fact that lots of people stand to be out of work, and are terrified at that prospect, can't be denied. It can't be overlooked. And the way they feel about it can't be discounted. You maybe can't change their reality, but you certainly don't do any good by just discounting how they feel about it.

I came here in 1969 from San Francisco. I grew up mostly in Colorado. I was born in Kansas. We left the farm in Kansas when I was about eight and a half years old. It was the post-Dust-Bowl Dust Bowl going out of Kansas at that time. It ran a huge number of farmers off their farms. My father was just one of virtually all of his peers had to sell out and leave. So we left and went to Colorado. My father got a job in the oilfields, which at that time was booming in eastern Colorado. We began to move around. We moved from Brush, Colorado, on the eastern slope of the Rockies, to North Dakota, then Montana, then ended up back in western Colorado—high plains, sagebrush kind of country. Cold, really cold.

So then I ended up in San Francisco after dropping out of college in 1967. Ended up in San Francisco like any other hippie. Ended up becoming part of the commune movement. That's where I met Paula.

Paula I'm from Smithfield, Rhode Island. My father was a cook, my mother worked in different mills. Or as a waitress. My mother's ambition was that I go to college. So I did. Then I ended up marrying this guy who got a job in California, so we came to California. And we got divorced instantly after we got there—sixty-seven. Eventually I

ended up in the same commune with Art. And they had already
bought property in Oregon.

Art   We went on a land search the early part of 1969. It was kind
of one of those things that was happening among the subculture that
existed around the Bay Area — everybody wanted to leave the city and
go to the country. This is around the time of the *Life* magazine article
about a commune in Sunny Valley. We ended up buying this really remote, really impossible piece of land way up on the hill. I mean, it was
like it would have made a good ski resort if you had a billion dollars to
develop it.

We were supposedly the country branch of this city commune. We
were going to have a country retreat. We invested several years and a
lot of money into it. And then eventually there was kind of a spiritual
breakdown of the original dream. And a lot of people went different
ways.

In 1969 we bought this thing, and we had no sooner inked the paper than we got a letter and a visit from the Bureau of Land Management. Saying that they would gladly pay us one dollar for the privilege
of subordinating our easement to theirs, and using our property for access to their timber holdings above us on the drainage.

It kind of triggered the whole process. That property was so high
on the drainage that we had a real unique perspective. We were right
up with the fire lookout. We used to go up there and hang out with
him, and look at this panorama, and contemplate what was going on.
And it was when I was first beginning to become aware of what was
going on with forest practices, you know? I mean, I had been into the
same illusion that lots of people were under at that time, which was
that national forest land was park. Like nobody could touch it. I was in
the process of having my eyes opened. Roundtop Mountain is the hub
of a really large complex, which includes a lot of drainages. I got to
looking at it and studying this topography, and realizing that if they
took what they wanted, there wasn't any left. This was it. It occurred to
me, maybe it wasn't right. So I got inspired and said, "Well, you know,
I don't know if we have to cooperate with these guys or not."

I had been kind of the person who was pushing the land movement, and I was the only country boy in the group — that had any kind
of country background. So being young and eager — How young was I?
Twenty-one or twenty-two. One of the nice things about communal
living at that time, you were basically free from the normal financial
responsibilities that people have. I had a roof, I didn't have any attach-
ments, so I kind of devoted my life to it for a while.

We went back to the BLM guy. The guy made us this offer of a dollar, and we said, "We don't think so. It just doesn't seem right."

And he said, "Well, I guess you could write a letter of protest if you wanted to."

In the process of writing this letter, I had some thoughts crystallize. We did a little bit of research, and I got my first taste of forestry textbooks and the idea of forestry.

We began to research alternatives. And I started looking for a lawyer. Of course, back then, we figured in order for it to work, it had to be free. One of the things that distinguished our commune is that we were a free commune. The old Digger Paper philosophy: If you do what you do for free, and everybody did what they do for free, for fun, then it would be a wonderfully utopian society.

And we were trying to make that a reality. We did all kinds of stuff for free. So I went looking for free lawyers. And then I went looking for free scientists, and one thing led to another. I was in a unique position to be able to do it. In looking for the land, we'd made dozens of connections with people all over the Northwest who were doing the same thing. We'd visited all the other communes that were buying property, and I just kind of had these connections.

So we filed a protest which ended up being an administrative appeal. We learned how to do it kind of on the fly. And managed to hook in our first lawyer.

Paula   One of the people in the commune belonged to the Sierra Club when they were first trying to figure out what they could do. So they went to the Northwest representative, who was Brock Evans. And he helped. He came and spent a week.

Art   And they encouraged us to go to the DEQ and look into the law, and told us how to do environmental appeals.

Eventually I broke off from the commune and decided to go ahead with this work. So I was kind of free and on my own. I thought, Well, I'll go up and visit ol' Brock Evans up in Seattle. By the time I got up there, I hatched a scheme. If he would give me a little bit of front money, and an Abne level and an increment borer . . .

An Abne level used to be a real valuable timber cruiser's tool. It's been replaced now by more sophisticated equipment. But it's a little level that, between that and an increment borer, you can begin the process of determining what the yield capacity for a given site is. I knew that if I could prove that they were violating sustained yield, and really breaking the law in that sense, that I could make this into more than just an environmental issue. It was a bottom-line economic issue. OK?

So I said, "If you'll give me these things, I'll do this work." And he did. He wrote me a check for two hundred and fifty dollars, and I went and bought an Abne level and an increment borer and I started.

B. B.   The easement was no longer the issue.

Art   No, we were appealing their decision to cut.

Paula   And without having written an environmental impact statement.

Art   NEPA happened in seventy,* and by this time it was getting to be seventy-one and seventy-two, and they still hadn't even begun to file a statement. They were due to have one filed by the end of seventy-one.

We didn't really pick up on the NEPA thing as being a real core issue for a little while. We just started out protesting what they were doing, and then protesting their decision to go ahead. We did good. We made the "decision of record" broad enough to really address what we thought were the central issues. And the central issue ended up being sustained yield. We tried to make the case that what they were doing was typical, and we got them to admit that it was typical of what they had to cut. In fact, one of their rationales for not making an exception was that this is what they had to do if they were going to meet their commitments.†

We were then living on a piece of property called the One-Twelve. It was a hundred-and-twelve acre piece. There were a couple of guys who had bought land. They invited me to live on their property while I did this thing. Because they said, "You know what? You're hot. And it affects us, too. So here. Build yourself a little cabin. Bring your girlfriend. Whatever you want to do, but do the job."

So we were there. It became clear that we needed to go out and connect up with the other interests that were out there that we had in common. We went and got affidavits. We tried to get some old-timers. We tried to get some younger.

Paula   Everybody in the drainage.

Art   We were getting down to the deadline. We had a Deux Chevaux, a little French two-cylinder Citröen car. Little sardine-top kind of thing. I spent a whole day and a half driving all over southern Oregon

*The National Environmental Policy Act of 1969 went into effect in 1970. *B. B.*

†That is, meet the allowable sales quantity (ASQ) set by Congress for that fiscal year. *B. B.*

collecting affidavits and signatures. I was in Takilma and Williams and Ashland and Wolf Creek and just everywhere. And that was the original Headwaters Association.

Paula The fun part about those days is that it was so wide open. The BLM, the Freedom of Information Act, we could go in and we looked in their file drawers. And we found out so much information. Now they're very guarded and all that.

Plus the appeals process was so wide open. It's so structured and restricted now. But it stopped the whole thing for years. They couldn't do it. So we really had a lot of freedom to investigate and know what was going on.

Art Two women friends had research skills. I didn't know the hell what I was doing. But I had the chutzpah, because I was on fire, to go to the BLM office and say, "Tell me about this. Come on. Account for this. Explain this to me and explain it now!".

And they would say, "Well, if you really want to know, OK." And they'd bring me down to their little room, and I would bring these two women friends and Paula, and we'd research. They'd leave us alone, sometimes for days. And we'd dig into their charts and their files. God! For a long time they didn't even charge us for photocopies. [*Laughs*] After a while they wanted to charge us ten dollars a page!

Paula We found out things about them that they didn't know about themselves. Regulations that they were supposed to live up to that they didn't live up to. That's how we found out, really, about the allowable cut. They would say, "Yeah, we're cutting eight times as much as we're growing. Yes, we are." And I have that on tape! And they just told us all those things. It was just so open at that point.

And then we appealed. Headwaters appealed the timber plan sale for one year. Up to that point we didn't act as an organization.

They gave us a hearing. If we had had any political brains, we would have made a lot of it public. But nobody knew about it. [*Laughs*] The BLM didn't tell anybody, and we didn't tell anybody. But we had a three-day hearing. They sent a judge and all that.

Art That was basically on the Roundtop appeal. The ruling at that hearing was: Well, basically you're right. We're making a mistake here. And we see that you're reaching toward a broader issue, but this is not the right format. If you want to raise those issues, you're going to have to go to federal court.

Paula We were trying to reduce the allowable cut. That was our goal.

Art   We wanted to raise the sustained yield issue as a violation of the Environmental Policy Act. And a violation of sustained yield. For the Medford District. And by this time it's becoming 1976.

B. B.   How were you supporting yourselves?

Paula   We probably lived on a couple hundred dollars a month. We didn't have to pay rent. I crocheted some things. I sewed little things. And some people would donate money to us. Fifty bucks here and there.

Art   We had food stamps. We didn't have any welfare, but we had food stamps. And somewhere in there, about seventy-five, is when I started selling poles. There were some donations coming in. Head-waters got some donations. A friend of mine in the Bay Area who was well off had funneled money our way occasionally, for key expenses. I know it's hard to believe, but we really didn't need any money. Hardly.

Paula   Got fifty miles to the gallon.

Art   We built a cabin out of poles and cardboard. [*Prolonged laughter*] Refrigerator boxes.

Paula   Lots of plastic. And roofing.

Art   So we didn't have much. We were living on almost nothing. We didn't want to live that way for very long. Especially once we had a baby. That didn't happen for a while.

The next wave was when we raised the major issue. They were going to publish the allowable cut that year, and we had already raised all the issues in the other appeal. We had the goods. We knew that they were overcutting by a huge factor. We had pretty well proved that.

Instead of an individual sale, we said, "You know what? Your al-lowable cut is illegal. It violates NEPA, and it violates sustained yield. And you'll see our statement of reasons in thirty days." [*Laughs*]

By that time we had gathered up [Randall] O'Toole. We had got-ten a lawyer from Portland, and it was pro bono. We had gathered to-gether a panel of expert witnesses.

During the Roundtop appeal, we got wind that they were going to show up at the hearing with five Ph.D.s, you know? The forest hydrol-ogy, the forest geology, soil geology, soil science, silviculture, dendrol-ogy. They were going to show up with the big guns.

And so we thought — maybe we ought to have a couple experts of our own. So for want of a better idea, I got in the Two-C-V and went to Corvallis, Eugene, and Seattle. I went wherever the experts were. By this time I was really well read, and I just followed my nose. I man-aged to put together a panel of five really solid experts willing to come down and testify. Mostly they were the graduate students of the Ph.D.s who we were facing.

Paula They were their best students, too.

Art Well, the judge saw the point. And he made probably the best ruling he could under the circumstances and wrote really in our favor without actually giving up all the issues. But he did force us to go to federal court. And we did.

It's hard to believe, looking back on how it happened. That somehow or other people without money managed to be in federal District Court, Judge [James M.] Burns. We had a case.

Paula The BLM, the industry — there were like twelve industry lawyers who had intervened.

Art It took a long, involved process. By the time it actually got to court, we'd managed to get a temporary restraining order, and they did not cut. The allowable cut was held in suspense for about six months.

There were headlines, but I don't think it caused quite the stir that it would now. Though I don't know. It caused a stir, believe me. Reporters came and tracked us down. Friends were afraid that we were going to get snuffed by bad-assed loggers.

We showed up in Portland. There wasn't room at the table for both our attorneys and me. [*Laughs*] We had one corner of this table, and all of our papers and briefcases had to be on the floor. Because the rest of the table was covered with attorneys for the interveners. It was just interveners coming out the doors.

None of them knew what the hell they were talking about. They didn't have any concept of the issues, for the most part. All they could do was argue that *x* number of jobs were going to be down the tube. And of course the judge had to be sensitive to that. They managed to politicize the issue to the extent where he made what really ended up being a pretty real political decision.

B. B. So these "bad-assed" loggers — were you hearing from them?

Art We never heard from them. Not that I'm aware of. One of the things we did when we first formed Headwaters, we put forth our position: We're Headwaters for the identification and protection of critical watershed. And here are the issues we're concerned about.

We called town meetings all over Wolf Creek, Williams, Cave Junction, Grants Pass. I offered to go and represent Headwaters at these town meetings. I went to the Soil and Water Conservation Districts. I went wherever anybody would have me. Little town board meetings. The Williams town council invited me out.

We basically took the approach of being really up front. We were just as concerned about jobs and the economy as anybody else is. We're just trying to make sure we all see the handwriting on the wall. That was our approach.

By that time I was able to say, "Hey! I work in the woods, too." Which I did, you know. I had a little pole business and I looked like somebody that worked in the woods. I talked like somebody that worked in the woods. And I was sincere.

So I was able to talk directly to a couple local mill owners. Various other people who ended up deciding I wasn't just a wildlife fanatic. That we weren't just crazy people.

B. B. What difference do you think it made that you came from a working-class background?

Art Oh, it made a big difference. Some of the other environmentalists — they come from inside their heads.

Paula Um-hmm. Education. Intellectual. To me, the allowable cut is, by definition, an economic issue. And there wasn't anybody who didn't know that what we were saying was true.

Art We ended up in court. We won but we lost. We got co-opted in a sense by the National Resources Defense Council. They, at the last minute, realized we had a real case, and it all pivoted on NEPA. They at that time considered themselves the main people behind NEPA. If there was going to be any major rulings on a NEPA issue, they wanted to be in it. And we were short on resources, and our lawyers were fried. Out of time, out of patience. Out of energy. Certainly out of money. They were looking for a way to unload all that responsibility. I was burned. I had reached this plateau, this objective, that I never thought I would get to, and I was suddenly hit with: Ha! What do I do now?

So when someone marched in and said, "Hey! We know what to do!" I thought, Well, OK. Maybe they do. So we chose to allow NRDC to become the negotiating party. And allowed them to negotiate the settlement on the NEPA issue.*

---

*Two cases, with interrelated issues, were being pursued: NRDC picked up the Headwaters case focusing on the lack of an environmental impact statement by the BLM and took it to U.S. District Court for the District of Columbia. The BLM chose to settle, agreeing to prepare an EIS. Parallel with the NRDC case was *Downing v. Frizzel*, filed in U.S. District Court for Oregon. In this case Headwaters chose to press the overcutting, or sustained yield, issue, which the NRDC was not interested in litigating. Judge Burns in Oregon declared the issue of the case moot after the BLM settled with the NRDC, but testimony at the hearings resulted in a BLM agreement to cut the ASQ for the Medford District by at least 30 percent (P. Downing, personal communication, 1994). *B. B.*

In retrospect, I really think it was a real mistake. We lost control of the case. A lot of important issues got lost in the wash. And, unfortunately, the sustained yield issue was one of them. If the NRDC had had it together, they would have put their weight behind that one.

Paula Well, they wanted victory. They wanted something they could put in their brochure which said, "We did this and we won."

Art Right. They really never even hardly gave us credit.

Paula It's just how those environmental organizations are. They took it on because they thought they could win. They didn't think they could win on sustained yield — that's why they dropped it. But NEPA was so clearcut — it was obvious that they would win that.

Art They hadn't filed an environmental impact statement.

Paula And there was this major impact going on, and we had documented it and proven all that.

Art And the sustained yield issues didn't end up getting addressed.

Oh! I forgot a real important part. Donald Scofield. Who was at the time the District Manager. We considered him our archrival. He was distant, aloof, cold, and hostile.

But as a result of getting to federal court, we had turned up all this evidence having to do with how they inventoried, and how much they were overcutting. And the goods were in. And right at that point Donald Scofield said, "You know what? They're right." And he went to Eric Allen of the *Medford Tribune,* and Eric Allen wrote this incredible editorial which encapsulated the issues and laid it out real clearly.

Paula And Scofield lost his job because of it. They "moved" him — three years away from retirement. And he said, "Screw you. I'm going to get out." Actually, that move got investigated, too. Representative [Jim] Weaver got a Congressional committee to investigate what happened with that.

Art But he knew we were right. It turns out, in retrospect, the guy was a man of principle. He had to choose whether he was going to go down with the ship, or do something in keeping with his integrity. And he ended up being our expert witness. In federal court! We subpoenaed him, and he testified on our side.

It's really sad, because in some ways — it's youthful folly in a way. I mean, we tended to think in "good guy/bad guy." I overlooked some really important stuff about Donald Scofield and what he had done back then. I don't think we fully appreciated what a gem he was until we had to deal with his successor.

He instituted the whole idea of shelterwood cutting in this district before anyone else did. He was the first to recognize that they couldn't succeed with clearcuts. The only thing he couldn't do was reduce the allowable cut. His hands were tied. He was still forced to try to produce his allowable cut.

B. B.   That was during a time we were reaching an all-time high in the cut in the area, too. Were people concerned about jobs? Mills were spinning away, right?

Art   There's always, ever since I can remember, mills closing and people worried about supply. Mills have always shut down. Historically mills close, and others conglomerate. Small mills go out of business. It's the nature of the industry. It takes lots and lots of real capital invested in research and development and upgraded technology to stay on top of it.

And there's always been the perception of shortage. They are always pushing to increase the allowable cut. There's never enough. Never enough wood! It's always because the government won't sell the timber to us, or it's because of this or that.

The environmentalists stepped into the fray and just became the convenient scapegoat for a process that had been going on for a long time. Like the spotted owl. You get to be the scapegoat for what basically is betrayal on the part of the relatively inhumane corporations. Who don't really give a shit. It's not in the accounting to be concerned about social issues — it just isn't, you know? Unemployment? It's not a consideration.

When we were cutting more timber than had ever been cut in the history of the world, there were fewer jobs in the woods industry than there had ever been in the history of the world. It's mechanization. It's a change in the type of the supply, from big logs to smaller logs. Primarily it's mechanization, it's conglomeration. Technology has advanced to the point where they can do so much more with so much less manpower.

The other issue is that they're running out of the supply anyway. They're cutting and running on the largest scale possible — and pretending that they're not. There has been a shortage of timber for a long time. There will only continue to be a shortage of workable, harvestable, cheap timber.

B. B.   But to be devil's advocate for a moment: The environmentalists say, "Trees, trees, trees!" And never talk about people.

Art   That's right. You're damn right. We end up being a real convenient strawman. I think we have played right into their hands. It distresses the piss out of me. That's what I was getting at originally, talking about core issues of fear and ignorance.

We don't address those issues by being intellectual snobs. And by being bright and smart and clever and well-informed or any of that stuff. None of that stuff addresses any of that. It's always been a people issue. It will continue to be. It's not a question of aesthetics. It really is an economic issue, and it's the same issue the rest of the world is facing. It's a Third World kind of issue. It's economic terrorism.

We got just enough people on the street, starving, just enough homeless people, to put the fear in all the rest of us who aren't. You know? Anything that's challenging to the vested interests that are doing well, it's been convenient to couch the arguments politically in terms of a choice between poverty and environment. Right? Anytime they can make that equation, everybody backs off. All they got to do is put the squeeze on just a little bit.

B. B. So the court case happened. Then what happened with you?

Paula We were retired for a couple of years.

Art One of our objectives was met. The environmental impact statement was going to be filed. The other objective was, we wanted to see a reduction in the allowable cut. And that happened, as a result of the testimony of Donald Scofield and the issues aired in that forum. They chose to reduce the allowable cut by thirty percent.

George Francis was the new District Manager. And his new policy was: We can go to intensive management practices. We can get it all back by using herbicides and fertilizer. Mostly herbicides. And so we had a new battle on our hands. Then we had SOCATS and NCAP.

B. B. What happened to Headwaters?

Art SOCATS was kind of the same people.

Paula It was the same people, right? We just stopped doing Headwaters. Art was speaking at a thing at which George Francis was also a speaker. He and the Forest Service guy were bragging about the herbicide programs. And Art said, "You know, we didn't know you had an herbicide program." That's how we found out about it. They had never told anybody they were using them.

Art People were scared about herbicides. We gathered a lot of support for SOCATS real quickly.

Things had changed for us a lot. At least they had for me. Toward the end of the early Headwaters, the pole business had become more and more of a preoccupation. I had chosen that as my thing to do. I was going to manifest an economic alternative, and practice excellent forestry, and try to make a living practicing excellent forestry, and be some kind of a model. I was using mules, and small equipment. I started with the drawknives, bowsaws, and burros, you know?

Paula   I went to bed. I was pregnant. Everybody ended up at my house one night, and they wrote a letter of protest: You can't spray herbicides if you haven't written an environmental impact statement. Of course they knew that was true. So it shut them down pretty much. Then they went through their process and sprayed a little bit one season. We all went—

Art   — occupied sites and did the alternative —

Paula   — brushing and stuff. *Nobody* wanted the spraying. Nobody did. The loggers didn't want it, nobody wanted it. There was such broad-based support. And then basically what happened with the herbicide thing was, it just went away.

Art   The primary battles were won at that time in Alsea, Oregon. We knew those people. They had the test case. And they managed to raise a credible case that there was a cause and effect relationship between the spraying and the birth defects.

Paula   There's some strong people involved in the herbicide issue in the Northwest, so we kind of backed out.

And then more time passed. And you started looking around Selma, and they were clearcutting. And we knew that they had committed to partial cutting.

Somebody from the neighborhood came and said, "They're going to clearcut in our back yard." These are just neighbors in Selma. So we had a meeting, and the whole neighborhood showed up. Across social lines. A lot of people. One of the people who showed up, he lost his job at a local mill, where he had worked since he was sixteen years old, because he was involved.

We talked about it and what should we do. When it came down to writing the appeal, I wrote it. The BLM came several times, and people walked all over this timber sale with them. And said, "We don't want you to do that. This is my farm, this is my father's farm. We've lived in this valley for a hundred years. We don't want you to do this." There was a lot of that. But when it came down to it, I was the only one who knew how.

Art   And because we had a pole business, we bought poles from a lot of the local people. When they weren't logging, they would go cut poles and bring them to us. So we had that kind of working relationship.

Paula   Everybody knew who we were. We got people talking to us. They know what's true, the local people. About what's being done in the woods. I'm really convinced of that.

Meanwhile there was another pocket of interest in the same issues over in the Applegate. I said, "Look, they're clearcutting here, they're clearcutting over there. Let's get together and have a meeting." So we started meeting in the Applegate. They had already been five years into the allowable cut, so it was 1984.

And we started writing more timber sale appeals. Two other women and I are going: "Jesus, we don't want to keep doing this! We already did five years of this. We're sick of this."

And this other guy is new. He's real energetic, you know? [*Laughs*] And he wants to be king of the mountain anyway. So we're going: "Let's have a Headwaters meeting. Let's revitalize the name." We put out the word: We were going to have a meeting. Picked a date. And reestablished Headwaters at that meeting. And a lot of people came. And it just started to mushroom. Maybe twelve or fifteen people would show up. Intellectual people. I did it for a couple years. Art was doing the pole business.

Well, there was conflict. Between me and this one man who was taking a leadership role. The BLM said, "Oh, let's work out a compromise and an agreement. We will do this and make you happy."

And we were paying a lawyer. Which was sitting in my craw. That he was getting all that money. I was working for free. Because we were poor. I was tired. The kids were growing up, and all that.

So I'm going: "No, they don't want to compromise with us. They are leading us down the garden path." And this one man and I went: Kewweww! Over that. Because they thought they were going to save everything by getting into this arrangement with the BLM. And there were endless meetings, and the lawyers talked and charged money, and talked and charged money. It was just so clear nothing was going to happen.

Art To go back to the original terminology I was putting forth before, we had gone back to a real intellectual perspective on it. It's a double-edged sword. 'Cause on the one hand, those legal, intellectual strategies can be effective. They have been very effective, and they probably will be again. On the other hand, they're like good drugs. They're addictive, and they're all about control. And they put the control in the hands of people who are very intellectual. Who'll go right into their heads and deal with things in their heads. Which is unfortunate for all the people who don't work that way. And it's also unfortunate for movements, because very often the legal strategies wear out. They're not effective anymore.

Like from my point of view right now, the issues are no longer legal. The issues that the environmentalists should be addressing right now are not legal, they're political. They're political in the deepest sense: They're economic.

And that means they need to engender the support of people who can identify from the purse-strings, from the gut, from the heart. Because that's really where it's at.

There was a time when legal strategies were appropriate. It seems like the way it works in history — just taking a look at our system of government. We have the checks and balances system — we have the executive, judicial, and the legislative. At different times in history, different branches tend to dominate and make changes. Either moderating changes, or reforming changes, or creative changes. Different eras, different branches become the movers.

Well, there was a period when environmental law was being written and established and tested. Lots of test cases. It was all new ground. The ink wasn't even dry, and the door was wide open.

That era is past. It's time to break some new ground. And it takes a lot of politics to do that. Politics is education — and communication, really. It's going to take a lot of that. It's going to take honest, sincere willingness to go right to where people are and talk about what matters to them, and communicate heart to heart.

It's going to take a certain amount of intelligence to do that. But it's going to take a lot more than that. It's going to take some kind of unifying spirit. More than a unifying issue. Whatever put together the original beautiful democratic coalition, you know? That kind of stuff.

I don't know if we're moving closer to that or not. It has been done in this country. I think in terms of the aftermath of the Depression and the Second World War. There's lots and lots of examples. The whole Populist movement. The whole Labor movement. Liberalism was alive and well there for a while. It didn't used to be a dirty word, it really didn't.

So it's possible. It's really possible. That's what it's going to take — people looking for the similarities instead of the differences. And not discounting the issues that are important. Not discounting the fear that's associated with facing being out of a job. And being terrified by your lack of skills. There are not very many people in the world that can just ride that one out with equanimity, you know?

Paula   There's all these people you can see are going to be out of work. But then there's this whole second growth. I mean, there's tons of work in the woods. You can put everybody to work in the woods if you put your energy into figuring out how to do that, how to pay for it, what they need to do. But that would take a united political effort.

That would take the industry and the politicians and everybody going, "Here's the reality." We have all this second growth. We have almost no old growth left.

And the real truth about the old growth and the owl is that it's an indicator species of what's happening to *us*. [*Laughs*] They're talking about the number, you know: "Well, we can do this and we won't have to reduce the allowable cut." Who are you kidding? Maybe you don't have to reduce it this year, but that means you will have no wood in five years. Whereas if you reduce it this year, you might have wood for the next ten years.

Art   There's enough political pressure from above to make it real uncomfortable for anybody to take a stand. There always are good pockets among the professionals and among the people in the agencies that see truth and see how it is and will take a stand and will speak out. But they don't last. So they're victim of the same fear that everyone else is. They're just as scared as anyone else. That's their job.

Paula   That's what a friend was telling me this afternoon at lunch — that the BLM called a meeting of the whole agency and said, "Fifty percent of you will be out of work in eighteen months."

Art   It's just fear. Same economic terrorism that everybody's victim of right now. Hey, college-educated people can be homeless, too. And often are, in modern times.

I mean, there's been more unemployment here than practically anywhere in the country — from forever. When we moved here, this was the second-highest unemployment rate in the country. Was right here.

▍▍▍ Postscript

Conflicts in the Rogue Valley over the environment, the economy, and cultural dominance proceeded without resolution into the mid-1990s. Environmental struggles took a new turn, briefly reviewed in this chapter. The greater struggle — to reestablish some level of social well-being and community civility — muddled along in the face of a worsening economy and intensifying local divisions.

THE APPLEGATE PARTNERSHIP: A MODEL?

In the early 1990s, seeking new strategies to resolve timber harvest problems in southwest Oregon, the North Applegate Watershed Protection Association tackled the BLM's Bluefoot timber sale in a spirit of negotiation. When logging was complete, Bluefoot yielded the same amount of timber as BLM's initially proposed clearcut, but through much more environmentally benign harvest methods. This cooperative solution set a precedent for BLM lands in the Pacific Northwest.

With this success under their belts, members of environmentally oriented neighborhood associations worked to create a wider cooperative network that would include industry as well as the federal agencies and private land owners. Skepticism abounded among all parties. A local mill owner's first words on the project to a local environmentalist were: "You're walking a fine line with me, you son-of-a-bitch" (Shipley and Bratt interview, 1993).

But, as all parties recognized, "the handwriting was on the wall" (Shipley and Bratt interview, 1993). Spotted owl injunctions and the threat of preservationist victory brought the principal parties to the table, and in November 1992 the 400,000-acre Applegate Partnership formally convened in an atmosphere of hope (Shipley and Bratt interview, 1993).

President Bill Clinton, soon after taking office in 1993, announced his intention to break the deadlock over the Northwest forests. On April 2, 1993, Clinton, Vice President Al Gore, and seven cabinet members, including Secretary of the Interior Bruce Babbitt, attended a Forest Conference in Portland, Oregon. Clinton announced that he would have a new forest proposal in sixty days, and by July a thick, two-volume analysis and draft environmental impact statement was produced by the Forest Ecosystem Management Assessment Team (FEMAT) (1993) and the Interagency SEIS Team (1993). Oregon will be the state most profoundly affected by the outcome of these proposals.

The Applegate Partnership came to the attention of Secretary Babbitt, who has a reputation for seeking out cooperative solutions. After a whirlwind visit through the Applegate watershed with Partnership members, Babbitt praised the experiment. The Partnership was spotlighted at the Forest Conference, and the concept was used as a model in proposing "adaptive management areas" (AMAs) throughout the Northwest. National environmental groups railed against the very idea of cooperation among environmentalists, agencies, and industry (KenCairn interview, 1993; Norman interview, 1993; Shipley and Bratt interview, 1993), but if the AMAs prove successful, they could be a new model for forestry throughout the nation.

WHOSE AGENDA?

Whether the Applegate Partnership will succeed remains to be seen. By the summer of 1994, purportedly under pressure from large regional and national environmental groups, Headwaters had pulled out. The Forest Service withdrew soon after, over concerns that Partnership meetings might violate the Federal Advisory Committee Act of 1972 (FACA), which requires meetings with federal officials to be closed to the public or open to everyone. The Forest Service may have chosen to pull out because Clinton's FEMAT report was challenged in court earlier in the year with allegations that the teams that assembled it violated FACA by inviting only selected experts for consultation.

The weakening of the Applegate Partnership followed the decision in June 1994 by federal District Court Judge William Dwyer in Seattle to lift the several-year-old injunction against most logging in national forests in the range of the northern spotted owl. Dwyer held that Clinton's revised FEMAT forest plan provided adequate habitat preservation for spotted owl recovery. Environmental groups allowed the lifting of the injunction without much outcry, in part because the narrow focus on the spotted owl restricted strategies with broader objectives, and immediately sued to prevent the implementation of a revised Option 9, the FEMAT "preferred option," which would reduce logging to about one-quarter of 1980s harvests, on the grounds that it inadequately protects not just spotted owl habitat but a much larger concept of forest ecosystems.

Many powerful public lands environmental groups supported a zero-cut option for forest policy. In addition to further old-growth concerns, new environmental efforts emphasized watersheds and salmon habitat, criticizing impediments to annual fish runs, especillay dams. Critics countered that oscillations in weather and massive overfishing by international trawlers in the Pacific may account for declines in anadromous fish runs.

In the Rogue Valley, the efforts of the Applegate Partnership continued despite the absence of crucial representatives. A fundamental goal is to bring to the table "whoever walks in the door" (Shipley and Bratt interview, 1993) from the Applegate River watershed community. Jack Shipley expressed frustration with the Forest Service withdrawal, since the whole idea of the Partnership was to conduct open meetings.

The Applegate Partnership succeeded in bringing diverse interests to the table for over a year—something no one had achieved before. Still, the representation of poor and blue- and pink-collar working people was thin to non-existent, and Latino workers, who constituted the majority of treeplanting crews, were entirely unrepresented. Who, indeed, lived in the Applegate River watershed after more than a decade of out-migration by working people and in-migration by city people? There are no incorporated areas within the watershed, and therefore no provisions for low- or moderate-income housing. Although there are still low- and middle-income residents in the Applegate Valley—thanks to the low real estate values before the early 1970s—land prices and multi-acre parcel minimums keep access limited. How would a functioning Partnership avoid consolidating itself as a middle-class property owners' protection association, pursuing its own interests with federal agencies and industry?

Public lands environmentalists continue to hope that the blue- and pink-collar public will sign on to their cause. But as Rich Rhode, one of the rare community development activists in the region, points out, getting poor and working people at the same table with middle-class people is difficult. (Rhode is Director of Rogue Valley Fair Share, Medford.) Besides the coordination of childcare, transportation, and time, these individuals are taking a different kind of risk: "[Lower-income] people have had experiences where when they tried to make a change, they've been slammed. So they've learned . . . 'If I get too far out, I'm going to get cut off'" (Rhode interview, 1993). Several blue-collar workers who became involved in environmental issues in the 1980s lost their jobs, as I learned through personal contacts as well as interviews (Cribby interview, 1993; Shipley and Bratt interview, 1993).

Unemployment stayed in the high single digits in Jackson County through the first years of the 1990s, while Josephine County's unemployment rate was stuck above 10 percent. Low-quality employers pose new problems for people making the transition from wood products work. One former lumber-hauler indicated his hands, fissured and reddened by exposure to chemicals in an ill-ventilated local factory: "Now, if your environmentalist friends would pay attention to some of these kinds of problems, they might start getting some support."

Many long-time locals are discouraged. In recognition of the mood of the community, a few activists are nursing fledgling community development groups. But the conditions they address are different from those of even a decade ago. In referring to the newer urban-flight immigrants, and the increasing dominance of their city-based culture over the previous rural culture, one activist said simply, "They've already won."

William E. Shands (1991) and Kenneth P. Wilkinson (1991) question whether the term "rural" should be applied to areas like the Rogue Valley in the 1990s, where good roads and good cars allow middle- income country-dwellers the same access to urban amenities and jobs that they would enjoy in a metropolitan area. Although high-poverty rural areas remain, mostly on the western and northern edges of the Rogue Valley, they, too, are on an upward trajectory, appealing to urban people accustomed to commuting an hour or an hour-and-a-half to work. Fred Buttel, past president of the Rural Sociological Society, mused, "I cannot help but wonder whether . . . environmentalism might over time lead to a fundamental shift in how rural spaces are symbolized, and accordingly how we define and deal with rural problems. . . . Will we, in other words, witness a further erosion of commitment to improving the livelihoods of the rural poor and to rural development? Can we think meaningfully of 'sustainable development' in nonmetropolitan contexts of the advanced countries?" (Buttel, 1992, pp. 22–23).

The Rogue Valley has already undergone much of the transition from a rural to a "dispersed-urban" area with little regard for low- and moderate-income rural and small-town people. If the issues of contention in the area look more and more similar to national metropolitan debates over neighborhoods, racism, and fiscal or religious ideologies (often aggravated by economic polarization), the need for poor and working people of all colors to organize to rediscover a democratic community has not diminished — it has expanded.

Organizing for social justice in the Rogue Valley has focused in the recent past on issues chosen by activists of middle- and upper-middle-class origin. This book offers an alternative approach to rural advocacy: Ask poor and working people what matters to them. As Myles Horton of the Highlander Center never tired of saying, "Start where people are" (personal communication, 1986; also see Adams, 1975).

This book indicates some of the places "where people are." Among many issues is the sense that the transition from rural to urban culture has cut people out of their own community. But, again quoting Myles Horton, "The future is out there; it's malleable. Whatever is fixed can be un-fixed." (See the film *You Got to Move* [1985], directed by Lucy M. Phenix and Veronica Selver, distributed by First Run Features, New York.)

What is a just and ecologically sound relationship between working people's communities and forests? Does the national interest in forests supersede a local interest, as many national environmental organizations argue in the United States? This question is an international one, unsettled in many more nations than our own.

The gulf between lower- and upper-income people increases in the United States and the world, as well as in the Rogue Valley. Whether in Brazil, Indonesia, India, Africa, or the Pacific Northwest, rural workers have been portrayed as enemies of the forest environment. Industry and more privileged citizens have asked poor and working people to accept, in exchange for environmental protections, contempt, low wages, and relocation. Working citizens who believe in saving both the trees and the people do not have to submit to the request to leave quietly. Instead, the first task is to resist false choices; the second is to work with optimism towards a future that embraces both healthy forests and inclusive democratic community.

References

Interviews

All interviews were conducted by the author and taped. Cassette tapes and partial transcriptions are in the author's possession.

Casebeer, Robert. 1993. Local historian and Professor of English, Southern Oregon State College. Sept. 24.

Cribby, Phyllis. 1993. SOCATS Coordinator. Jan. 23.

KenCairn, Brett. 1993. Executive Director, Rogue Institute for Ecology and Economy (Ashland, Oreg.). Sept. 29.

Lang, Linda. 1993. Professional land-use planner. Sept. 10.

Norman, Julie. 1993. Projects Coordinator, Headwaters (Ashland, Oreg.). Oct. 1.

Owens-Stevenson, Mollie. 1993. Coordinator of Training Resources for Women, Rogue Community College, and master's candidate in history, Southern Oregon State College. Oct. 1.

Peters, Boyd. 1993. Former president of Headwaters. Jan 2.

Rhode, Rich. 1993. Director, Rogue Valley Fair Share (Medford, Oreg.). Sept. 23.

Shipley, Jack, and Chris Bratt. 1993. Jack Shipley, Applegate Partnership, and Vice President, Headwaters Board of Directors (Ashland, Oreg.); and Chris Bratt, Applegate Partnership, Headwaters Board of Directors, Rogue Institute for Ecology and Economy Board of Directors (Ashland, Oreg.). Sept. 29.

Sturtevant, Victoria. 1993. Professor of Sociology, Southern Oregon State College. Sept. 24.

Written sources and presentations

Adams, Frank, with Myles Horton. 1975. *Unearthing seeds of fire: The idea of Highlander.* Winston-Salem, N.C.: John F. Blair.

Adams, Nancy, Marijean Badger, and John Todaro. 1989. *A profile of the recent Ashland homebuyer, June 9, 1989.* Ashland, Oreg.: Southern Oregon Regional Services Institute, Southern Oregon State College.

Allen, Mary Beth. 1987. Five counties join forces to study the economy. *Medford [Oreg.] Mail Tribune,* Dec. 13.

Alston, Dana A. 1994. Program Officer, Public Welfare Foundation, Washington,

D.C. Presentation to the Rural Development Leadership Network Institute, Davis, Calif. June 6.

Anderson, John. 1992. *Oregon Employment Division business and employment outlook, Volume 1: Economic structure and analysis, District 8.* Salem, Oreg.: Labor Market Information, State of Oregon.

————. 1993. *Labor trends, Grants Pass local office.* Salem, Oreg.: State of Oregon, Employment Division, Department of Human Resources. June.

Ansell, Phill, et al. 1992. Accidental tourism: A critique of the Los Angeles tourism industry and proposals for change. Manuscript. Urban Planning Department, University of California at Los Angeles.

Beckham, Stephen D. 1971. *Requiem for a people: The Rogue Indians and the frontiersmen.* The Civilization of the American Indian, vol. 108. Norman: University of Oklahoma Press.

Behan, R. W. 1990. The RPA/NFMA: Solution to a non-existent problem. *Journal of Forestry* 88 (5): 20–25.

Brock, Richard. 1993. Tree growth survey contradicts BLM projections. *Headwaters Journal* (Summer): 18–20.

Brothers, Robert. 1993. SAT Report: 667 old-growth species need protection. *Headwaters Journal* (Summer): 6–8.

Buttel, Frederick. 1992. Environmentalization: Origins, processes, and implications for rural social change. *Rural Sociology* 57:1–27.

Caldwell, Lynton K., Charles F. Wilkinson, and Margaret Shannon. 1994. Making ecosystem policy: Three decades of change. *Journal of Forestry* 94 (4): 7–10.

Carroll, Matthew S. 1989. Taming the lumberjack revisited. *Society and Natural Resources* 2:91–106.

Carroll, Matthew S., and Robert G. Lee. 1990. Occupational community and identity among Pacific Northwestern loggers: Implications for adapting to economic changes. In Robert G. Lee (ed.), *Community and forestry: Continuities in the sociology of natural resources,* pp. 141–55. Boulder, Colo.: Westview Press.

Centaur Associates and James M. Montgomery Consulting Engineers. 1981. *Socioeconomic and environmental impacts of forest-based activities.* Study Module IV. Pullman: Washington State University.

Chambers, Robert. 1987. Sustainable livelihoods, environment, and development: Putting poor rural people first. Discussion Paper 240. Brighton, U.K.: Institute of Development Studies, University of Sussex.

Chapman, Jeffery. 1981. *Proposition 13 and land use: A case study of fiscal limits in California.* Lexington, Mass.: Lexington Books.

Clephane, Thomas P. 1978. Ownership of timber: A critical component in industrial success. *Forest Industries* (August): 30–32.

Culhane, Paul J. 1981. *Public lands politics: Interest group influence on the Forest Service and the Bureau of Land Management.* Baltimore: Johns Hopkins University Press, for Resources for the Future, Inc.

Daniels, Steven. 1994. Professor, School of Forestry, Oregon State University, Corvallis, Oreg. Correspondence. June.

Davis, Mike. 1991. *City of quartz: Excavating the future in Los Angeles.* London and New York: Verso.

Davis, Steven. 1994. Pluralism and ecological values: The case of the Siskiyou National Forest 1983–1992. Ph.D. dissertation. Loyola University, Chicago.

Downing v. Frizzel. U.S. District Court, Oreg. 1975 (75–1128). Filed Dec. 9, 1975.

Fattig, Paul. 1986. Mill boss rips environmentalists. *Grants Pass [Oreg.] Daily Courier*, Aug. 8.

———. 1987a. Tree spiking stirs timbermen's ire. *Grants Pass [Oreg.] Daily Courier*, May 26.

———. 1987b. EarthFirst! digs in for blockade. *Grants Pass [Oreg.] Daily Courier*, June 13.

———. 1987c. Timber battle turns violent. *Grants Pass [Oreg.] Daily Courier*, June 22.

———. 1989. Oregon yells 'yes' to log export ban. *Grants Pass [Oreg.] Daily Courier*, June 28.

———. 1990. Feds: Spare that owl. *Grants Pass [Oreg.] Daily Courier*, June 22.

Fitchen, Janet. 1991. *Endangered spaces, enduring places: Change, identity, and survival in rural America.* Boulder, Colo.: Westview.

——— (presenter). 1992. Poverty in rural America: An holistic overview of causes, characteristics and changes. Corvallis Conference on Rural Poverty, Oregon State University, Corvallis, Oreg., Oct. 23, 1992. Conference sponsored by the Western Rural Development Center and the National Rural Studies Committee.

Flacks, Richard. 1989. *Making history: The American left and the American mind.* New York: Columbia University Press.

Forest Ecosystem Management Assessment Team. 1993. *Forest ecosystem management: An ecological, economic, and social assessment: Report of the Forest Ecosystem Management Assessment Team, July 1993.* Pub. no. 1993-793–071. Washington, D.C.: U.S. Government Printing Office.

Fortmann, Louise, and John W. Bruce (eds). 1988. *Whose tree: Proprietary dimensions of forestry.* Rural Studies no. 71. Boulder, Colo.: Westview.

Frohnmayer, Dave. 1993. The new pioneers. *Old Oregon: University of Oregon Alumni Magazine* (Autumn): 23–27.

Gamboa, Erasmo. 1991. Mexican mule packers and Oregon's Second Regiment Mounted Volunteers, 1855–1856. *Oregon Historical Quarterly* 92 (1): 41–59.

Grants Pass [Oreg.] Daily Courier. 1986. Atiyeh proposes swap: Owl land for wilderness. Nov. 18.

———. 1991. Is Bush letting owl impact hit jobs too hard? May 21.

———. 1992. Census: Oregon natives a minority. May 1.

Gregory, Gordon. 1989a. Battle over old growth reaches summit: Politicans must sift through conflicting facts and figures. *Grants Pass [Oreg.] Daily Courier*, June 24.

———. 1989b. Timber shortage raises log export issue. *Grants Pass [Oreg.] Daily Courier*, Nov. 13.

———. 1990. Timber woes go beyond the owl. *Grants Pass [Oreg.] Daily Courier*, July 28.

———. 1992a. Lujan's latest owl team. *Grants Pass [Oreg.] Daily Courier*, Feb. 19.

———. 1992b. Lujan's latest owl team to be packed with political types. *Grants Pass [Oreg.] Daily Courier*, Mar. 10.

Grier, Norma. 1984. A chronology of NEPA-based "Spray" cases. *NCAP News* 4 (1): 35.

Halle, David. 1984. *America's working man: Work, home, and politics among blue-collar property owners.* Chicago and London: University of Chicago Press.

Harrison, Bennett, and Barry Bluestone. 1988. *The great U-turn: Corporate restructuring and the polarizing of America.* New York: Basic Books.

Hawkins, Ann. 1991. The politics of claiming voice: Development and the rhetoric of environment. Manuscript. Ciriacy-Wantrup Postdoc Papers, University of California at Berkeley, Natural Resource Studies.

Hawkins, Ann, and Frederick Buttel. 1989. The political economy of sustainable development. Paper presented at the American Sociological Association Meeting, San Francisco. Aug.

Hibbard, Mike. 1993. Associate Professor of Planning, Public Policy, and Management, University of Oregon. Presentation at Lane Community College. Nov.

Hill, Edna May. 1976. *Josephine County historical highlights.* Grants Pass, Oreg.: Josephine County Library System and Josephine County Historical Society.

Huntington, Howard. 1989. Commission signs owl proclamation. *Grants Pass [Oreg.] Daily Courier,* June 7.

Interagency SEIS Team. 1993. *Draft supplemental environmental impact statement on management of habitat for late-successional and old-growth forest related species within the range of the northern spotted owl.* Pub. no. 1993-793-234/82403, Region no. 10. Washington, D.C.: U.S. Government Printing Office.

Israel, Tom. 1980. *The southern timber industry: History, profile, analysis.* Thomastown, Miss.: Southern Woodcutters Assistance Project.

Johnson, Olga Weydemeyer. 1978. *They settled in Applegate country: Frontier days along the lower Applegate River in Southern Oregon.* Grants Pass, Oreg.: Self-published.

Kusel, Jonathan. 1991. It's just like baseball: A study of forest community well-being. Ph.D. dissertation, University of California at Berkeley, Wildland Resource Science.

Labor Trends. 1991–93. *Labor Trends, Grants Pass local office.* Salem, Oreg.: State of Oregon, Employment Division, Department of Human Resources.

Lee, Robert G. 1991. Four myths of interface communities: Rural localities do not epitomize idealized conceptions. *Journal of Forestry* 89 (6): 35–38.

Levitan, Lois, and Shelley Feldman. 1991. For love or money: Non-monetary economic arrangements among rural households in central New York. *Research in Rural Sociology and Development* 5:149–72.

Loveman, Gary W., and Chris Tilly. 1988. Good jobs or bad jobs: What does the evidence say? *New England Economic Review* (Jan./Feb.): 46–65.

Lowenstein, Steven. 1987. *The Jews of Oregon, 1850–1950.* Portland, Oreg.: Jewish Historical Society of Oregon.

Lowi, Theodore. 1986. The welfare state, the new regulation, and the rule of law. In Allan Schnaiberg, Nicholas Wats, and Klaus Zimmermann (eds.), *Distributional conflicts in environmental-resource policy,* pp. 109–49. New York: St. Martin's Press.

Lyson, Thomas A. 1988. Economic development in the rural South: An uneven past — an uncertain future. In L. J. Beaulieu (ed.), *The rural South in crisis: Challenges for the future,* pp. 265–75. Boulder, Colo.: Westview.

Machlis, Gary E., and Jo Ellen Force. 1988. Community stability and timber-dependent communities. *Rural Sociology* 53:220–34.

McLogan, Esther. 1980. *A peculiar paradise: A history of Blacks in Oregon.* Portland, Oreg.: Georgian Press.

Money from timber sales pays many of Josephine County's bills. 1992. In *Josephine County: A report to the citizens* [tabloid handout]. Grants Pass, Oreg.: Josephine County Commissioners. Feb.

Nelson, Robert H. 1977. *Zoning and property rights: An analysis of the American system of land-use regulation.* Cambridge, Mass.: MIT Press.

Norman, Julie. 1989. USFS/BLM ignore substitutes for old growth and trigger political bail-out that threatens U.S. Constitution. *Headwaters Journal* 1 (Aug.): 12–15.

NRDC v. Kleppe. U.S. District Court, D.C., 1975 (75-1861). Filed Nov. 7, 1975.

Oliver, Gordon. 1992. 1000 Friends are watching: Checking out the record of Oregon's pace-setting public interest group. *APA Planning* 58 (Nov.): 9–13.

O'Toole, Randall. 1988. *Reforming the Forest Service.* Washington, D.C.: Island Press.

Plotkin, Sidney. 1987. *Keep out: The struggle for land use control.* Berkeley: University of California Press.

Ratner, Shanna. 1984. Diversified household survival strategies and natural resource use in the Adirondacks: A case study of Crown Point, New York. M.A. thesis, Cornell University.

Retrain for what? 1993. *The Nation* 257:519–20.

Richmond, Henry R., III. 1975. Land use and economics. *1000 Friends of Oregon Newsletter* 1 (1): 1.

————. 1976. LCDC's urbanization goal cuts the tax cost of public services. *1000 Friends of Oregon Newsletter* 1 (12): 1.

Rodriguez, Sylvia. 1987. Land, water, and ethnic identity in Taos. In Charles L. Briggs and John R. Van Ness (eds.), *Land, water, and culture: New perspectives on Hispanic land grants*, pp. 313–403. Albuquerque: University of New Mexico Press.

Rogue Valley Fair Share. 1989. Can we afford decent housing in Jackson County? Medford, Oreg.: Rogue Valley Fair Share. June.

Sadler, Russell. 1994. Outlook: Where did the money go? *Jefferson Monthly*, membership magazine, KSOR, Southern Oregon State College, Ashland, Oreg. (Jan.): 8–9.

Salazar, Debra J., and Frederick W. Cubbage. 1990. Regulating private forestry in the West and South. *Journal of Forestry* 88(1): 14–19.

Salo, Kauko. 1992. Yields of wild berries and edible mushrooms in North Karelia, Finland. In Marjatta Hytönen (ed.), *Proceedings of the IUFRO interim meeting and excursion in Finland, Estonia and Russia, 25 August–8 September, 1991*, pp. 129–35. Helsinki: Finnish Forest Research Institute.

Scott, James C. 1990. *Domination and the arts of resistance: Hidden transcripts.* New Haven: Yale University Press.

Shands, William E. 1991. Problems and prospects at the urban–forest interface: Land uses and expectations are in transition. *Journal of Forestry* 89 (6): 23–26.

Shannon, Margaret A. 1991. Resource managers and policy entrepreneurs: Governance challenges of the urban–forest interface. *Journal of Forestry* 89 (6): 27–30.

Sievänen, Tuija. 1992. Outdoor recreation in Finland. In Marjatta Hytönen (ed.), *Proceedings of the IUFRO interim meeting and excursion in Finland, Estonia and Russia, 25 August–8 September, 1991*, pp. 103–15. Helsinki: Finnish Forest Research Institute.

Smith, Michal. 1989. *Behind the glitter: The impact of tourism on rural women in the Southeast.* Lexington, Ky.: Southeast Women's Employment Coalition.

SOCATS Staff. 1983. *SOCATS v. Watt:* The evolution of a court case. *NCAP News* 3(3): 7–9.

SOCATS v. Clark. 1983. 720 F.2d 1475 (9th Cir. 1983), *cert. denied,* 469 U.S. 1028, 105 S.Ct. 446, 83 L. Ed. 2d 372 (1984).

Southard, P. A. Dee. 1993. Non-recreational campers: Homeless people who use public lands. Paper presented at the Pacific Sociological Association Meeting, Portland, Oreg. April 1.

Southern Oregon Regional Services Institute. 1992. Population for southern Oregon counties: 1970–2000. Flyer. Ashland, Oreg. Aug. 17.

State of Oregon. 1993. *Oregon's statewide planning goals, 1993 edition.* Salem, Oreg.: State of Oregon.

State of Oregon, 1992. *Oregon Employment Division business and employment outlook, Volume 3: Job Training Partnership Act planning data.* Salem, Oreg.: State of Oregon, Employment Division, Department of Human Resources Labor Market Information.

Sturtevant, Victoria. 1991. Impacts on neighborhoods/communities of the Bureau of Land Management Medford District Office's Resource Management Plan/Environmental Impact Statement Alternative. Paper, contracted with Medford District BLM. Dec.

Tollenaar, Kenneth, et al. 1981. *The O & C lands.* Eugene: University of Oregon, Bureau of Governmental Research and Service, School of Community Service and Public Affairs, in cooperation with the Association of O & C Counties.

Tourism notable for its part-time, low-pay jobs. 1993. *Grants Pass [Oreg.] Daily Courier,* Jan. 30.

University of Oregon. 1984. *Guide to local planning and development.* Eugene: University of Oregon, Bureau of Governmental Research and Service. Oct.

U.S. Census. 1992. *1990 census of population and housing.* Washington, D.C.: U.S. Census Bureau.

Weber, Bruce. 1992. How does Josephine compare with other Oregon counties? In *Josephine County: A report to the citizens.* Tabloid handout. Grants Pass, Oreg.: Josephine County Commissioners. Feb.

White, James Boyd. 1984. *When words lose their meaning: Constitutions and reconstitutions of language, character, and community.* Chicago and London: University of Chicago Press.

Wilkinson, Kenneth P. 1988. The community crisis in the rural South. In L. J. Beaulieu (ed.), *The rural South in crisis: Challenges for the future,* pp. 72–86. Boulder, Colo.: Westview.

———. 1991. The future of the community in rural areas. In K. E. Pigg (ed.), *The future of rural America: Anticipating policies for constructive change,* pp. 73–89. Boulder, Colo.: Westview.

Wondolleck, Julia. 1988. *Public lands conflict and resolution: Managing national forest disputes.* New York: Plenum Press.

Zippay, Alison. 1991. *From middle income to poor: Downward mobility among displaced steelworkers.* New York: Praeger.

Index